Human Resources and Income Distribution

Human Resources and Income Distribution

Issues and Policies

Edited by

Barry R. Chiswick
and June A. O'Neill

W · W · NORTON & COMPANY · INC ·
NEW YORK

Library of Congress Cataloging in Publication Data

Main entry under title:

Human resources and income distribution.

    Bibliography: p.
    Includes index.
    1. Income distribution—United States—Addresses,
essays, lectures. 2. Public welfare—United States—
Addresses, essays, lectures. I. Chiswick, Barry R.
II. O'Neill, June.
HC110.I5H85   1977   331.1'1   77–9031
ISBN 0–393–05623–6
ISBN 0–393–09131–7 pbk.

To the memory of Robert J. Schanzmeyer

Contents

Introduction

Over the past forty years the role of Government in the economic and social affairs of the country has undergone profound change. Government is of course much bigger, in both absolute and relative terms, and if for no other reason its actions are bound to have wide ranging effects. But there has also been a change in the Government's responsibilities. The Government is now expected to promote a high and stable level of economic activity. It is also expected to be a major agent for providing an equitable distribution of our national income.

Views regarding the effectiveness and desirability of Government intervention in these two areas are not unanimous however, and they have varied over time. The role of Government in economic activity may well undergo further change, perhaps in quite different directions, as our programs are re-evaluated on the basis of experience.

This volume is concerned with the underlying factors that determine the distribution of income in the United States and the Government policies that have been introduced or proposed to alter this distribution either directly or indirectly. The cores of the chapters are taken from sections of the Annual Reports of the Council of Economic Advisers (referred to as the Economic Report) mostly written during the 1970s. During these years the Economic Reports reflected the need for careful analysis in areas where emotion may have too often been the primary guide to policy. The essays drawn from the Economic Reports discuss the basic economic factors which determine differences in earnings and unemployment, and the effects of public policy on these and other aspects of the income distribution.

THE GOVERNMENT AND INCOME DISTRIBUTION

The role of Government in affecting the distribution of income has been the subject of considerable public debate over the past 10 years.

Just how much economic equality can be achieved or is even a desirable goal in a democratic, free-enterprise economy has not, and may never be resolved. There is a general acceptance of the view that all Americans should be enabled to maintain some minimum standard of living and that it is appropriate for Government to redistribute income to achieve that end. However, there is much debate over the way this goal should be achieved in practice. Some of the important questions that have been raised are: Should everyone, including able-bodied adults, be eligible for benefits on the same basis? What is the minimum level of income to be provided? Should it be provided in cash or in the form of particularly essential goods and services?

Government concern with income maintenance can be traced back to the programs initiated in the Great Depression. There is, however, a fundamental difference between the goals of the programs of the 1930s and those developed in the 1960s. The emphasis in the 1930s was on programs to protect the income of families from declining because of factors outside their control, such as old age (social security), unemployment (unemployment compensation) or the death or disability of the father (Aid to Families with Dependent Children). These programs basically provide a measure of social insurance, which helps families who are not necessarily poor to maintain the income position they have achieved on their own.

The programs introduced in the 1960s and the 1970s have different, broader goals. They aim to produce greater equality of income among the population by raising the income of those at the lower end of the income distribution. The approach to this goal shifted, however, from the 1960s to the 1970s. The programs that made up the "War on Poverty" of the middle 1960s were directed largely at removing the causes of poverty perceived to be related to factors such as poor skills and racial and sexual discrimination. In introducing the concept of the Great Society in May 1964, President Johnson said that, ". . . We have the opportunity to move not only toward the rich society and the powerful society, but upward to the Great Society. The Great Society rests on abundance and liberty for all. It demands an end to poverty and racial injustice, to which we are totally committed in our time."

Underlying the Great Society programs was the belief that if all individuals were given "equal economic opportunity", earnings, and therefore income, would eventually be more equally distributed. Substantial emphasis was placed on the usefulness of education or training programs in providing the skills to overcome poverty. Because the results of education would not be instantaneous, and because there were substantial numbers of people who could not be expected to work, income transfer programs were to be expanded, partly in the form of more generous cash benefits and partly in the form of goods and services in-kind (e.g., medical benefits, public housing).

Since 1964 there has been a substantial reduction in the number of persons in poverty, at least as it is measured by the U.S. Bureau of the Census.[1] In 1964, 36 million people, or 19.0 percent of the population, were in poverty; by 1973, the most recent year of low unemployment, the number was 23 million or 11.1 percent.[2] However, the primary factor accounting for the decline appears to be the rapid growth of the economy which raised the real income of families at all points in the income distribution. Indeed, because income increased at about the same rate in all parts of the distribution, there was no decrease in measured relative income inequality over the period. Moreover, a rise in real average family income, with no change in relative inequality, has been the pattern since the late 1940s when the annual series on family income was started. The effectiveness of economic growth as a factor in reducing poverty, combined with increasing questioning of the usefulness of the efforts of the Great Society, has motivated a general rethinking of the Government's programs.

First, it became evident that for Government to try to equalize the earnings distribution by raising the earnings capacity of particular individuals was a most difficult and uncertain task. Although education, on average, has a large and positive effect on earnings, its contribution to differences in earnings between individuals is small. Many factors create differences in earnings among individuals: diversity in talents for varying occupation activities, ease of access to labor market information specifically relevant to the individual; the non-monetary aspects of jobs (which create compensating differentials), and, the effects of luck (e.g., choosing an occupation which happens to become much in demand later on). The effect of education also differs because it interacts with factors associated with individual and family background characteristics. Education also interacts with technology, and as technology changes, the overall effects of education can change, as can the differential effects for individuals. Providing "equal" resources for schooling and other training is not only difficult to define—it does not necessarily produce more equal outcomes.

Because education and training play an adaptive role with regard to

1. The poverty threshold is the income considered necessary to provide an adequate diet and other necessities and is adjusted for family size and composition and for inflation. See the discussion in Chapter 3 for further detail.

2. Following the typical cyclical pattern, poverty increased during the 1974–1975 recession. In 1975, 26 million people, or 12.3 percent of the population were in poverty. This is not strictly comparable to the earlier data as revised procedures reduced the number in poverty by 0.9 million in 1974.

so many other factors, it would be difficult for the Federal Government to design the "right" programs for particular individuals.[3] The results of the manpower training and education programs for the disadvantaged did not live up to expectations; starting in the early 1970s the Federal Government curbed the growth of subsidies to these programs, many of which were combined into general training funds distributed to the States to be used at their discretion.

At the Federal level there has been a relative shift away from programs which aim to eliminate or mitigate the *causes* of poverty, while at the same time there has been a shift towards those aimed at alleviating the *effects* of poverty. Thus, since the late 1960s there has been an expansion of funding for those programs which simply transfer income to families in the form of cash or in-kind benefits. The latter include medical care, housing and, more recently, the cash-like food stamps.

The income transfer programs have created a new set of problems. Most visibly, costs to the taxpayer have escalated. In addition to an increase in the number of programs, eligibility was generally liberalized, contributing to large increases in participation. Also, training programs always put an implicit cost on the trainee, who must invest his time. Income transfers make smaller demands on the recipient, and as a result those who would be able to qualify are more likely to apply for benefits.

Defining eligibility remains an extraordinarily difficult issue. Much publicity has been given to individuals portrayed as abusers of the programs, i.e., persons who scheme to qualify or who falsify income and other data on their applications. On a more scientific level, many economists and others who study the welfare "system" have questioned its equity in giving too much to some and too little to others.

Another criticism of the transfer programs is that they may induce people to alter behavior in a way that can be viewed as contrary to the best long-term advantage of the program recipients. Research has indicated that some of the programs create work disincentives which not only lead to higher program costs but also discourage the recipients from obtaining the training and experience which could increase their future earnings. A number of programs, by their very nature, encourage the splitting up of households or create impediments to remarriage. This may adversely affect not only the adults, but their children as well.

---

3. It is possible, of course, for Government to subsidize training without designing and running the programs by providing grants or vouchers to individuals. The GI bill has taken that approach and recently some college-level subsidies are in the form of grants and loans to individuals. However, the bulk of the "manpower" and education subsidies for the disadvantaged are essentially given in the form of publicly controlled and operated training.

Many believe that the adverse effects of dependency replacing self-reliance, although difficult to quantify, are significant.

THE ROLE OF THE COUNCIL OF ECONOMIC ADVISERS

The Employment Act of 1946 directed the Federal Government to "use all practicable means consistent with its needs and obligations . . . for the purpose of creating and maintaining . . . conditions . . . to promote maximum employment, production and purchasing power." To assist the President in carrying out his responsibilities under the Act, it also created the Council of Economic Advisers within the Executive Office of the President.[4] The Council, or CEA, was given the responsibility for analyzing and interpreting current and prospective economic developments and for developing and recommending economic policies to the President to further the objectives of the Employment Act. The CEA is independent of the Office of Management and Budget, the Treasury Department and other Government agencies. As the scope of economic policy has expanded in the last three decades to include microeconomic and distributional issues, as well as the macroeconomic (aggregate) issues mentioned in the Employment Act, the responsibilities of the CEA have also increased.

As one of its responsibilities under the Employment Act, the CEA submits an Annual Report to the President, usually in late January. A brief report, called the Economic Report of the President, is combined with the CEA's more lengthy Annual Report and is submitted to Congress. Because both are submitted under the title, *Economic Report of the President,* the CEA's report is commonly referred to as the Economic Report and is the main "outside" or public document of the CEA. As such, it is given considerable scrutiny in the press and among the members of the economics profession as reflecting the views of this group of Presidential economic advisers.

OUTLINE OF THE VOLUME

Part I focuses directly on the distribution of income. Chapter 1 reviews the problems of measuring income, the historical pattern and sources of income inequality, and the impact of Government policy. Chapter 2 analyzes differentials in earnings between groups—men and women, blacks and whites—with emphasis on the role of discrimination versus productivity factors. The measurement of poverty, a description of the characteristics of the poor, and the factors behind the decline in poverty are discussed in Chapter 3. Chapter 4 looks at the programs

4. The Council is composed of three persons—one chairman, and two members—who are nominated by the President and serve at his pleasure, although they are confirmed by the Senate. From its founding, the Council members have all been professional economists.

for supplementing income that have been developed over the past four decades. Some of the problems concerning the equity and the behavioral effects of the programs are discussed. Proposals for welfare reform are also considered.

Unemployment affects differences in income among families and individuals as well as changes in income over the business cycle. Part II considers unemployment issues. Unemployment is defined and examined in Chapters 5 and 6 from several dimensions, including the various types (or causes) of unemployment, the differences among demographic groups, and the variation in unemployment among nations. The unemployment compensation system is described and its impact on the economy is analyzed (Chapter 7). Part II closes with an analysis, in Chapter 8, of the effectiveness of alternative Government programs to increase employment—including public service employment.

There are several special topics closely related to income distribution issues that form the basis of Part III and IV. The social security system is described and the effects of the program on the income and work of the aged are analyzed (Chapter 9). Several problems of the system, including the treatment of the non-working wife, the "indexing" of benefits, and the system's financial viability are discussed. This is followed (Chapter 10) by an analysis of the economic role of women, with particular attention given to their labor market behavior and earnings, and to their changing role in the economy. A consideration of the *effects* of education permeates the entire study. Chapter 11, in particular, considers aspects of the determination of the level of education. The volume closes (Chapter 12) with an analysis of the health status of the population and of the system of providing and financing health services in the U.S. This includes the current public programs (medicare and medicaid) and a discussion of proposals for a national health insurance program.

The chapters of the CEA Economic Reports which form the basis of the book have been updated by the editors where more recent data are relevant. Explanatory notes have also been added to clarify the original text. In some sections (e.g., those on welfare reform and health) longer notes have been inserted to provide material not included, or too briefly treated, in the CEA Reports, but which seemed relevant for a full understanding of the issues. There explanatory notes and additional discussions can be identified by the square brackets that enclose them.

Preface

From 1971 to early 1977, as Senior Staff Economists at the Council of Economic Advisers, we were in a position to observe the making of policies affecting the accumulation of Government programs that now distribute to individuals huge amounts of cash and in-kind benefits. The programs have a multiplicity of goals: to provide income security, to improve health, nutrition and housing, to provide jobs, to provide education and other training. They assist retired, disabled and unemployed persons and those who for other reasons cannot earn enough to support their families.

We became acutely aware that all too often the many participants in the formulation of these programs—the Government agencies, the press and the public—ignored, or seemed to misunderstand many basic economic factors that could seriously affect the outcome of the programs. And since the outcome of these programs have a significant effect on the way the nation's income is distributed, and also perhaps on the rate at which its income grows, this was an important omission.

In recent years the CEA's Annual Reports have included special chapters devoted to analyzing the income distribution and the various income security, unemployment, health and other issues under the general label of human resources. These chapters attempt to synthesize economic theory, data analysis and the description and analysis of economic institutions. They provide a unique framework for understanding the economic conditions that government is trying to affect, and for evaluating the success of those efforts. Because of the importance and timeliness of these issues we felt the need for combining these analyses in a single, readily accessible volume.

This volume includes the CEA analyses of issues in human resources and income distribution, primarily from the 1973 to 1976 Economic Reports. Where important subsequent changes have occurred, we have brought the data and institutional description in the original material up to date. Explanatory notes intended to clarify the analysis of policy issues have also been inserted as needed. In a few instances pertinent issues, not explicitly treated by the CEA, such as welfare reform and national health insurance, have been dealt with in new sections.

We will view this volume as a success if it helps bring public discussion away from the more dramatic but often unfounded assertions about the distribution of economic well being and how to improve it, and toward a more informed discussion of the realities.

April 1977
Barry R. Chiswick
Stanford, California
June A. O'Neill
Washington, D.C.

Sources of Chapters in This Volume

Chapter	1	Economic Report, 1974
Chapter	2	Economic Report, 1974
Chapter	3	Economic Report, 1974
Chapter	4	Economic Reports, 1974 and 1976
Chapter	5	Economic Reports, 1975 and 1976
Chapter	6	Economic Report, 1975
Chapter	7	Economic Report, 1976
Chapter	8	Economic Reports, 1975 and 1976
Chapter	9	Economic Report, 1976
Chapter	10	Economic Report, 1973
Chapter	11	Economic Report, 1965
Chapter	12	Economic Report, 1976
Statistical Appendix		Economic Report, 1976

Human Resources and
Income Distribution

Part I

Income Distribution

I MPLICITLY OR EXPLICITLY, MOST DISCUSSIONS of the performance of the American economy and the economic role of the Government are concerned with the growth of national income and the way it is distributed.

Three fundamental principles of equity concerning the distribution of income are widely accepted: those who produce the same amount should be rewarded equally (horizontal equity); those who produce more should be rewarded more (vertical equity); and no individual or household should be forced to fall below some minimum standard of consumption regardless of productive potential. Although there is fairly general agreement on these principles, the desirability of any given amount of inequality in the income distribution remains a matter of personal judgment and of social and political debate.

One of the principal social debates has been about the extent to which those having high incomes should share with those having less. Among its chief objectives, the Government seeks the proper balance between redistributing income to the disadvantaged so that they may have the basic amenities of life and allowing a reward system which gives individuals incentives to work to their fullest capacity.

OUTLINE AND SUMMARY

Part I looks at the distribution of income among families and individuals and examines some of the Government policies which have influenced it. It considers the distribution of income among individuals and families and among various classifications of the population: age, sex, and race.

While the inequality of family income is quite stable over the long term, it varies over the business cycle. Inequality increases during a recession and decreases in an expansion. This is a consequence of the variation in weeks worked that occurs because of changes in the unemployment rate.

Because the concept of income used to measure inequality is es-

1

sentially limited to money income before taxes, these measures need not reflect the true inequality of economic well-being. Some sources of income which are omitted would increase measured inequality and others would decrease it, and estimates of some of these effects are given. While those omitted sources which would decrease family income inequality have been growing in importance over time, there exists no such presumption concerning the omitted sources that would increase it.

Many factors, such as schooling and on-the-job training, determine the inequality of earnings among workers. Differentials in the earnings of whites and blacks, and of males and females, are analyzed with respect to the contribution to the differential made by training and other factors that influence productivity. Past discrimination has contributed to current differences in productivity because of the once widespread barriers to equivalent schooling and on-the-job training. Because of the difficulties of measuring productivity, no conclusion could be reached about the magnitude of current labor market discrimination against blacks or women. For the same reason it is difficult to determine whether labor market discrimination has declined with time, although there is a strong presumption that it has. For men, the black-white earnings differential has narrowed, and much of the change may be due to a narrowing of educational differences. The narrowing of the differential has been much more dramatic for black women, however, and outside the South black women now receive a higher wage rate than white women. This development is largely due to black women's greater lifetime attachment to the labor force, and hence their greater level of experience and training.

The differential in hourly earnings between men and women has widened over time, and this change reflects the relative decline in education and experience of women in the labor force. With the rapid increase in the labor force participation of women, the female labor force has become increasingly composed of recent entrants with fewer years of schooling and of experience. Younger women are, however, showing less tendency to withdraw from the labor force for a prolonged period; as the age of these cohorts increases and they come to comprise a larger proportion of women in the labor force, the experience and earnings differential between men and women should decrease.

Widespread concern is felt about those whose incomes fall below a level needed to maintain an adequate living standard. There has been a marked decline in poverty, as conventionally defined, from 39 million persons in 1959 to 24 million persons in 1972, in large part because of economic growth, which increased wage rates and employment opportunities for men and women, and permitted larger social security and pension benefits. Increasingly the poor are living in families in which there is no adult worker, and increasingly the family is headed by a female. The number of persons in poverty decreased to 23 million in 1973 and then increased by 700,000 in 1974 and by 2.5 million in 1975 as a result of the recession.

The Federal Government has several programs—some operated on its own, others in conjunction with the States—which are intended to decrease poverty. Aid to Families with Dependent Children (AFDC) is the most important Federal-State program designed explicitly for poor families in which there is no employed male head. The 3.1 million AFDC families in 1972 represent nearly a threefold increase in the number of AFDC families since 1965. This increase can be partly explained by the spread of knowledge about the program and the lessening of the social stigma attached to it. In addition, the faster rate of increase of benefits to AFDC families, compared to average wages, contributed to the change by making the incentives greater for an existing female family head to apply for benefits, as well as giving women an incentive to head a family.

Social Security is the largest single Federal transfer program, with 28 million recipients of old age, survivor, or disability benefits in fiscal 1973. Many of the recipients of old age and survivors' benefits were in families classified as in poverty. For many others, however, social security kept their income above the poverty level.

The Federal Government also transfers economic resources to aged and low-income families by subsidizing the price of food, medical care, and housing. The Food Stamp Program, initiated in 1961, subsidized the purchase of food for 12.6 million recipients from low-income families in fiscal 1973. The average monthly subsidy (of $15.30 per individual recipient in July 1973) represents a substantial contribution to the economic well-being of many low-income families, although the food stamp subsidy is not counted in the measure of income used to define poverty.

A rapidly growing source of Federal transfers to the aged and the poor is medicare and medicaid, which lower the cost of medical care to the recipients. In fiscal 1973, 10.6 million people received medicare benefits, and 23.5 million received medicaid benefits.

Participation in the income transfer programs has increased since fiscal 1973. Some of the increase was due to the spread in coverage of food stamps to all of the counties of the United States. The 1974–75 recession also contributed to program growth, particularly for food stamps. And, in 1974, a new Federal program, Supplemental Security Income, became operative which provided benefits to low-income persons who are aged, blind or disabled, and replaced the State programs for these groups.

The combined effects of the tax and transfer mechanisms of Federal,

State, and local governments appear to redistribute income toward low-income families. Various studies have concluded that when accrued capital gains are included in income the tax system is roughly proportional in the income ranges in which most Americans are located, but regressive for very low incomes and progressive for very high ones. However, some government transfers have a strong effect of redistributing income to low-income families. These include public assistance programs, social security, food stamps, medicaid, and medicare.

CHAPTER 1

Determinants and Trends in the
Distribution of Income

Between 1947 and 1972 median family income, adjusted for the rise in prices, doubled.[1] This rapid increase in the overall level of income tells us much about the change in living standards, but it tells only part of the story. The extent to which the gains from economic growth have been diffused throughout the population is also important.

SECULAR CHANGES

There are various ways of illustrating the distribution of income among persons and of measuring the amount of inequality in the distribution. Since family members typically pool their incomes, the distribution of family income is a particularly useful indicator of the distribution of economic well-being. One common measure of inequality shows the percentage share of aggregate money income before taxes received by each fifth of families ranked by income. Quite remarkably, relative income shares measured in this way have hardly varied in the 25 years between 1947 and 1972 (Table 1–1). Thus in a relative sense the rich were not getting richer and the poor were not getting poorer. In this period the average income of each quintile increased at much the same rate. If anything, there seems to have been a slight tendency towards greater equality, since the share of measured income received by the top 5 percent declined somewhat from 1947 to 1972. The decline in the income share of the top 5 percent may be a con-

1. Although median family income increased from 1972 to 1973 (by 2 percent after adjusting for inflation), since 1973 the economy has experienced a sharp rise in the price of imported oil, and an unprecedented post-World War II inflation and recession. As a result, median family income adjusted for price changes declined by 4 percent from 1973 to 1974 and by 2.6 from 1974 to 1975. As a result of improvement in the economy, real incomes can be expected to be higher in 1976.

TABLE 1–1.—*Share of Aggregate Income Before Taxes Received by Each Fifth of Families, Ranked by Income, Selected Years, and Median Family Income, 1947–1975* [1]

(Percent)

Income Rank	1947	1957	1967	1972	1974r	1975r
Total families	100.0	100.0	100.0	100.0	100.0	100.0
Lowest fifth	5.1	5.0	5.5	5.4	5.5	5.4
Second fifth	11.8	12.6	12.4	11.9	12.0	11.8
Third fifth	16.7	18.1	17.9	17.5	17.5	17.6
Fourth fifth	23.2	23.7	23.9	23.9	24.0	24.1
Highest fifth	43.3	40.5	40.4	41.4	41.0	41.1
Top 5 percent	17.5	15.8	15.2	15.9	15.5	15.5
Median family income (in 1975 dollars)	$7,303	9,496	12,788	14,301	14,081	13,719

1. The income (before taxes) boundaries of each fifth in 1975 were: lowest fifth, under $6,914; second fifth, $6,914 to $11,465; third fifth, $11,465 to $16,000; fourth fifth, $16,000 to $22,037; highest fifth, over $22,037; top 5 percent, over $34,144.

Note.—Detail may not add to totals because of rounding. r designates data under revised procedures are not strictly comparable with principals. The table has been updated by the editors.

Source: Department of Commerce, Bureau of the Census.

sequence of the secular decrease in the share of national income received by the owners of nonlabor factors of production.

[From 1972 to 1974 there was a very small reduction in family income inequality. The proportion of aggregate income received by the top 5 percent declined by 0.4 percentage point, while the proportion received by other income groups either increased or did not change. The rapid growth of the in-kind food stamp subsidy would have improved the relative income of the lowest income groups in 1974, but the value of food stamp income is not included in the income measure. The data for 1974 indicate some reversal of the very small increase in inequality from 1967 to 1972. In general, the 1974 data provide further evidence that relative family income inequality has been fairly constant in the postwar period, although it does appear (Table 1–1) that the share of the top 5 percent has declined while that of the bottom quintile has increased by small amounts.

Since early 1974, the economy has undergone the most severe recession in the post-World War II period. The downturn was particularly strong in the last quarter of 1974 and the first half of 1975, after which economic recovery began. There was a small rise in family income inequality from 1974 to 1975.

An interesting exercise is to compare one's own family income in 1975 with the income brackets given in the footnote to Table 1–1. Nearly everyone believes that they are in a lower quintile in the income distribution than is suggested by the data.]

The general impression that no significant trend has developed in the relative inequality of income among families is confirmed by other measures of inequality. For example, the variance of the natural logarithm of income, a measure which takes into account dispersion throughout all ranges of income, shows no trend in the dispersion of family income throughout the post-World War II period. (See the supplement to this chapter for an explanation of this measure.)

A family's income depends on the amount of work the different family members perform, on the earnings they receive, on the monetary return from property owned by the family, and on transfers received from the Government. Underlying the distribution of family income then is the distribution of individuals' incomes. For males 35 to 44 years old or those 25 to 64 there is no trend during the post-World War II period in income inequality. However, in all years inequality is greater for the 25–64 age group than for the 35–44 age group, and this reflects the change in earnings with age. Thus, measures of inequality for broad age groups merge the inequality resulting from differences between lifetime incomes with the inequality that results because individuals do not earn the same income in successive phases of their lives.

An increase does occur over time, however, in the inequality of income for males 14 years of age and over, and in the inequality of income for all members (male and female) of the labor force. The increasing inequality for all male workers and all workers results mainly from the greater proportion of workers with part-time and part-year work schedules, rather than from an increase in the inequality of wage rates. The growth of part-time and part-year work may to some extent be attributed to a shift in industrial composition towards the service industries, where flexible hours are more common, and partly to the increasing desire among workers for flexible schedules with shorter hours. Such schedules are particularly attractive to students, semi-retired older workers, and married women. Associated with the increasing importance of these groups in the labor force has been a secular increase in the variability of annual hours worked and consequently in the variability of annual income for the labor force as a whole.

Since most families (75 percent in 1972) are husband-wife families with a working husband, the stability in the dispersion of adult male incomes has been one factor leading to stability in the distribution of family income. The increase in the proportion of wives with earned income evidently did not lead to increases in the relative inequality of family income, partly because husbands' and wives' annual earnings have not been positively correlated.[2] In the future, if a strong positive correlation between husbands' and wives' annual earnings should de-

---

2. Although men and women with high earning potential are more likely to marry each other, a woman is more likely to work the lower the income of her husband, other things being the same. [Editor]

velop, this correlation could be a factor in increasing the relative income inequality among families.

Stability of Income Inequality Among Adult Males

It is striking that there has been no change in the relative inequality of income among adult males. The greater opportunities for schooling among persons at all income levels and the larger subsidies for training less advantaged persons might have been expected to reduce earnings inequality in the past 20 years, but the relation between equal access to training or schooling and earnings inequality is not so straightforward.

The post-World War II period has brought a narrowing of differences in years of schooling among adult males, and this alone generally decreases the inequality of lifetime income. In the same period, however, the level of schooling has greatly increased. A recent study suggests that at higher levels of schooling the relative dispersion of wage rates tends to be greater than at lower levels, and that the effects on income inequality of the higher level and of the smaller variance in years of schooling have somewhat offset each other.

Greater equality of opportunity could also lead to increases in income inequality if investments in schooling or training became more closely related to ability. Generally, more able people receive a higher money return on an equal investment in education. In a world where financial access to schooling and training depend on family income (and assuming that family income and ability were not perfectly correlated), extending equal financial access to such investments for all people, regardless of income, could result in those with more ability investing more. In that case inequality could increase.

Obviously many factors other than education influence earnings. However, the distribution of adult males by age, marital status, health, and union membership, and the profitability of investments in school and post-school training, have been essentially stable over the past 25 years, and this stability has undoubtedly contributed to the stability of the income distribution.

CYCLICAL CHANGES

The inequality of income among families and among individuals fluctuates with the business cycle. Inequality increases in a recession and decreases in an expansion. During a recession, wage rates tend to be sticky, and there is no substantial change in the inequality of wage rates. However, layoffs increase and there is an increase in the relative inequality of weeks of employment, and hours worked per week for those who are employed. The increase in the relative inequality in weeks worked during a recession shows up both within and across demographic groups (age, sex, race, and schooling).

During a recession, unemployment within a group of the same skill, age, and other characteristics is not experienced uniformly; rather, in any one year it is likely to affect some workers to a disproportionate degree. Thus, an increasing rate and duration of unemployment have a greater effect on the weeks of employment of some workers than on others and result in a greater inequality of employment within the group.

A recession also intensifies the inequality of weeks of employment among groups with different characteristics. Workers with higher levels of skill—that is, more schooling and longer labor market experience—usually work more weeks per year at all stages of the business cycle. During recessions, however, the disemployment is relatively greater for workers with less skill. For this reason, in a recession one finds a larger inequality of weeks worked between skill groups than during a business cycle peak.

Because of the expansion of income transfer programs, income inequality may not have increased in the 1974–75 recession as much as in past recessions. However, while income from the expanded unemployment compensation programs will be counted, transfer income is apparently subject to greater under-reporting in the Current Population Survey (CPS) than is earned income. Income received in-kind from other programs such as food stamps and medicaid would not be included in the income measure.

OMITTED SOURCES OF REAL INCOME AND
THE INEQUALITY OF WELL-BEING

Because the concept of income used in the measures of inequality just presented omits some sources of real income, it gives an imperfect description of the resources that families actually command. The omitted items can be very important. They include the imputed value of rental income received by homeowners living in their own homes, as well as capital gains. Employee fringe benefits paid by the employer are omitted, and so is the monetary value to the recipient of Government transfers in kind, such as food stamps, medical benefits, and housing allowances. Many goods and services are produced at home and are excluded from these income measures because of the difficulty of placing a value on production outside the market. Families with a working husband and wife may thus have more measured income than some families in which the wife confines her work to caring for the home and children, although the extra expenses or loss of leisure time of the working couple could mean that they are really less well off. Finally, the data used here refer to income received in one year before payroll and income taxes.

The reason for not including these sources of income in census surveys of consumer income is that they are all extremely difficult to measure for individuals or families. Several studies have attempted to measure the magnitude and distribution of the different items, but so far the net effect on income inequality of all the items cannot be stated with complete confidence. Nor can we say how past changes in the importance of the different omitted sources may have affected the true trend in income inequality.

Table 1–2 presents estimates of the effect that some of these omitted sources of income would have had on measured income inequality. For convenience the basic measure of income dispersion used in the calculation is the variance in the natural logarithm of income (see supplement to this chapter). The measure is zero when there is perfect equality of income, and it increases for greater income inequality. However, while a reduction from 0.7 to 0.6 conveys an acceptable suggestion about a decline in inequality, and a decline from 0.7 to 0.5 an acceptable suggestion about a greater decline, the statement that the second of these two declines is twice the first would not be meaningful.

The rental value of owner-occupied dwellings can be imputed by assuming that it is proportional to the value of the house. When the imputed rental value of owner-occupied dwellings is added to money income, the inequality of family income does not change significantly. Although the imputed rental value of housing rises with money income, it does not rise as a percentage of income.

Farm wages and farm income received in kind (such as food and

TABLE 1–2.—*Income inequality under alternative definitions of income, 1968*

Definition of income	Income inequality [1]
1. Money income	0.75
2. Line 1 plus rental value of owner-occupied homes	.74
3. Line 2 plus nonmoney wages and nonmoney farm income	.69
4. Line 3 plus medicare payments	.62
5. Line 4 plus imputed interest from banks and insurance companies	.61
6. Line 5 plus other imputations [2] equals money income plus imputed income	.61
7. Line 6 less direct taxes equals disposable family personal income	.52

[1] Income inequality is measured by the variance in the natural log of income. (See supplement to this chapter.)
The income classes used are: Under $2,000; $2,000–$3,999; $4,000–$5,999; $6,000–$7,999; $8,000–$9,999; $10,000–$14,999; $15,000–$24,999; $25,000–$49,999; and $50,000 and over.
[2] Other imputations include services furnished without payment by banks and insurance companies, military clothing, and miscellaneous other items.

Sources: Department of Commerce (Bureau of the Census) and Council of Economic Advisers.

lodging) and medicare payments are generally concentrated among the poor, and they reduce income inequality. The inclusion of imputed interest from banks and insurance companies does not significantly change inequality. When personal income taxes and payroll taxes are deducted from money income plus imputed income, the dispersion of income declines.

Because of the extreme difficulties involved, no effort was made to compute the distribution of capital gains or losses among families. Nor was an effort made to remove the effect of transitory influences on income in any one year. Capital gains and losses, however, tend to be concentrated among upper-income families, and for years of net capital gains their inclusion in the income concept would clearly increase family income inequality. Several studies suggest that if accrued capital gains are included in income a very high proportion of families earn incomes falling in ranges in which the tax system is essentially proportional.

The huge growth in Federal food, medical, and other in-kind subsidies to the poor during the past 10 years would certainly reduce inequality if they were included in the income measures. In addition, families differ in their use of government-subsidized goods and services, such as manpower training programs, public schools, national parks, and roads, but the incidence of benefits by income level is not known.

Family Composition and Work in the Labor Market

Families vary considerably in the hours they work in the labor market to produce measured money income. The difficulty of imputing a value to work done at home has already been noted. The fact that a wife does not work in the market can be taken to mean that she considers her productivity at home to be of more value than what she could earn in the market. Knowing that she does not work in the labor market is not sufficient, however, to determine the money value of the wife's work at home.

Table 1–3 indicates roughly how families at three levels of income differ in their composition and work in the labor market, and how this has changed. In both 1952 and 1974, families in the lowest fifth were much more likely to be headed by a woman or by a person either less than 25 years of age or older than 65 years. Partly because of these differences in age and sex, the heads of lower-income families are less likely to participate in the labor market, and so are the other family members.

Such families consequently depend more on income from sources other than earnings, such as social security, other retirement incomes, and public assistance. By contrast, upper-income families generally have many earners per family and are more likely to include a wife who

TABLE 1–3.—*Selected characteristics of the lowest, middle, and highest fifths of families ranked by money income, 1952 and 1974.*

(Percent)

Family characteristic	Lowest fifth		Middle fifth		Highest fifth	
	1952	1974	1952	1974	1952	1974
Total families	100.0	100.0	100.0	100.0	100.0	100.0
Female head	22.0	33.3	7.1	8.1	4.8	3.1
Head under 25 yrs. of age	7.1	13.1	6.0	7.8	1.3	0.8
Head 65 yrs. of age and over	30.1	31.6	7.8	9.9	7.9	5.9
No earners	25.3	39.0	1.2	3.4	.6	1.0
2 earners or more	22.4	19.7	36.7	56.1	66.3	76.9
Husband-wife families	100.0	100.0	100.0	100.0	100.0	100.0
Wife in paid labor force	18.9	19.9	21.2	42.9	38.1	54.2
Mean number of children	1.14	1.06	1.43	1.25	1.10	1.19

Source: Department of Commerce, Bureau of the Census.

Note: Updated by the editors.

works. Presumably these families have less time for work at home, and they must buy with their earnings some of the services that would otherwise be produced at home.

These differences in the characteristics of families by income class have become more intense. They raise problems of interpretation which are important for public policy designed to influence the distribution of income. Some of these issues are discussed below in Chapter 3.

DETERMINANTS OF DIFFERENCES IN EARNINGS

Wage rates and annual labor market earnings of individuals vary considerably. Much of this variation can be related statistically to individual differences in measurable characteristics—schooling, post-school training, region of residence, and other demographic characteristics, as well as restrictions on entry into occupations. How far such unmeasurable characteristics as innate ability, diligence, personal attractiveness, and contacts explain the remaining differences is not known. Nor can it be ascertained how important luck is in determining the distribution of income.

Other aspects of earnings are not included in earnings data. Psychic earnings from having a pleasant job or living in a pleasant locality are not measurable. Earnings received by individuals in kind, such as free lodging and fringe benefits purchased by the employer, are measurable in principle, but difficult to measure in practice.

SCHOOLING

Schooling is an important determinant of the distribution of earnings. Table 1–4 shows average usual weekly earnings for males 35 to

TABLE 1–4.—*Average usual weekly earnings of male workers 35–44 years of age who worked full time, by years of schooling and race, 1973*

Years of schooling	White	Negro and other races
0–4	$150	$96
5–7	173	149
8	202	165
9–11	211	165
12	231	178
13–15	265	209
16	321	241
Over 16	333	284

Note.—Data are from a survey made in May 1973.
A full-time worker is defined as one who usually works 35 hours or more per week.
Source: Department of Labor, Bureau of Labor Statistics.

44 years of age who worked full time. Those with more schooling have substantially higher earnings; and this relation has been persistent in many different sets of data.

One suggested reason why schooling and earnings are positively related is that schooling increases a worker's productivity. A mobile labor force and competitive markets translate the increased productivity into higher income for the worker. To test the hypothesis that schooling increases productivity and thereby increases income, one must have some measure of productivity other than income itself. Several studies have investigated the association between schooling and the productivity of self-employed farmers, efficiency in household activities, interregional migration and scores on standardized ability tests. They indicate that, controlling for other variables, those people with more schooling are more productive.

Some say that those capable of higher productivity receive more schooling and that business firms use the amount of schooling as a means of sorting out those capable of better performance. It is therefore important to distinguish between schooling as a means of changing productivity and schooling as a means of identifying the more productive members of the population. The sorting hypothesis implies that firms regard the number of years of schooling as an index of individual qualities that the educational system can identify more efficiently than they can. The educational system, according to this theory, is effective in attracting persons possessing these qualities and discouraging the schooling of those without these qualities. Empirical tests of the sorting hypothesis have not been conclusive.

[The data in Table 1–4 indicate a $90 per week difference ($4,693 per year) in pay between white male high school and college graduates, 35–44 years of age. Suppose schooling had no effect on ability, but was only a means of identifying ability or some other characteristic that employers prefer. What would be the cost of a battery of tests for high school graduates designed to acquire the same information about them? Even if it cost $5,000 to identify one high school graduate with the desired characteristics (i.e., those associated with success in college), a system of certification via tests would be less costly than employing college graduates at the existing wage differential. This suggests that sorting by ability is not likely to be the reason for college schooling in our economy. However, credentials which are a by-product of schooling undoubtedly play a role in the initial job placement.]

Chart 1–1

Real Income Profiles of Cohorts of Men Born in Selected Years

REAL ANNUAL INCOME (1967 DOLLARS) 1/

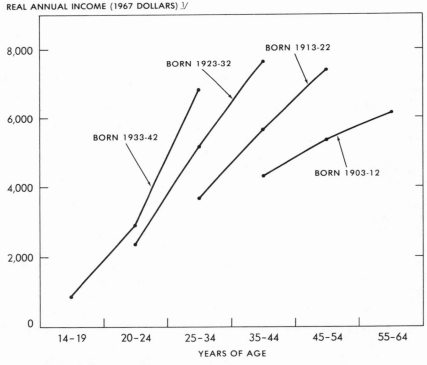

1/MEDIAN TOTAL MONEY INCOME FOR EACH AGE DEFLATED BY THE CONSUMER PRICE INDEX.

SOURCES: DEPARTMENT OF COMMERCE AND DEPARTMENT OF LABOR.

POST-SCHOOL TRAINING

Another important aspect of training is experience acquired on the job after schooling is completed. On-the-job training can vary from formal training programs within the firm to the informal process of learning by doing. Thus, particularly at younger ages, a worker may be involved in a process of investment with returns accruing later on. For this reason earnings would rise as age increases.

Charts 1–1 and 1–2 give the results of two different procedures to find the relation between age and income for males. Chart 1–1 presents the

Chart 1–2

Real Incomes for Men in Different Age Groups

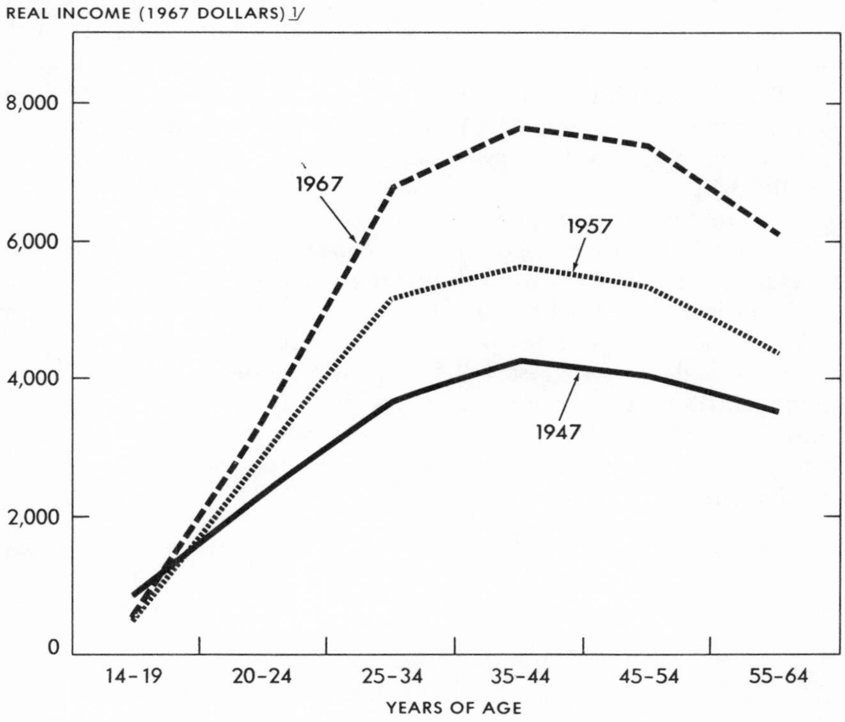

REAL INCOME (1967 DOLLARS) 1/

YEARS OF AGE

1/ MEDIAN TOTAL MONEY INCOME FOR EACH AGE DEFLATED BY THE CONSUMER PRICE INDEX.
SOURCES: DEPARTMENT OF COMMERCE AND DEPARTMENT OF LABOR.

age-income profiles of a group of men over time (cohort profile). For a cohort, income increases with age, but for adults it does so at a decreasing rate. Income increases with age because the workers are acquiring experience and because of the rising productivity of workers as technology improves and physical capital grows. The cohort profiles are higher for younger workers because they have not only more years of schooling but also the benefits that accompany a growth of technology and physical capital.

Chart 1–2 presents the age-income profiles obtained from plotting the income of males of different ages in the same time period (cross-sectional profile). The tipping down for the oldest age groups (45 to 54 and 55 to 64 years of age) of the cross-sectional profile for annual income reflects the lower income of retired persons and, compared to younger males, the lower level of schooling and obsolescence of knowledge of those older males still in the labor force.

There are too few comparable data to determine whether the cohort profiles are becoming steeper over time for adult males, although there are some hints to that effect. Increased high school and college attendance has increased the slope of the age annual income profile for younger males. If better data in the future indicate a steepening over time in the slope of the age-income profile, a constant income inequality within a broad age interval would imply a narrowing of income inequality for each age in the interval.

The relation between age and usual weekly earnings in 1973 for males with 12 and 16 years of schooling is shown in Table 1–5. For the same level of schooling, usual weekly earnings generally increase with age. The age-earnings profiles are steeper for those with more schooling and thus suggest a positive association of schooling and on-the-job training. Because women are more likely to participate discontinuously in the labor force, entering and leaving several times during their lives, their post-school training does not necessarily rise steadily with age.

TABLE 1–5.—*Average usual weekly earnings of males who worked full time, by age and years of schooling, 1973*

Age	Years of schooling	
	12	16
20–24 years	$158	$170
25–34 years	201	238
35–44 years	226	317
45–54 years	227	347
55–64 years	227	323

Note.—Data are from a survey made in May 1973.

Source: Department of Labor, Bureau of Labor Statistics.

EMPLOYMENT

The annual labor market earnings of a worker are a function of the worker's weekly earnings and the number of weeks of employment during the year. Weeks of employment can vary because of unemployment; but they also vary because of voluntary withdrawals from the labor force.

The number of weeks worked is greater for male workers 25 to 54 years of age than for younger, older, or married female workers. Younger persons work less because of school attendance and a greater incidence of unemployment. Students, who are about 60 percent of the teenage labor force, ordinarily work during vacations or have part-time jobs for a few months during the year. Most new entrants and re-entrants to the labor force are young people or married women, and most also experience some unemployment before taking their first job. One reason for the higher unemployment rate for young workers is that they voluntarily leave jobs to acquaint themselves with the labor market and to gain experience in various jobs. In addition, the instability of their employment is increased by the fact that their productivity is very close to the legal minimum wage, and they have a smaller amount of specific job training.

Employers make investments specific to the firm for some workers. Specific investments include the component of training a worker receives that is useful only in that firm, and also hiring and placement costs. The more important specific training is, the more costly it is for both the firm and the worker if the worker is separated from the firm. Workers with more specific training are therefore less likely to be subjected to layoffs or to quit, and they will work more weeks during the year. Workers with advanced schooling ordinarily work more weeks during the year, partly because their higher wage makes absence from work more costly, and partly because they have more specific training.

Married men work more weeks per year than men who have not married, but married women work fewer weeks than those who have never married. Most married women work less if they have young children. Older workers work less because of deteriorating health and partial retirement.

The weekly wage and the number of weeks worked are related. Those who work more weeks per year tend to have a higher weekly wage, partly, because they have acquired more experience. On the other hand, it has been suggested that the weekly wage for each week worked is higher in some seasonal occupations in which there are fewer weeks of employment during the year.

The Variance of the Natural Logarithm of Income

The "variance of the natural logarithm of income" is the measure of overall income inequality used in the analysis of the distribution of income in this chapter. It can be written as:

$$S^2(\ln Y) = \frac{\sum_{i=1}^{N} (\ln Y_i - \ln Y)^2}{N} \tag{1}$$

where Y_i is the income of the i th observation (individual or family), ln designates natural logarithm, and there are N observations in the data. Larger values of S^2 mean greater inequality of income, and S^2 equals zero if there is no inequality. While a reduction of the measure from 0.7 to 0.6 conveys an acceptable suggestion about a decline in inequality, and a decline from 0.7 to 0.5 an acceptable suggestion about a greater decline, the statement that the second of these two declines is twice the first would not be meaningful.

The variance of the natural logarithm of income is a commonly used simple measure of relative inequality. A measure of relative inequality does not change in value if all of the observations have the same percentage change in income. If

$$Y^*_i = Y_i(1 + k), \tag{2}$$

where k is the percentage change in income, the natural logarithm of both sides of equation (2) is

$$\ln Y^*_i = \ln Y_i + \ln(1 + k). \tag{3}$$

Computing the mean of both sides of equation (3),

$$\overline{\ln Y^*} = \overline{\ln Y} + \ln(1 + k). \tag{4}$$

Then, subtracting equation (4) from equation (3),

$$\ln Y^*_i - \overline{\ln Y^*} = (\ln Y_i + \ln(1 + k)) - (\overline{\ln Y} + \ln(1 + k)) = \ln Y_i - \overline{\ln Y}, \tag{5}$$

and

$$S^2(\ln Y^*) = S^2(\ln Y). \tag{6}$$

Thus, a proportional tax on income or a proportional cash subsidy does not change relative income inequality.

Relative inequality decreases (increases) if the income of each observation is increased (decreased) by the same dollar amount. A $100 per year grant to a poor family constitutes a larger percentage increase in income than an equal dollar grant to a wealthy family. Such a grant reduces the relative inequality of income.

A progressive tax is one in which the higher the level of income, the larger the proportion of income paid in taxes. In a regressive tax a smaller proportion of income is paid in taxes as income increases. A progressive tax reduces, and a regressive tax increases, relative income inequality ($S^2(\ln Y)$).

CHAPTER 2

Earnings Differentials:
Black/White, Male/Female

In the last quarter century there has been substantial public concern
with the causes and consequences of the observed earnings differential
between groups differentiated by race and sex. This discussion has
focused on investments in training and current and past discrimination, as factors that may explain the differential.

DISCRIMINATION

Discrimination is said to exist when two or more groups that are
differentiated on the basis of some characteristic irrelevant to an objective measure of productivity are not granted equal treatment in a
particular activity. The differentiating characteristic may be race, sex,
ethnic origin, marital status, age, or physical appearance. Obviously
some forms of discrimination give rise to more social concern than others. Discrimination may also take several forms: the way individuals
and business firms behave in the market place for jobs, housing, credit,
and other goods and services; and discriminatory taxation or public
expenditure policies by government. It may be so closely interwoven
with the culture of a society that the stereotyping of roles is accepted
by all with little or no question.

The income and employment of an individual can be influenced by
past and present discrimination. Past discrimination affects the years
and quality of an individual's schooling and the path to his present
occupation and training. Current discrimination affects incomes when
two workers are given a different wage for the same productivity and
restrictions are placed on a worker's occupational mobility.

It is important to distinguish between the differences caused by discrimination and those from other causes. Observed differences between
the wages or occupational distribution in two groups of individuals may
be due to discrimination or to factors entirely unrelated to discrimination. Because many important variables are not measurable, one cannot

fully quantify the effects of past or present discrimination on earnings and occupational choice. What can be quantified, however, is the extent of observed differences between groups that remain after making allowance for what is measurable.

RACE DIFFERENTIALS

Data on the income or occupations of white and black males and females indicate a substantial racial difference that has persisted for the last century.[1] The relative income difference widened in recessions or depressions and narrowed during periods of economic expansion, particularly during World War II. Evidence is accumulating, however, that there has been a long-run narrowing of the racial income difference. According to one recent study, for example, the median wage and salary income of black males increased at an annual rate of 3.2 percent from 1917 to 1971, compared to an annual increase of 2.6 percent for white males. For black and white females the rates were 4.9 percent and 1.7 percent respectively. In spite of this narrowing, substantial racial income differences continue, particularly for males.

Why the Differential Narrowed

There are several reasons for the narrowing of the black-white earnings differential. Important changes have occurred in the relative schooling of blacks and whites. The substantial discrimination against blacks that was evident in the public school expenditures of many States appears to have ended. For this and other reasons there has been a dramatic increase in the level of schooling for blacks. The median number of years of schooling among black males 18 years old and over in the labor force increased between 1952 and 1971 by 4.2 years, to 11.4 years. For white males the increase was 1.7 years, to a level of 12.5 years. During the same period, black females in the labor force increased their level of schooling by 4 years, to 12.1 years, compared to an increase for white females of only 0.4 year, to 12.5 years.

The substantial migration of blacks out of the South and into States in the northern and western regions may also have influenced the relative increase in the earnings of blacks. In 1940, 77 percent of the black population lived in the South; by 1970, the proportion was 53 percent. Earnings are lower in the South than in other regions for all workers, but the difference is particularly great for black workers, and in the past the difference between earnings in the South and elsewhere was even more pronounced. Thus blacks could increase their earnings by moving out of the South. Although whites have an even greater propensity than blacks to migrate between States or regions, this greater regional

---

1. Almost 90 percent of nonwhites are blacks, but many of the available data do not distinguish between blacks and other nonwhites. [Editors]

earnings differential for blacks, coupled with their greater concentration in the South, provided an important way for blacks to improve their earnings. Blacks are likely to have increased their earnings relative to whites through migration, despite their somewhat lower geographic mobility.

The changing occupational structure and labor force status of the population was another factor influencing the rate of growth of earnings. The labor force participation rate of married white females increased at a faster rate than that of married black females. The entry into the labor force of white females with little experience and the growth of part-time employment slowed the rate of growth of earnings among white females. The proportion of black females employed as household workers declined from 43 percent in 1949 to 18 percent in 1969.

Two important factors served as catalysts enabling these changes to take place. First, the American economy is highly competitive, and business firms whose owners or white workers have less discriminatory attitudes toward blacks will be likely to employ more blacks. These firms prosper if blacks receive lower wages. When such firms expand, the demand for black workers increases and the discriminatory differential declines.

Competition may not be a fully effective weapon against discrimination, however, if prejudice is very widespread. The second factor, working with the first, was a change in attitudes toward discrimination against blacks. This development improved the relative income and occupational status of blacks by directly reducing labor market discrimination. It also facilitated the passage of the 1964 Civil Rights Act and other Federal and State legislation as well as court decisions prohibiting discrimination in wages and employment. Such changes in the legal system made discrimination more costly and therefore lessened it. The reduction in discrimination in housing and in public accommodations brought about increased contact between blacks and whites and presumably expanded the information sources and job opportunities for blacks.

Dead-End Jobs

There is a widespread belief that, compared to white males, black males are relegated to poorly paid, dead-end jobs—that is, jobs in which earnings are initially low and do not rise with experience. This view originated as a result of examining the relation between age and income for white and black males at a moment in time (cross-section). For example, reading down the columns of Table 2–1 indicates a substantial decline for older age groups in the income of black males relative to white males. The appropriate procedure for a study of life-

TABLE 2–1.—*Income of Negro males as percent of income of white males, by type of income and age, 1949, 1959, and 1969*

[Percent]

Type of income by age group	1949	1959	1969
Annual income:			
25–34 years	57	57	65
35–44 years	48	52	56
45–54 years	46	49	53
55–64 years	45	48	51
Weekly income:			
25–34 years	61	61	67
35–44 years	52	57	58
45–54 years	48	52	55
55–64 years	47	51	53

Note.—Data for 1949 and 1959 relate to Negro and races other than white end therefore are not strictly comparable with data for 1969 which relate to the Negro race only.

Sources: Department of Commerce (Bureau of the Census) and Council of Economic Advisers.

cycle income, however, is to follow a group (cohort) as it ages, as is shown along the diagonals of Table 2–1. For each cohort, the ratio of black to white annual and weekly incomes either did not decline at all with age from 1949 to 1969, or declined at an appreciably slower rate than in the cross-section. Thus, experience appears to have a similar relative effect on the incomes of white and black males. Although some black and some white males may be in dead-end jobs, this is not the situation of the average black or white worker.

Current Differentials

Although the earnings differential between black and white females has become quite small, the differential that still exists between the earnings of black and white males is substantial. It does narrow, however, when the comparison is restricted to the States outside the South, and when differences in years of schooling are taken into account (Table 2–2). A further narrowing of the differential occurs if the comparison is restricted to married men. There are large differences in marital status between blacks and whites. In March 1972, 78 percent of white males 20 years old and over were married and living with their wives, compared to 61 percent for black males. Among both white and black males, marital status is closely related to earnings, married men having higher earnings than those not currently married. How the division of labor within the family affects the earnings of married men and women is discussed at greater length in the next section.

Several factors can be mentioned to explain why black males still receive lower earnings than white males after adjustment for schooling, age, region, and marital status. Prior investments made in the child

TABLE 2-2.—*Earnings of Negroes as a percent of earnings of whites, for persons 25–64 years of age, 1969*

[Percent]

Type of earnings by sex and region	All persons			Married, spouse present		
	All levels of schooling	High school graduate	College graduate or more	All levels of schooling	High school graduate	College graduate or more
EARNINGS OF MEN						
Annual earnings:						
All regions	60	68	71	61	61	72
South	53	60	64	55	61	(2)
North and West [1]	69	74	78	70	76	79
Hourly earnings:						
All regions	67	73	79	68	76	81
South	60	64	71	60	65	(2)
North and West [1]	77	81	87	79	85	93
EARNINGS OF WOMEN						
Annual earnings:						
All regions	80	93	104	88	102	108
South	69	80	105	75	88	112
North and West [1]	94	102	111	105	112	108
Hourly earnings:						
All regions	89	99	119	91	107	95
South	82	76	128	76	79	88
North and West [1]	101	118	109	111	128	107

[1] Includes Northeast and North-central.
[2] Fewer than 50 persons in the sample.

Note.—Education, region, marital status and age relate to 1970.

Sources: Department of Commerce (Bureau of the Census) and Council of Economic Advisers.

at home are important in determining the extent to which a student benefits from schooling. Black youths are more likely to come from poorer homes where the parents have less schooling, to have poorer diets, and to be less healthy. They are likely to start school with fewer advantages and skills than the typical white youth. Moreover, at least in the past, there was discrimination against black youths in public school expenditures. Later on, as adults, blacks have poorer health, and may have poorer information about better jobs. Some of the current wage differences may thus be a consequence of past discrimination. Many factors, such as health and information about labor markets, are difficult to measure, however, and their actual effects on earnings differences between blacks and whites have not been quantified. One cannot then reliably measure the extent of the occupational and wage rate discrimination that now exists, or the effect that current discrimination has on earnings.

SEX DIFFERENTIALS [2]

In 1972 the median annual earnings of women 14 years old and over who did full-time, year-round work were about 58 percent of that of fulltime, year-round male workers. This low ratio cannot be taken as a measure of current market discriminating, however, since the average full-time work-week is shorter for women than for men, and their life time work experience has been vastly different.

Specialization and Working Women

Although the pattern is changing rapidly, the traditional economic organization of the family has been marked by a specialization of function: women tend to specialize in the work associated with child care and keeping up the home; men tend to specialize in labor market employment. In the past, when it was typical for families to have more children than they now do, this specialization of function was undoubtedly an efficient arrangement. Whether it now reflects societal discrimination or efficiency is a matter for speculation.

In many families a lesser degree of specialization and a greater sharing of home and labor market activities have come to be the preferred form of family organization, and women's participation in the labor force has increased greatly. In 1950, 28 percent of married women 35 to 44 years of age were in the labor force; in 1972 the proportion was 49 percent, in 1975, the proportion was 52 percent. However, most married men still work nearly continuously during their prime working years; and the labor force participation rate of married men from 25 to 55 years of age is over 95 percent.

The work histories of individual women cannot be ascertained from current labor force rates; special surveys are needed to provide information about lifetime work experience. The National Longitudinal Survey (NLS), a large data source sponsored by the Department of Labor, has recently become available and provides much more detailed information on the work histories of women than has ever been previously compiled. The survey indicates that in 1967, among married women 30 to 44 years old with children, only 3 percent had worked at least 6 months every year since leaving school. On the average, married women worked at least 6 months in 40 percent of their years after leaving school, but the work was not likely to be continuous.

One study which used the NLS showed that earnings of women do rise with experience and that continuity of experience, as opposed to intermittent participation, commands a premium. Withdrawal from the labor force for a time resulted in a decline in earnings when work

2. For further discussion see Chapter 10. [Editors]

resumed, since previously accumulated skills, or human capital, actually depreciate during extended periods away from work. For the married women in the sample, the hourly wage rate was about 66 percent of that of married men in the same age group (30–44 years) in the same year (1966), after controlling for differences in years of schooling. At least half of the 34 percent differential resulted from differences in their measured experience. The remaining differential is unexplained.

It is not known to what extent current discrimination, as opposed to other unmeasured factors, contributed to this differential. For example, the study could not provide direct measures of the nature of the investments made in the productivity of women and men, other than years of formal schooling. Women do not appear to obtain as much training on the job as men for the same length of time in the labor force. Thus, although women's earnings rise with experience, the study found that they do not rise as steeply as men's. This difference could result partly from a faulty measurement of a year's experience for women; as noted above, in these data a year's work could be as little as 6 months of part-time employment. However, the measured effect of experience could also be interpreted as the result of discrimination. That is, employers may deny a woman on-the-job training or a promotion because of her sex, sometimes from sheer prejudice, sometimes because they think a woman is more likely to quit for personal reasons. One can also surmise that women themselves may not choose to invest in training at a cost of either lower current earnings or additional hours of work, when the payoff might be lost because of the uncertainty of their future work patterns.

For example, women in school have a lower enrollment rate in programs oriented toward the labor market—engineering, accounting, electronics—and a higher enrollment rate in courses that may be more applicable to work or leisure in the home—child development, languages, literature. This pattern may reflect greater uncertainty among women about their future attachment to the labor force. A choice of field of study may also be influenced by social pressures, however, which make women feel less feminine and men feel less masculine if they enroll in courses traditionally selected by the other sex.

The study also relates lifetime work history to earnings for women who never married. A year's experience has a much greater effect on single women's earnings than on those of married women. Single women work much more continuously than married women, though less so than married men. Some single women may choose not to make investments related to work because they expect to marry. But many look forward to careers and may therefore delay marriage or never marry at all. This career orientation is consistent with the relatively greater number of years of schooling completed by single women compared to those who marry. It is also consistent with their observed higher earnings. Estimates of hourly wage and salary earnings from 1970 census data show that women 45 to 54 years of age who had never married earned 20 percent more than married women, and 28 percent less than married men, but only 2 percent less than men who had never married.

There is then also a differential between the earnings of married and single men, and it may be taken as another illustration of how specialization within families may affect career patterns and earnings. Single men have somewhat lower labor force participation rates; they also work fewer hours per year than married men. In part this may result from a higher incidence of disability, which influences both marriage and work. Although they have greater work participation than married women, single women also have higher disability rates than married women.

Because of differences in life-cycle participation in the labor force by women and men, the experience of women does not bear the same relationship to age as it does for men. Many women who have entered or reentered the market at older ages are really beginners. Men's earnings are at their peak when the men reach an older age, but women's earnings will represent a mixture in which a small minority have high earnings because of their considerable experience, but the majority have earnings closer to those at the start of a career. As age increases, it is therefore not surprising that the earnings differential between women and men widens. For example, a comparison of usual weekly earnings of workers who worked 35 hours a week or more in 1973 shows that the ratio of women's earnings to men's earnings declined from 0.70 at ages 20–24 to 0.59 at ages 45–54 for high school graduates. Of course the earnings ratios at older ages reflect the work histories of different cohorts of women. If the younger women maintain a greater attachment to the labor force during their lifetime (and there is some evidence that this is the case), then the ratio of women's earnings to men's may not decline as much with age in the future.

Differences in lifetime work experience also seem to explain why the ratio of black women's earnings to those of white women exceeds the ratio of earnings of black men to those of white men (Table 2–2). Indeed, in the regions outside the South, within educational levels, black women earn more than white women. The differential between whites and blacks in quality of schooling, family background, and discrimination can be assumed to be similar for women and men. Black women have a much greater life-cycle attachment to the labor force, however, than white women do, although this differential is largely confined to married women. For example, in 1972 among women 35 to 44 years of age, with 4 years of high school or more, 71 percent of the black women were in the labor force, compared to 53 percent of the white women.

The greater tendency of black married women to work, compared to white married women, may be due in part to the relatively lower earnings of their husbands. Partly because of the relatively high earnings and work participation of black wives, the ratio of annual income of black husband-wife families to that of white husband-wife families is higher than the ratio of black men's to white men's income. For families headed by males 35 to 44 years old the ratio in 1969 was 75 percent, compared to 56 percent for males alone (Tables 2–1 and 2–3).

TABLE 2–3.—*Median income of Negro husband-wife families as percent of white husband-wife families, by region and age of husband, 1959, 1969, and 1972*

[Percent]

Age of husband	1959	1969	1972		
			Total	South	North and West [1]
All families_____	57	72	76	69	86
Under 35 years_____	62	80	85	84	93
35–44 years_____	60	75	76	67	80
45–54 years_____	55	66	71	63	78
55–64 years_____	51	62	59	53	79
65 years and over_____	57	65	72	67	98

[1] Includes Northeast and North-central.

Source: Department of Commerce, Bureau of the Census.

Trends in the Earnings Differential

Much has been made of the rather puzzling observation that the ratio of earnings of all women to those of all men has declined during the past 20 years. This observation refers to annual earnings, or the earnings of full-time, year-round workers who are not necessarily representative of the total. But average hours and weeks worked during the year fell for women relative to men from 1949 to 1969. If annual wages and salaries are divided by total hours worked during the year, the result is a much modified decline in the hourly wage of women relative to the hourly wage of men (Table 2–4).

An additional factor which would produce a relative decline in women's earnings is the relative decline in their general educational level and their labor market experience during the period. In 1950, women in the labor force had on the average more schooling than men did; but this advantage was eliminated by 1970. Since education has an effect on earnings—both men's and women's earnings increase with education—it is important to take these changes into account. An approximate adjustment for educational level increases the differential

TABLE 2–4.—*Relation of wage and salary earnings and of total money earnings of women to those of men, 1949, 1959, and 1969*

Type of earnings	Earnings of women as percent of earnings of men		
	1949	1959	1969
Mean wage and salary earnings: [1]			
Annual_____	56	50	47
Hourly_____	67	66	63
Hourly adjusted for education [2]_____	63	65	63
Mean total money earnings: [1]			
Annual_____	([3])	48	46
Hourly_____	([3])	65	62
Hourly adjusted for education [2]_____	([3])	64	62

[1] Earnings for any year are for those in the experienced labor force the following year.
[2] Approximate adjustment based on differences in the educational distributions of men and women in the labor force in 1950, 1960, and 1970.
[3] Not available.

Source: Council of Economic Advisers.

in 1949 and 1959, because women in the labor force then had more education than men. After the educational adjustment, the differential shows little change from 1949 to 1969.

What has not been accounted for is the experience differential between men and women. As has been explained above, this difference seems to be the most important factor causing a divergence in hourly earnings. But since the labor force participation of women, particularly married women, was increasing rapidly during the period, it is very likely that the constant flow of entrants into the labor force resulted in a decline in the average experience of women in the labor force during the 20 years.

The foregoing suggests that if we could compare women and men with a given amount of experience and education the ratio of women's hourly earnings to men's might well show an increase over the 20 years—a narrowing in the gap. This would, of course, be compatible with the fact that women have dramatically increased their participation in the labor force during the past 20 years. The rapidly increasing opportunities offered them would be one reason why they have done so.

OCCUPATIONAL DIFFERENCES

The occupational distribution of blacks differs from that of whites. In 1970, for example, 27 percent of employed white males and 9 percent of employed black males were managers or professionals, whereas 7 percent of white males and 19 percent of black males were hired farm or nonfarm laborers; and 18 percent of employed black females were domestic household workers, compared to only 2 percent of white females. There is also considerable occupational segregation by sex, and some believe that the sex segregation is even greater than the racial segregation. For example, 83 percent of managers and 87 percent of farm laborers were men; but only 3 percent of nurses and 16 percent of elementary school teachers were men.

Occupational segregation by race derives partly from differences in schooling and partly from the geographical distribution of blacks, who disproportionately live in the South. Moreover, there has been substantial discrimination against blacks who entered, or tried to enter, certain occupations. This discrimination, stemming from the attitudes of white employers, employees, and consumers of services, resulted in a smaller proportion of blacks entering these occupations. In some professions—for example, medicine, law, and the ministry—blacks were generally restricted to practicing in segregated black markets. In addition, blacks were not always granted equal opportunity to move up the occupational scale—for example, from laborer or operative to foreman or manager.

Some of the differences in occupational composition by sex can be attributed to differences in physical attributes. Undoubtedly, however, jobs requiring physical strength are on the decline, and it is questionable whether this factor was ever very important. One may also argue that prejudice on the part of employers, fellow employees, and consumers operates to exclude women from some activities in the labor market and to favor them in others.

Another hypothesis stresses the difference in role identification that leads to differences between the work careers and training of women and men. That is, women who anticipate combining some work with marriage seek occupations and work situations which are most complementary to home responsibilities, such as those in which hours are shorter or correspond to the children's school hours, or those offering work close to home. Another criterion is the penalty for interruptions in work. For example, women might avoid situations with rigid seniority rules, or they might choose careers in which skills are least likely to depreciate during a period spent at home. Some of the occupations stereotyped as women's, such as elementary school teaching and nursing, are indeed those where the same skills can be utilized in the home. According to this view occupational differences arise from choice, although the choice may be induced by a pervasive societal bias which dictates that home responsibilities are the women's major work. It is quite difficult to separate empirically the effects of discrimination in the labor market from the effects of personal considerations in women's occupational choices.

One may question whether the wage rates received by blacks and women have been affected by the occupational segregation. Earnings differ from occupation to occupation. If blacks or women were clustered in occupations that were low paying for all groups, including white males, then the lower average hourly earnings of blacks and women could be attributed to differences in their mix of occupations, rather than to earnings differences within individual occupations. To estimate the effect of occupational mix on the earnings of black males, indexes were calculated to measure what black males would earn if they had the white male occupational distribution but the earnings of black males within each occupation. Similar indexes were computed to measure what white women would earn if they had the same occupational distribution as white men, but the earnings of white women within occupations.

Preliminary results, using 1970 census data on 443 detailed occupations, indicate that black males would have hourly earnings about 18 percent higher if they had the white male mix of occupations. Since white males earned 50 percent more than black males, occupational differences would appear to "explain" 35 percent of the differential. However, those with high levels of education have a very different occupational distribution compared to those with lower levels of education. Hence it may be that in adjusting for occupation one is really adjusting for education. Indexes calculated for separate education groups indicate a much smaller explanatory power of occupation. For example, among males who completed 12 to 15 years of schooling, the earnings of black workers would be increased by only 8 percent if they were given the white occupational distribution, and this would account for 22 percent of the race differential in earnings.

Comparing white women and white men 25 to 64 years old, the preliminary results for 1970 indicate that women would increase their earnings by about 11 percent if they had the occupational mix of men, and this would account for about 21 percent of the gross earnings differential between women and men. Since women have completed roughly the same average years of schooling as men, education would not be expected to interact so strongly with occupation. Within education groups, occupational mix seems to explain less for women below the college level than for women as a whole, but relatively more at the college level.

Since occupation alone does not explain very much of the overall earnings differential between men and women, it would seem that earnings differentials within occupations, as they are now defined, must be more important than earnings differentials between occupations. In other words, if custom or overt barriers to entry have relegated women to different occupations from those of men, this factor has not been the major one in lowering their earnings.[3]

It has already been noted that earnings differences between women and men are in large part a consequence of differences in lifetime labor market experience. Since earnings differences between occupations may also be influenced by sex differences in the extent of post-school training between occupations, it may be necessary to make a distinction between the explanatory power of occupational mix per se and the explanatory power of occupational differences in experience. This requires data not currently available.

In conclusion, it appears that the different occupational distributions of white men, compared to black men and white women, explain at most about one-fourth of the existing earnings differentials between them. Because occupational differences can also be explained by other factors that differ between the races and the sexes, such as labor market experience (post-school training), and region, the true effect of occupation may be much smaller.

3. Many find this conclusion startling. The stereotype has developed that women are secretaries and clerks and men are managers and professionals. However, women are also "under-represented" at the lower end of the occupational distribution. Women are "under-represented" among farm and non-farm laborers and operatives. [Editors]

CHAPTER 3

The Low-Income Population

The Government has assumed an ever larger role in helping to see that those in need reach an adequate standard of living; and a considerable share of the Federal budget is now devoted directly and indirectly to that end.

THE DEFINITION OF POVERTY

There is not, and probably never will be, a consensus on any one definition of poverty. Many programs require, however, that we distinguish those who fall below a minimum income standard; and, accordingly, the concept of the low-income or poverty threshold has been developed. The Government concept is defined essentially as an amount about three times the estimated cost of a nutritionally adequate diet.[1] The standard is adjusted for differences in family size, sex

1. The cost of a nutritionally adequate diet is based on the U.S. Department of Agriculture's (USDA) Household Food Consumption Survey which prices the diets of households. However, this survey shows much higher expenditures on food than are shown in the Consumer Expenditure Survey conducted by the Bureau of Labor Statistics (BLS). For example, the USDA's Thrifty Food Plan, emerging from their Household Survey, supposedly reflects the lowest feasible expenditure for a nutritionally adequate diet. However, the Thrifty Food Plan for a family of four came to $30 a week in 1972–73 while the actual expenditure for the *average* family was also $30 a week for food at home and $40 a week for food at home and away from home, in the same year.

The decision to multiply the food expenditures by three to derive the total poverty income is based on the proportion of income spent on food by the *average* family as shown in the USDA survey for 1955. However, since food falls as a percentage of income as income rises, food would be a larger proportion of income for families with poverty level food expenditures. Moreover, if the multiplier were to be automatically tied to current surveys, it would continuously rise, thereby pushing up the poverty line expressed in real dollars. This is because although the average family income rises over time, food expenditures do not rise as fast. Because of the difficulties of objectively setting a standard for non-food expenditures it was felt that the multiplier approach was the most reasonable procedure. It is, however, quite an arbitrary one. [Editors]

of family head, number of children, and farm-nonfarm residence; and different schedules are set for each group. The standard for each group is adjusted each year for changes in the overall consumer price index. Thus, the average threshold for a nonfarm family of four increased from $2,973 in 1959 to $4,275 in 1972; $5,500 in 1975.

Because the poverty threshold is, in real dollars, an absolute standard, it cannot be used to measure changes in the relative inequality of income. Indeed, as the average real income level of the population increases, the poverty standard lags farther behind the average. Thus the poverty threshold for a family of four declined from about 55 percent of median family income in 1959 to 38 percent in 1972; and due to the recession increased to 40 percent in 1975.

Only cash income is used in determining low-income status, although a crude implicit adjustment is made for food grown at home by farm families. It has not been feasible to take account of the tremendous growth in the number and size of transfers in kind, such as public housing, food stamps, child care, and medical care. For example, in 1972, Federal and State government expenditures per poor person on the food subsidy and medicaid programs alone, valued at cost, were equal to about 50 percent of the money income of the average person in the low-income category. [Income security programs are discussed in greater detail in Chapter 4.]

It would be extremely difficult to determine the exact incidence or value of all the benefits. The programs for the low-income population are administered by different agencies and jurisdictions, they also have different aims and are distributed to somewhat different target populations. Moreover, the income in kind cannot be considered a perfect substitute, dollar for dollar, for cash income. For example, a public expenditure of $100 a month for public housing may be valued by the poor family at considerably less than $100. Nevertheless, it seems safe to conclude that some low-income families with in-kind benefits are receiving real incomes in excess of the low-income threshold and that the proportion exceeding the threshold has increased with the growth of the programs. On the other hand, some persons classified as above the low-income threshold, who receive no in-kind benefits and who have unusual expenses—for example, because of poor health—may have their real income position overstated.

THE DECREASE IN POVERTY

There has been a rapid decline in the number and proportion of persons in families with a cash income below the poverty line (Table 3–1). In 1972, 12 percent of all persons were classified as low income, compared to 22 percent in 1959. In all years the incidence of poverty is greater among blacks than among whites and much greater among female-headed families than among male-headed families. Since 1959 the decline in poverty has been particularly marked for both black and white male-headed families.

[The increase in the overall number and proportion of the population in poverty from 1973 to 1975 was most severe among persons in families headed by a male under age 65. This is attributable to the slow rate of increase of wages (which did not rise as fast as prices) and the rising unemployment that accompanied the recession. Persons over 65 years and families headed by women depend more heavily on income from social security and other transfers which remain a more stable source of real income during recessions.

Given the severity of the recession, the rise in poverty is smaller than what would have been predicted on the basis of previous recessions. This appears to be the result of the expansion of income transfer programs, particularly unemployment compensation.]

TABLE 3-1.—*Persons below low-income level and percent below the low-income level by family status, selected years, 1959–75*

Family status	1959	1966	1972	1973	1974	1974r	1975r
Total persons below the low-income level (thousands)	39,490	28,510	24,460	22,973	24,260	23,370	25,877
Group below low-income level as percent of all persons in group:							
Total persons	22.4	14.7	11.9	11.1	11.6	11.2	12.3
65 years and over	(1)	28.5	18.6	16.3	15.7	14.6	15.3
Unrelated individuals	46.1	38.3	29.0	25.6	25.5	24.1	25.1
Persons in families with male head:							
White	14.7	8.0	5.6	4.9	5.5	5.2	6.1
Negro and other races	51.0	31.2	18.5	16.5	15.9	15.8	17.3
Persons in families with female head:							
White	40.2	29.7	27.4	28.0	27.6	27.7	29.4
Negro and other races	75.6	64.6	57.7	55.5	55.2	53.2	52.6

1. Not available.

Note.—Updated by Editors.

Note.—Persons below the low-income level are those falling below the poverty index adopted by the Federal Interagency Committee in 1969. See text for explanation of index.
Years are not exactly comparable because of changes in definition and methodology. r designates the latest revision in procedures.

Source: Department of Commerce, Bureau of the Census.

The principal factor behind the decline in poverty is economic growth. The basic forces underlying economic growth have raised the productivity of even the least skilled worker and have enabled millions of workers to rise above the low-income threshold through higher wage rates for those in the labor force. In addition, economic growth has increased the labor force participation of wives by increasing their

TABLE 3–2.—*Work experience of family heads below the low-income level by sex, 1959 and 1972*

Work experience of head	Total		Male head		Female head	
	1959	1972	1959	1972	1959	1972
Total families (thousands)_____	8, 320	5, 075	6, 404	2, 917	1, 916	2, 158
Total families (percent)_____	100. 0	100. 0	100. 0	100. 0	100. 0	100. 0
Worked [1]_____	67. 5	53. 5	74. 9	64. 9	42. 9	38. 1
50–52 weeks, full time_____	31. 5	19. 8	37. 6	29. 4	10. 9	6. 9
1–49 weeks, part time or full time_____	31. 0	30. 1	32. 1	31. 3	27. 1	28. 5
Worked part of year because unemployed_____	14. 4	11. 1	17. 3	14. 9	4. 9	5. 8
Did not work_____	30. 5	45. 9	22. 5	34. 0	57. 1	61. 9
Unable to find work_____	1. 2	2. 2	1. 0	1. 9	1. 5	2. 6
Keeping house_____	10. 9	19. 0	[2]	[2]	47. 5	44. 7
Ill, disabled, retired, and other_____	18. 3	24. 6	21. 5	32. 2	8. 1	14. 6
Head in Armed Forces_____	1. 9	. 6	2. 5	1. 0	[2]	[2]

[1] Includes those who worked part-time hours for 50–52 weeks, not shown separately.
[2] Not reported.

Note.—Persons below the low-income level are those falling below the poverty index adopted by the Federal Interagency Committee in 1969. See text for explanation of index.
Data for 1959 and 1972 are not exactly comparable because of changes in definition and methodology.
Detail may not add to totals because of rounding.

Source: Department of Commerce, Bureau of the Census.

labor market wage relative to the cost of consumer durables and other substitutes for time in the home. Thus the decline in poverty has been most pronounced for the working poor. In 1959, 14.6 percent of family heads who worked at all, and 9.4 percent of those who worked full time, year round were classified as low income; by 1972, the percentages had dropped to 6.0 and 2.9 percent respectively. Those heads of families who do not work but are no longer in poverty have benefited from increases in social security and pension income, which were made possible by economic growth.

More and more the low-income population is composed of families headed by a person who does not work because of disability, age, responsibilities in the home, or perhaps simply inability to cope with work (Table 3–2). Unemployment, perhaps surprisingly, does not play a major role in withdrawal from the labor force. Of those low-income family heads who did not work in 1972, 4.8 percent cited inability to find work as the reason for not working. Thus, the vast majority of the poor who do not work seem to be in a situation where work is not a feasible alternative. For some the inability to work is a permanent condition, but for others it may be temporary.

THE CHARACTERISTICS OF THE POOR

As the population in poverty has come to include a smaller proportion of families with a working adult, the demographic characteristics of the poor have changed. Male-headed families have decreased as a proportion of all poor families—dropping from 77 percent in 1959 to 57 percent in 1972—because male family heads are more likely to work than female family heads. The proportion of low-income families headed by a female has increased sharply from 1959 to 1972, from 23 to 43 percent for all females and from 8 to 20 percent for black females. In part this trend results from an increase in the proportion of all families headed by a woman, from 10 percent in 1959 to 12 percent in 1972. However, while the incidence of poverty among female-headed families declined in this period, it did not decline nearly as fast as for families headed by a male.

The Male-Headed Family

Among male-headed families, the presence of children has a direct influence on poverty status, since for a given income the more children there are, the higher the poverty-income threshold. Children also indirectly affect the family's income, because it is more difficult for a wife to work outside the home when young children are present. In 1972, 31 percent of low-income families with a male head had three or more children, compared to 17 percent for families above the poverty line. The presence of a working wife can bring an otherwise poor family above the poverty line. Only 22 percent of the wives in low-income families headed by a male worked in 1972, compared to 48 percent of wives in families above the poverty line.

The number of children and the work experience of wives are also important variables affecting the ability of the poor to move up from poverty. One longitudinal survey which followed the poverty status of a cohort for 5 years, starting in 1967, found that about 20 percent of nonaged families headed by a male experienced steady income increases and ended the period out of poverty. This group had significantly fewer children than those who remained poor during those 5 years, and a larger proportion of wives who increased their labor market work over the period. However, a period of 5 years is too short to determine whether this group is permanently upwardly mobile or simply experiences long-term fluctuations in its income position.

Low earnings, per se, are still an important reason for poverty among male-headed families. Educational levels are very low for this group. In 1972 only 29 percent were high school graduates or better, compared to 63 percent among other male family heads. As might be expected, the poor were also much more concentrated in low-income jobs, particularly farming: 20 percent of employed men heading low-income families were farmers or farm laborers, compared to 4 percent among those not poor. In the future, as the level of education rises and as productivity change continues to increase earnings, one would expect that the incidence of poverty (under a fixed standard) may come close to disappearing for this group.

The Aged Poor

The population 65 or more years old increased as a percentage of the poor from 1959 to 1970. Since then, however, the incidence of poverty has dropped sharply for this group, from 24.6 percent in 1970 to 18.6 percent in 1972 to 15.7 percent in 1974 and the aged represent a declining proportion of the poor. This rapid change is primarily due to across–the–board increases in social security benefits of about 50 percent from 1970–72. Since 1972 there has been further expansion in social security benefits. The increase in a widow's benefits to 100 percent of her deceased husband's benefits should reduce the extent of poverty among widows.

Undoubtedly, however, cash income understates real consumption by the aged poor compared to that of the other poor. Many of the aged have income in the form of imputed rents from owner-occupied homes. Elderly people often consume out of past savings, and many widows receive life insurance benefits which are not included in income data. In addition, compared to others classified as poor, the aged poor derive a larger proportion of their measured income from sources which are not taxed, such as social security and some pension income. The aged also have fewer expenses related to employment. The aged benefit disproportionately from medicare and medicaid, which are not counted in money income statistics, although in this case obviously their need is often greater because of poorer health. Even excluding the benefits of medicare and medicaid, however, it would appear that on average a two-person aged family may have a higher level of consumption than a two-person family which has the same measured cash income but whose members are under age 65.

The Female-Headed Family

Perhaps the most important issue concerning poverty status in this country is the increasing identification of poverty with the female-headed family. Future progress in eliminating poverty will depend in large part on the extent to which poverty can be reduced for this group. If the proportion of families headed by women continues to increase, the problem may become still more difficult. Among families with a female head, 33 percent were classified as in poverty in 1972, compared to 6 percent for male-headed families. Among black female-headed families the proportion was 53 percent. The factors behind this very high incidence of poverty among families headed by women are complex.

As discussed earlier, the average married woman has not had the same labor market experience or vocationally oriented training as her husband. Since the incidence of marital breakup is greater among less educated couples, the woman who becomes a family head is more likely to have assumed during her marriage the traditional role of caring for children and the home, and she is less likely to have had work experience. Women who have children without having married tend to be young, with little work experience or formal education. Earnings for women in these circumstances tend to be much lower than for men of the same age and to be lower even than the earnings of other women, particularly those with considerable education. Moreover, the expenses of going to work are higher for a person with sole responsibility for child care. It is thus clear that if work is to be a sensible option in the single-parent family, earnings (after taxes) must be sufficiently high to cover the additional costs of child care and other home expenses.

Not surprisingly, poverty status among women is strongly related to presence of children and to work participation. As noted above, among women in general the presence of children, particularly young children, has a strong inhibiting effect on work participation. About 70 percent of female family heads under 65 years of age have children under age 18. As one would also expect, mothers who head families are more likely to work than mothers living with their husbands. In 1972, 30 percent of the former and 17 percent of the latter worked full time, the year round. However, mothers heading families are much less likely than men to work full time, the year round. Among males heading families, the proportion was 68 percent.

Of the small proportion of female family heads with children who did have full-time, year-round jobs in 1972, 9.5 percent were in poverty, a markedly lower incidence than the 42 percent for all female family heads with children. One cannot, however, infer from this statistic that poverty would fall to that level for all women with children if they did full-time, full-year work. It is likely that those women who work extensively are relatively more productive in the labor market because of higher educational attainment, greater work experience in the past, or greater ability.

The poverty status of female-headed families is often the result of a marital breakup, and this situation is temporary for many. One longitudinal study which followed the poverty status of a cohort over a 5-year period, starting in 1967, discovered that of those persons in non-aged female-headed families who were poor at the start of the period, 27 percent experienced consistent increases in income and had moved out of poverty by the end of the period. (The comparable percentage for male-headed families was 20 percent.) Remarriage of the female family head was the primary factor associated with this upward mobility.

About 32 percent of the persons in female-headed families who started as poor in 1967 remained poor throughout the 5 years. The demographic characteristics associated with this more permanently poor group were low education, a large number of children, and residence in low-wage, rural areas with low public assistance payments. For this group, the high costs of child care and poor prospects of high earnings suggest that training and increased work in the labor market by the female family head could not be relied on as a route out of poverty.

The remaining 41 percent of persons in female-headed families who started in poverty moved in and out of poverty during the 5-year period. A large part of this change in poverty status was associated with a change in household arrangements.

Because of the lower work participation of low-income female heads of families, the major source of income for this group is public assistance. In 1972, public assistance accounted on the average for 51 percent of the income of low-income, female-headed families. Many in-kind benefits are given automatically to families receiving public assistance, specifically those in the Aid to Families with Dependent Children program, which is largely a program for female-headed families. Moreover, because public assistance income is not taxed, the real consumption of female-headed families is probably understated, compared to that of husband-wife families whose income depends more heavily on earnings.

The increase in female-headed families may, per se, be an important variable in determining the size of the poverty population in future years. There is some evidence, discussed below, that our system of welfare payments, which has been an important way of increasing income for mothers heading families, may itself have promoted some of the increase in female-headed families through the structure of incentives. This is clearly an important issue in the future design of transfer payments to the poor.

CHAPTER 4

Income Security Programs

Income security programs redistribute income in cash or in kind to individuals and families. Some may have the effect of increasing future earning potential, but that is not their primary purpose. The Federal programs having that purpose, such as those for schooling, job training, and rehabilitation, are not considered in this chapter.

Income security programs have been a major factor in the growth of the Federal budget. As classified in the national income accounts (NIA), Federal transfer payments to persons (excluding Federal pensions for military and civilian Government employees and for veterans and railroad workers) amounted to $120 billion in 1975, 34 percent of Federal expenditures. As a source of income to persons, Federal, State, and local government transfers (again excluding all the above items and their State counterparts) accounted for 13 percent of disposable personal income. The magnitude of income transfers in 1975 was, of course, unusually high because of the recession, during which earnings were depressed and the cyclically responsive transfers high. But even in 1973 net Federal transfers were 28 percent of Government expenditures and net Federal, State, and local transfers 10 percent of disposable personal income. This represents a substantial growth from the middle 1950s. In 1957 these percentages were 14 percent and 5 percent respectively.

Although all the income security programs involve the redistribution of income, they differ considerably in their specific goals, the people they serve, and their sources of funds (Table 4–1). Some programs are related to need and provide or supplement income so that particular groups may attain a higher level of purchasing power—supplemental security income (SSI) and aid to families with dependent children (AFDC). Others attempt to ensure an adequate or more nearly equal level of consumption of particular goods or services that are considered essential. Thus some programs supplement income with in-kind transfers of food, medical care, or housing. Another category of programs is not directly based on need but replaces a proportion of wages lost as a result of retirement, disability, death, or unemployment. In-

TABLE 4-1.—*Aspects of selected Federal income security programs*

Program	Basis of eligibility	Source of funds	Form of aid	Fiscal 1976	
				Expenditures [1] (billions of dollars)	Beneficiaries (monthly average; millions)
OASDI	Age, disability, or death of parent or spouse Individual earnings	Federal payroll taxes on employers and employees	Cash	71.4	32.1
Supplemental security income (SSI)	Age or disability Income	Federal revenues	Cash	6.0	4.3
AFDC [2]	Certain families with children [2] Income	Federal-State-local revenues	Cash and services	9.8	11.4
Food stamp	Income	Federal revenues	Vouchers	5.3	18.6
Unemployment compensation	Unemployment	State and Federal payroll tax on employers	Cash	18.3	12.5
Medicare	Age or disability	Federal payroll tax on employers and employees	Subsidized health insurance	16.9	25.1 [3]
Medicaid	Persons eligible for AFDC, or SSI and medically indigent	Federal-State-local revenues	Subsidized health services	14.7	9.1

[1] Expenditures by Federal and State and local governments; excludes administrative expenses.
[2] Families with children deprived of support because of death, absence from home, or incapacity of parent, or in some States, in certain circumstances, unemployment of father (AFDC-UF).
[3] Estimated number of enrollees with hospital insurance and/or supplementary medical insurance.

Source.—Council of Economic Advisers (based on program information).

cluded in this group are the unemployment insurance programs and the largest of all income transfer programs—old-age, survivors, and disability insurance (OASDI), commonly referred to as social security.

The sources of funds and administration of the programs differ. Social security is entirely federally funded and administered. The funding and regulations in the food stamp program are Federal, but the regulations are implemented by the States. AFDC is funded by the Federal Government and the States, but is largely State administered. There are, in addition, some programs not considered in this chapter that are State funded and administered, in particular general assistance and emergency assistance.

Forty years ago there were virtually no Federal income security programs. The programs that have since been introduced have expanded in number; coverage has been extended to additional groups in the population; and real benefit levels have increased. As a result of the program growth, a substantial proportion of the needy have been able to improve their level of consumption.

It has, however, been difficult to measure the precise contribution of the programs to reducing poverty. Many of the programs provide benefits in the form of medical care, food, or other in-kind services whose value to the recipient is not easy to determine. For this reason in-kind benefits are not counted as income for purposes of determining poverty status or for purposes of determining eligibility for other programs. However, in 1974, Federal, State, and local spending on medicaid, food stamps, and child nutrition programs came to $16.8 billion. These programs are not intended exclusively for those in poverty, although they are means tested and targeted to lower-income people. The combined outlays for these programs, however, were equivalent to about 118 percent of the gap between the aggregate incomes of those below the poverty threshold and what their incomes would be at the poverty threshold. This figure is raised to 130 percent if Federal subsidies for public housing and rentals are included. The Bureau of the Census has recently started collecting data on the Federal food stamp subsidy received by different families in the population. But additional work is needed before we can fully evaluate the contribution of the in-kind programs to the poor and their effects on the overall distribution of income.

This Chapter discusses two income security programs, AFDC and the Federal food programs (primarily food stamps). Unemployment compensation is discussed in Chapter 7, social security, in Chapter 9, medicare and medicaid in Chapter 11. Other programs such as housing subsidies and veterans benefits are not explicitly considered here.

AID TO FAMILIES WITH DEPENDENT CHILDREN

The AFDC program is administered by the States with Federal guidance, while funding is shared by the Federal Government and the States. In some States a part of the State portion is funded by local governments. Benefits are provided to families in which dependent children are deprived of the support of a parent, usually the father, through death, disability, or absence. In 26 States, benefits are also available under some circumstances if the father is present but unemployed.

Benefit Levels and Participation

The level of income now available to AFDC families, although low compared to that of the average family, is high relative to the potential earnings of AFDC participants. For example, in a sample of 100 representative counties in 1972, a hypothetical AFDC family of four (consisting of a woman and three children) with no earnings or other income was eligible for an average of $2,947 in AFDC benefits and $884 in food benefits. Since benefits are not taxed, this would be equivalent to $4,104 in taxable earnings if the families viewed the food benefits as equal to the same amount of cash. There were also medical care services available for virtually all AFDC participants. Although the average medicaid payment per AFDC family was $770, a low-income family might not value such care at that amount. Adding only $400 for medicaid results in a taxable equivalent income of about $4,550. This does not include any housing subsidies or child care services that might have been received, but does include greater benefits than would have been received if the family had earnings or other income. Moreover, as with all averages, these data mask considerable variation among States. Thus in 1972, 63 percent of the poor lived in counties where AFDC cash benefits and food benefits were $3,000–$5,000 a year (before taxes) for a family of four with no private income; but 32 percent were in counties providing $1,500–$3,000 in benefits, and 5 percent in counties providing over $5,000 in benefits.

Since 1972, AFDC and food program benefit levels have increased. Incorporating increases in benefits for these programs and retaining the same medicaid benefits results in an equivalent taxable income of $5,348 in 1974 and $5,815 in 1975 for the hypothetical female-headed family considered above. This is not high compared to the median income of all families, which was $12,836 in 1974. But on the whole these benefit levels compare favorably with what many women earn. In 1974, women with the same level of education as those on AFDC, but who worked full time, year round, earned $6,175.

As indicated in Table 4–2, the number of families in the AFDC program has increased substantially over time, with the sharpest rise between 1965 and 1971 when the number of AFDC families almost

TABLE 4–2.—*AFDC families, recipients, and cash payments, selected years, 1950–76*

Year	AFDC recipients (thousands)	AFDC families [1]		AFDC cash payments		
		Number (thousands)	Percent of all female-headed families with children	Annual total (millions of current dollars)	Monthly average per recipient [2]	
					Current dollars	December 1975 dollars [3]
1950	2,233	651	51.3	547	21	46
1955	2,192	602	32.2	612	23	49
1960	3,073	803	38.3	994	28	53
1965	4,396	996	40.2	1,644	33	57
1970	9,659	2,394	81.8	4,857	50	70
1971	10,653	2,783	82.7	6,230	52	71
1972	11,069	3,005	83.5	7,020	54	71
1973	10,815	3,068	80.8	7,292	57	68
1974	11,006	3,219	78.9	7,991	65	69
1975	11,389	3,424	77.8	9,349	72	72
1976	11,248	3,408			73	71

[1] Excludes families with unemployed fathers. The number of AFDC families is for December of each year except 1976 which is for June. The percents are based on the number of female-headed families in March of each year except for 1955, which refers to April.
[2] Data are for December of each year except 1976 which are for June.
[3] Deflated by the consumer price index.

Note.—AFDC refers to the Aid to Families with Dependent Children program.

Sources: Department of Health, Education, and Welfare and Department of Commerce (Bureau of the Census).

tripled. Several complex factors seem to have contributed to the program's growth. First, information about the program became widespread, in part because of the efforts of various organizations concerned with poverty. In addition, participation in the program was facilitated by changes which raised the income eligibility standards and liberalized other provisions for eligibility (e.g., residence requirements). As a result, the proportion of families eligible for the program increased, as did the proportion of applicants accepted. The rising level of benefits also made participation more attractive. Between 1965 and 1971, AFDC payments per recipient, adjusted for changes in the consumer price index (CPI), increased by 22 percent, compared with the 10 percent increase in hourly earnings (deflated by the CPI) over the same period. The introduction of medicaid in 1966 and the growing availability of food stamps after 1965 also added to the benefits that could be obtained, particularly since AFDC families gain automatic eligibility for these additional benefits.

After 1971 the rate of increase in the number of AFDC families slowed as a result of several factors. No substantial gains could be achieved from the spread of information, which was already widely disseminated by the early 1970s. There was a slower rate of increase in the combination of real cash and in-kind benefits available to AFDC participants. In addition the liberalization of eligibility provisions that occurred in the 1960s appears to have ended. A few States, including California and Michigan, have instituted programs to locate absent parents who are liable for a child's support. (This type of program is to be made nationwide by the summer of 1976 under the Child Support Program enacted in 1975.)

Since the early 1960s there has been a rapid increase in families headed by a woman with children. It is possible that the rising benefit levels and more liberal standards of eligibility in the AFDC program made it easier for women to form their own households. Studies have found that women tend to form their own households when their earnings opportunities improve, while some respond in a similar fashion to increases in the AFDC stipend. However, AFDC provides an additional incentive for women to remain family heads, since eligibility for AFDC is conditional upon the absence of a husband. This may help explain why women on welfare have been observed to be about half as likely to remarry within a 4-year period as all women heading families with children.

Work Incentives

In response to the rapid growth in the AFDC program various measures were taken to encourage AFDC mothers to work and to become self-supporting. Starting in the early 1960s, training was made available and pecuniary incentives were granted through a modification in the reduction in benefits that occurred when an AFDC participant worked. Prior to this time, in many States, a dollar of benefits was lost for each dollar earned—a 100 percent marginal tax rate on benefits.

The Work Incentive Program (WIN), a result of the 1967 Social Security Amendments, further modified the implicit marginal tax rate—the amount by which benefits would be reduced when earnings increased—by providing that the first $30 of monthly income (net of work-related expenses) be disregarded, after which cash benefits were to be reduced by 67 cents for each additional dollar earned. Some States, however, allow a monthly income disregard greater than $30, and there is also considerable variation between States in allowable deductions for work-related expenses. For these reasons marginal tax rates are discontinuous as income rises and vary substantially between States. On average, however, the effective tax on AFDC cash benefits appears to be considerably below 67 percent, and even after taking account of additional in-kind benefits, the tax on total benefits has fallen below that of the pre-WIN era. By 1972 the study of 100 counties noted above indicated that an AFDC family consisting of a mother with three children could retain, in terms of a gross taxable equivalent, $3,236 in basic AFDC and food stamp benefits out of a potential basic benefit of $4,104, if the mother's earnings were as much as $3,200 for the year, an implicit average tax rate on benefits of 27 percent. If she earned another $800, she would lose $431 in benefits, a 54 percent marginal tax rate.

Additional measures to encourage work among AFDC recipients were introduced as a result of legislation implemented in June 1972. This program, known as WIN II, requires all employable AFDC recipients to register for training or placement services as a condition for receiving welfare payments. AFDC recipients aged 16 or more who are neither disabled nor students under 21 years, and women who do not have a child under 6 years are generally classified as employable. WIN II provides child care services for trainees as well as training, employment placement services, employer subsidies, and public employment. The WIN II program costs were about $314 million in fiscal 1975.

The effect on employment of the various work incentive programs appears to be very slight, although a full evaluation has not been made. Periodic surveys of mothers in the AFDC program have shown that the percentage who were employed fluctuated between 15 and 16 percent from 1961 to 1973 (the latest available data), although the proportion employed full time as opposed to part time has increased. These are low rates of employment compared to those for all women with children, of whom 41 percent were employed in 1973. The percentage of all AFDC mothers who were in the labor force, but unemployed, jumped from 5.7 percent in 1971 to 11.5 percent in 1973 even though

1973 was a year of lower unemployment for the population as a whole. This increase in reported unemployment, which resulted from a change in status from outside the labor force to unemployed, appears to be related to the provisions of WIN II requiring registration for job placement or training.

The weak response to the work incentives introduced over time is likely to have been the net result of different and offsetting factors. There is evidence that AFDC mothers respond to changes in benefit tax rates: holding benefit levels and labor market conditions constant, employment rates are higher in States where the effective benefit tax rate is lower. But the effect is not very strong. It is estimated that, holding other things constant, even with an effective tax rate on benefits of zero, the percentage of the current population of AFDC mothers who would work is unlikely to exceed 25 percent, compared to the 16 percent employed in 1973. However, benefit levels were not held constant during the late 1960s. While the effective tax rate was being reduced, rapidly rising cash and in-kind benefits were increasing the income level available to AFDC participants who did not work. It appears that the negative effect of these rising real benefits on employment almost completely offset the positive effect of lower marginal tax rates.

An increase in employment, it may be noted, would not necessarily lead to a reduction in AFDC participation, since liberalized marginal tax rates make it possible to remain on AFDC with fairly high earnings. The shift to more full-time employment among AFDC mothers does suggest that some AFDC participants, possibly those with higher earnings opportunities, did increase their work effort and remained in the program after an increase in work effort, in response to the lowered tax rates on earned income. On the other hand, a substantial proportion of AFDC mothers, either coming into the program or already there, may have decreased their work activities. Indeed, there is evidence that during the period of increasing work incentives, 1967 to 1970, the largest increases in female heads of families who were economically eligible for AFDC were among those with no earnings and those with earnings above $2,000, with virtually no increase among families in the $0-$2,000 range.

The generally weak work attachment of AFDC mothers would appear to be related to factors which contribute to their being on AFDC in the first place. One factor is their low level of education—in 1973 only 33 percent were at least high school graduates, compared to 71 percent for women 15 to 44 years old with children. Studies have also found a higher incidence of physical and mental disabilities among women on AFDC compared to all women. Thus as indicated above, considering taxes, child care, and other work-related expenses, an unskilled woman with two or more children may well find that the cash and in-kind benefits available through AFDC provide her with nearly as large an income as work.

Several aspects of the AFDC program have led to concern, including the uneven treatment of single-parent and intact families. Some of the disparities between States in AFDC benefit levels and between single-parent and intact families are mitigated by the food stamp program, which is available in all areas and to all families. Because the same schedule determining benefits applies to all localities, low-income families entitled to smaller or no AFDC benefits as a consequence of their State of residence or their family composition are eligible for higher food stamp benefits. Because the basic benefit level provided by food stamps is low and the marginal tax rate on benefits is low, work disincentives from the food stamp program alone are probably not substantial.

AFDC—UF

The AFDC program for unemployed fathers (AFDC–UF) provides aid to intact families with a nondisabled father who is unemployed, as long as other conditions of AFDC eligibility are satisfied. In the 26 States which have elected to participate, the father must have been unemployed for at least 30 days, have had sufficient work experience to satisfy a minimum requirement, be seeking and available for work, and be unemployed or working less than 100 hours per month. In addition, until a June 1975 Supreme Court decision, a family was categorically ineligible for AFDC–UF benefits if the father was eligible for benefits under a Federal or State unemployment compensation program. Most of the approximately 100,000 participating fathers in 1974 and 1975 had exhausted their unemployment compensation benefit entitlement or were in an uncovered sector.

In July 1975, 113,000 families received AFDC–UF benefits and an average monthly cash benefit per family of $311, in addition to categorical eligibility for food stamps and medicaid benefits for dependent family members. There is no limit on the duration of AFDC–UF benefits. The average AFDC–UF cash benefits are about the same as the average monthly benefit to a worker under unemployment compensation; but for low-wage fathers, particularly in families with several children and no other income, AFDC–UF benefits could be substantially greater than unemployment compensation.

The June 1975 decision can be expected to increase AFDC–UF participation. This may create problems because of the potential work disincentives for low-income, intact families. In addition, some of the cost of unemployment will be shifted from the employer-financed trust funds to general Federal and State revenues. However, the opportunity for this aid does provide more ample income maintenance for more low-income, intact families.

From June 1975 to June 1976 the number of families on AFDC–UF increased by 31 percent, from 112,000 to 147,000 families. It is still too early to know the extent to which this increase is due to the broadened eligibility attracting families from unemployment compensation and the extent to which it is due to persons exhausting their unemployment compensation entitlement joining the program.

FOOD PROGRAMS

Concern about hunger or inadequate nutrition has led to the development of an array of programs which supplement income by providing either meals or vouchers to buy food. Benefits from these programs are not counted as income either by the Bureau of the Census in its income and poverty statistics, or in determining eligibility for other income maintenance programs. Spending on the major food programs has increased from $365 million in 1960 to about $6.4 billion in 1975, with the most rapid increases occurring since 1970 (Table 4–3).

Food Stamps

The food stamp program is the largest of these programs. It was set up in 1964 as an alternative to the direct distribution of surplus food commodities. The stated intention was to provide for "improved levels of nutrition among economically needy households." Because of the difficulties in estimating nutritional levels, the effect of the program on the health of the poor has not been established. Food stamps have, however, become an important part of our income maintenance system.

In fiscal 1965 the food stamp and food distribution programs together served a monthly average of 6.2 million people at a total Federal cost of $262 million, or a cost per participant of $41. By calendar 1975, the food stamp program alone served a monthly average of close to 19 million Americans at a total Federal expenditure of about $5 billion and a subsidy per participant of $270. A major factor in the growth of program participation has been its expansion by 1975 to all counties and U.S. territories.

Eligibility for food stamps is based on the "net income" a household expects to receive during the coming month (prospective accounting). A family's net income is its gross income less Federal, State, and local income taxes, social security taxes, retirement contributions, and union dues. Some other allowable deductions are medical expenditures exceeding $10 a month; child care when needed for work; expenses related to fire, theft, or other disasters; educational expenses for tuition and fees; alimony; rent, utilities and mortgage payments above 30 per-

TABLE 4–3.—*Federal food programs, selected fiscal years, 1950–75*

Program	Unit	1950	1960	1965	1970	1974	1975	1976 [1]
Food distribution program for needy families:								
Number of participants...........	Millions [2]	0.2	4.3	5.8	4.1	2.4	0.3	0.1
Federal cost:								
Total.................................	Millions of dollars	6	59	227	289	189	36	11
Per participant.....................	Dollars	24	14	39	70	80	120	110
Food stamp program:								
Number of participants...........	Millions [2]	....	....	.4	4.3	12.9	17.1	18.5
Federal cost:								
Total.................................	Millions of dollars	....	....	35	550	2,728	4,396	5,640
Per participant.....................	Dollars	....	....	76	127	212	257	304
National school lunch program:								
Number of children participating.........................	Millions [3]	8.6	14.1	18.7	23.1	25.0	25.3	25.9
Percent of enrolled children:								
Total number of participants.........................	Percent	34.1	35.0	39.2	44.4	48.7	49.6	51.2
Participants receiving free lunches or lunches at reduced prices.....................	Percent	3.4	3.5	3.9	9.2	18.1	20.7	22.2
Federal cost.........................	Millions of dollars	120	226	403	566	1,377	1,785	1,936
Special milk program:								
Federal cost.........................	Millions of dollars	....	80.3	97.2	101.5	61.4	124.1	143.1
School breakfast program:								
Number of children participating.........................	Thousands [3]	....	....	....	536	1,550	1,993	2,334
Federal cost.........................	Millions of dollars	....	....	....	10.9	70.1	86.1	113.0
Special preschool food service program:								
Number of children participating.........................	Thousands [3]	....	....	....	93.4	346.4	457.1	463.1
Federal cost.........................	Millions of dollars	....	....	....	6.3	30.0	48.8	76.8
Special summer food service program:								
Number of children participating	Thousands [3]	....	....	....	461.9	1,415.2	1,784.7	2,421.6
Federal cost.........................	Millions of dollars	....	....	....	6.5	36.1	50.3	72.4

[1] Preliminary estimate.
[2] Monthly average.
[3] Daily average.

Note.—Federal cost excludes administrative expenses.

Source: Department of Agriculture.

cent of income after all other deductions have been subtracted. A household is excluded if it has liquid assets or certain property valued at $1,500 or more. The asset limitation is $3,000 for households with a member aged 60 years or more. The value of a home, a car, and any other personal effects is not considered in determining eligibility.

The stamps are vouchers which can be used to purchase most food items sold in grocery stores. The stamp allotment for a family is based on the current market cost of the foods that make up the Thrifty Food Plan developed by the Department of Agriculture to meet their nutritional standards. The cost of this food plan, and therefore the food stamp allotment, is equivalent to about 80 percent of expenditures made by the average U.S. consumer for food at home. The allotment is changed twice a year to reflect changes in the price of foods that make up the food plan. The permissible amount of stamps a household can purchase varies with the number of household members. In January 1976, the allotment for a four-person household was $166 a month in food stamps.

The amount a household pays for the stamps depends on its net monthly income. The difference between the food stamp allotment and the purchase price is the "bonus" or Federal subsidy. Families with less than $30 net income pay nothing; that is, their bonus is equivalent to the entire food stamp allotment. Households of four receiving AFDC or SSI are automatically entitled to a monthly subsidy of at least $24 regardless of their income.

On the whole, the food stamp program reaches relatively low-income households (Table 4–4). It is estimated that the benefits have been sufficient to raise the mean income of the recipient families by about 10 percent. The food stamp program, however, has been criticized because it provides income supplements for some who do not have low income, and because it distributes resources in a way that many consider inequitable. The deductions allow some families to qualify who have large discretionary expenditures on items such as housing, education, and child care, while other families with the same income but with different consumption patterns for deductible items do not qualify.

TABLE 4–4.—*Distribution of food stamp households by annual and monthly income, July 1975 and March and July 1976*

Income class	Percent of total food stamp households		
	July 1975	March 1976	July 1976
Annual income [1]:			
Total food stamp households	100.0	100.0	100.0
Less than $6,000	82.8	80.7	83.0
$6,000–$7,499	6.8	7.6	7.4
$7,500–$9,999	5.0	5.6	4.7
$10,000–$11,999	2.5	2.4	2.1
$12,000 and over	2.9	3.7	2.8
Monthly income:			
Total food stamp households	100.0	100.0	100.0
Less than $500	87.7	88.5	91.8
$500–$599	6.1	5.1	3.3
$600–$749	3.2	3.4	2.0
$750–$999	1.9	1.7	1.3
$1,000 and over	1.1	1.3	1.7

[1] Annual income is for 12 months ending in July 1975, March 1976, and July 1976. Households include single-person households. Annual income shown here may be understated compared to data derived from more detailed surveys of income.

Note.—Detail may not add to totals because of rounding.

Sources: Department of Commerce (Bureau of the Census) and Department of Health, Education, and Welfare.

Another important inequity follows from determining eligibility on the basis of income in a single month. As a result, some households qualify during a portion of the year, although their income over the year as a whole is sufficiently high to exclude them by any comparable annual standard (Table 4–4). For example, while only 1 percent of households in the program had a monthly income of $1,000 in July 1975, 3 percent had annual incomes of $12,000 over the year ending in July 1975.

Because of the 1-month accounting period, the food stamp program provides benefits to both the long-term poor and those whose incomes are temporarily low because of unemployment, sickness, a strike, or other reasons. The food stamp program provides countercyclical income maintenance benefits for the unemployed and participation rises with seasonal unemployment. Although the family income of many of the unemployed may be low enough to qualify for food stamps during a month of unemployment, their income over a longer accounting period, covering months with employment, may be substantially above the food stamp eligibility level. The annual income of food stamp recipients in March 1976 was higher than in July 1975 or July 1976, partly because March was a month of high cyclical as well as seasonal unemployment.

In 1975, President Ford proposed legislation for reforming the program. The proposal would change the method of determining eligibility by averaging actual income received over the past 90 days, rather than using the applicant's estimate of next month's income. It is estimated that the change from prospective to retrospective monthly accounting would save about 5 percent of the program's cost because of a better reporting of income. Lengthening the accounting period would save an estimated additional 4 percent of program costs, since families with high income over 90 days, but temporarily low monthly income, will not participate. Families with a 90-day income just above eligibility levels would quickly qualify in the event that their income deteriorated. Families whose usual incomes are sufficiently high that they would not qualify if their income declined for only 1 month are more likely to have assets that they can draw upon.

Another proposed change is to replace the present itemized deduction for determining net income with a single standard deduction of $100 a month, except for households with a member 60 years old or more, when the deduction would be $125 a month. As a result of the standard deduction, some families will be ineligible who now qualify because of large expenditures on certain deductible items. However, the deduction of $100 is higher than the present total deduction for the average family. This will benefit families with low incomes who formerly did not have many itemized expenditures.

There had been substantial concern that youths from high-income families were qualifying for food stamps while they were away from home at a college or university. A new regulation requires that when a student's parents claim him as a deduction on their Federal income tax, the family, not the student himself, is the relevant filing unit for food stamp purposes. In addition, the proposed changes from itemized deductions, including school fees and tuition, to a standard deduction will provide a more equitable treatment of families.

[The Ford proposal was not enacted. Most proposals for food stamp reform have included provisions which eliminate or reduce the number of itemized deductions and which use past income, whether for one month or longer, rather than expected income, to determine eligibility. Some proposals, like the Ford proposal, restrict the program to those with incomes below the poverty line. Depending on the specific structure of the program this could cause a discontinuity in the schedule relating additional income to the food stamp bonus and could have substantial work disincentive effects for individuals in that income range. Another feature of some proposals is to eliminate the purchase requirement for food stamps. This would have the effect of making the food stamp subsidy closer to cash and would probably encourage participation among those in the upper end of the eligible income range who now receive small bonuses, but face relatively large purchase requirements.]

Food Programs for Schoolchildren

The Federal Government provided about $2 billion in fiscal 1975 in subsidies for meals provided to children in nursery, primary, and secondary schools, and in some summer programs. These programs are implicitly based on the two presumptions that an adequate diet for children is important for their ability to learn and that many children are not able to obtain a nutritionally adequate diet at home.

In 1947 the Government contributed 8.2 cents in cash and 1.1 cent in commodities for each lunch served to any child, regardless of income. About 25 percent of all schoolchildren participated in the program, of whom about 12 percent received a free lunch subsidized by State and local sources. Until the middle 1960s, program growth was due mainly to increases in school enrollments and less to increases in participation rates. The Federal share in funding dropped during the period, while State, local, and student shares increased.

Starting in 1970 the Federal Government began additional subsidies to the lunch program targeted to children from lower-income families. As a result, the share of Federal funds increased sharply, and the percentage of students in the school lunch program increased. In fiscal 1976 the Federal Government contributes 12.5 cents in a cash grant and 11 cents in a commodity grant to all school lunches, regardless of the family income of the children. In addition, the Federal Government contributes almost 57 cents per lunch in cash for children who receive a free lunch and 47 cents for children receiving lunch at a reduced price.

The lunch program provides a free lunch to children from families whose income is at or below 125 percent of the poverty threshold. In 1974, about 17 percent of all schoolchildren received a free lunch.

Several new and potentially expensive programs have been introduced recently to expand the child nutrition programs. The Government school breakfast program is one example. It now provides an average subsidy of 31.4 cents per breakfast. If all eligible students participated, the annual cost would be $0.9 billion. Another is the Federal subsidy of 75.5 cents per lunch and supper provided to summer camps and day care institutions on the condition that the children come from an area defined as one where at least 33⅓ percent of the children are eligible for free or reduced-price school meals. Since 38 percent is the national average, a substantial proportion of institutions will qualify for the subsidy, regardless of the family income of the participating children.

Legislation enacted in 1975 would further increase Federal expenditures on the programs. Eligibility for the reduced-price lunch was extended to 195 percent of the poverty line (the equivalent of an income of $9,800 for a nonfarm family of four, using the 1974 poverty threshold), and it was made mandatory that all schools receiving Federal lunch money provide such a program. As a result, about 38 percent of children would become eligible for a free or reduced-price lunch. Participation is also likely to increase because of the mandatory provisions of the program. As a result of the new legislation, Federal expenditures are expected to increase by $0.5 billion more in fiscal 1977 than the $2.3 billion that was anticipated under the old legislation.

It is estimated that 31 percent of the Federal expenditures of $1.8 billion on the programs went to children from families above 125 percent of the poverty line in 1975. In addition, there is duplication of Federal benefits, with different programs subsidizing the same meal.

[The rationale for the child nutrition programs is that American children (including the non-poor) suffer from nutritional deficiencies because of improper diets in the home. There is no evidence, however, of widespread health deficiencies related to poor diets. Many of the studies that have been made suffer from methodological difficulties. For example, they often compare the nutrients of the food on the school lunch tray with those in the brown bag brought from home. But food put on the school lunch tray may be less likely to be eaten than food brought from home, and account must also be taken of what is eaten the rest of the day. The few studies which actually examine biochemical tests of blood samples or make other physical tests find no significant difference between those who eat school lunches and those who do not. In spite of the lack of scientific evidence that the programs fill a real nutritional need, the child nutrition programs have grown to provide ever larger subsidies to higher and higher income families.]

ISSUES IN WELFARE REFORM

[The welfare system has been described in "crisis" terms for the past ten years or so. Aspects of the system have been criticized by different groups, although not always for the same reasons, and the nature of the criticism and the perceived solutions for the problems have changed over the past few years.

In the late 1960s the rapid increase in the number of recipients and in program costs made AFDC the most controversial program, and the major target of public concern. Some objected to it simply because it had become large and included families that some taxpayers did not regard as needy. Others saw serious problems of equity in that benefits vary considerably among the States and are confined to families with children headed by a woman or a disabled man, or in some States, by an unemployed father. Families whose heads are working males are not eligible for AFDC benefits, even if their incomes are low enough to qualify. This aspect of the program had been viewed as not only inequitable, but also as leading to the breakup of families—breakups which may be real, or feigned in order for the wife and children to qualify for benefits.

In response to growing public concern over these issues and following a five-year period of extraordinary growth in the AFDC program, President Nixon proposed in 1969, as a complete reform of public assistance, a new program to be known as the Family Assistance Plan (FAP). A modified form of the President's proposal was passed in the House of Representatives twice (most recently in June 1971) but failed to pass in the Senate. The proposed legislation, H.R. 1, was a variant of what is often called a negative income tax.

Generally, a negative income tax is an extension of the positive income tax system whereby a portion of each additional dollar of income earned (the proportion is the marginal tax rate) is paid to the Government in taxes. Under the negative income tax, payments flow from the Government to individuals with qualifying low incomes. However, with each additional dollar of income earned a portion of the Government benefit is taken away. The fraction of benefits thus removed is the marginal tax rate to benefit recipients. Under a negative income tax, the Federal Government would fund and administer the basic welfare program, benefits would be uniform among the States, families with an employed male head would be eligible, and the demeaning notion of "welfare" would be replaced by a modification of the income tax system in which everyone participates.

For these reasons the concept of a negative income tax was appealing. As the idea was put into legislative form, however, numerous practical problems arose. These problems ultimately led to the defeat of H.R. 1 and have deterred any further legislative efforts at massive welfare reform.

One of the basic problems of a negative income tax scheme is that if all families confront the same benefit schedule, serious work incentive problems may arise and program costs may become prohibitive. For families in which the adults could not be expected to work on any consistent basis, it is important that the basic benefit (the full benefit when other income is zero) be set at a level which adequately provides for subsistence. For such families, a high marginal tax rate on earnings would not have a large disincentive effect on work since work effort could not be substantial in any case. Included in this type of family for whom the issues of work are not important are the female-headed families that now form the basis of the AFDC program. As a result of poor occupational skills, which limit earnings, and the high costs of child care, work is most often not a prudent option for the AFDC mother. The disabled and elderly poor, now covered by social security and supplemental security income (SSI), also fit into this category.

For intact families, where one adult can be expected to work, the guarantee of an adequate basic benefit combined with a high marginal tax rate could create strong disincentives to earn an income. If, to take an example, the basic benefit were $5,000 and the marginal tax rate 60 percent, the net gain from earning $8,000 (versus having no earnings) would be only $3,200.[1]

The work disincentive could be weakened with lower marginal tax rates. However, for the same basic benefit, a lower marginal tax rate substantially increases program costs because benefits would be received further up in the income distribution where the density of families is greater. For example, with a $5,000 basic benefit and a 60 percent marginal tax, benefits would cease when earnings reach $8,333; but with the same basic benefit and a 30 percent marginal tax, benefits would cease only when earnings were as high as $16,667. There could, however, be a 30 percent tax and an income cut off of, say, $10,000. This would create a notch at $10,000, with $2,000 in benefits received if annual earnings are $9,999 and zero benefits if earnings were $1 higher. The effect on work incentives for those near the notch would be substantial.

1. The basic benefit is reduced by 60 cents for each dollar earned. Hence, $0.6 \times$ $8,000 yields a total benefit reduction of $4,800 leaving $200 of benefits.

Thus, a negative income tax that provides a uniform schedule for all families and that provides an adequate basic benefit for those who cannot work, would have either very strong work disincentives for those from whom work can be expected, or it could cover a substantial proportion of the population and thus be very expensive. The proposed legislation, H.R. 1, tried to deal with the work incentive issue through work requirements. Recipients of benefits would be divided into employables and unemployables, with the latter including the disabled and mothers of young children (defined as under 3 years old) heading families. Penalties were to be imposed on employable adults who did not register for work or training. Those with earnings were to be subject to a marginal tax rate of 67 percent. The basic benefit was to be $2,400 for a family of four which at that time would have been above the level provided to welfare families in some States, although lower in others.

The need for a complicated administrative mechanism to supervise the work requirement and the fear that these work requirements would not really counter the work disincentives inherent in the program, or keep the scope of the public assistance bill to the nation within bounds, helped defeat H.R. 1. Moreover, many felt that the basic benefit was too low for those families who could not be expected to earn any supplementary income. There were also second thoughts about the wisdom of a uniform benefit in all States. There is a generally held belief that there are regional differences in the cost of living, although the problems of constructing regional price indexes preclude any reliable estimates of the differentials that could be used to adjust benefits.[2] Regional differences also exist in what people perceive to be a low standard of living.

Recently, students of our welfare system have begun to raise the question of whether the present welfare structure is not, after all, an acceptable alternative, at least in its basic outlines. Since 1971, the food stamp program has been expanded to cover all counties of the United States and now provides a basic minimum guarantee to all families and individuals, subject only to their access to income and assets. Because the basic benefit is fairly low, as is the marginal tax rate (roughly 30 percent), the Federal food stamp program in itself is not believed to produce strong work disincentives. AFDC-type families (low-income, female-headed households) are eligible for AFDC, food stamps, medicaid, public housing and other benefits, have a higher basic benefit, and face effectively higher marginal tax rates from the multiple benefits. However, work is generally not a feasible option for this group.

2. A basic problem is that the market basket of goods consumed varies considerably, particularly between urban and rural places, and the index would be very sensitive to the particular market basket chosen.

In 1974, the Federally operated and funded Supplemental Security Income (SSI) program replaced the State programs for the poor who are aged, blind and disabled. Although originally SSI recipients were categorically ineligible for food stamp benefits, since SSI was designed to incorporate them, this restriction was soon removed. By combining SSI, food stamps, medicaid and other programs, the low income, aged, blind, and disabled from whom work effort is not expected also have a higher basic benefit and marginal tax rate than able bodied intact families.

Thus, by dealing separately with different groups, the programs may be better tailored to their individual requirements. Moreover, while food stamps provide a uniform benefit in all States, AFDC medicaid and State supplementation under SSI provide variation in benefits controlled by State concepts.

This discussion is not intended to suggest that the current structure of categorical programs is ideal. There are major administrative problems of program coordination. There are also problems in determining eligibility, such as accounting for assets, measuring income (e.g., over how long a period should income be averaged?), verifying the number of dependents, and determining the financial responsibility of absent parents. All of these problems, however, would remain under a negative income tax, although program coordination would be eased.[3] What this discussion does suggest is that when the basic programs are viewed as part of an overall welfare system, there is more inherent logic and internal consistency than had been believed.]

THE MITIGATING EFFECTS OF THE INCOME TRANSFER SYSTEM IN THE 1974/1975 RECESSION

Unemployment compensation and other income maintenance programs have had an important dual role as automatic stabilizers and as a means of providing income to those who have lost earnings because of a recession.[4] This was very clear during the 1974–1975 recession. Data on the effects of the major programs during this recession are given in Table 4–5.

Largely because of these programs, per capita real disposable income

3. Since it is unlikely that some of the in-kind programs, such as medicaid and child nutrition, would be "cashed out" under a negative income tax, problems of program coordination would still persist.

4. Automatic stabilizers are programs that provide increased benefits as unemployment increases or incomes decline without requiring additional legislation or changes in regulations. They therefore tend to counter the fall in aggregate demand that accompanies a recession.

Income Distribution

TABLE 4–5.—*Income transfer programs, 1974–76*

Program	Unit	1974 IV	1975 I	1975 II	1975 III	1975 IV	1976 I	1976 II	1976 III	1976 IV
Unemployment:										
Total number of persons	Millions	5.6	8.3	8.0	7.8	7.2	7.9	6.9	7.3	7.0
Unemployment Compensation:										
Beneficiaries: Total	Millions [1]	2.3	5.1	5.5	5.3	4.8	5.2	4.3	3.9	3.6
Permanent programs	do	2.3	4.7	4.8	4.0	3.5	4.1	3.2	2.8	2.8
FSB and SUA [2]	do		.4	.7	1.2	1.3	1.1	1.1	1.1	0.8
Benefit payments: Total [3]	Billions of dollars [4]	7.8	17.3	19.0	18.4	17.6	20.6	16.0	13.3	
Permanent programs	do	7.8	16.2	16.7	14.7	13.2	15.6	12.2	11.1	
FSB and SUA	do		1.1	2.3	3.7	4.4	5.0	3.8	2.2	
Food Stamp Program:										
Beneficiaries	Millions [5]	15.9	18.6	19.2	18.6	18.5	18.8	18.2	17.3	17.2
Benefit payments	Billions of dollars [4]	4.0	4.9	5.0	5.2	5.1	5.6	5.4	5.1	5.0
Aid to Families with Dependent Children:										
Beneficiaries: Total	Millions [5]	10.9	11.3	11.3	11.3	11.4	11.5	11.3	11.2	11.2
Unemployed fathers	do	.4	.5	.5	.5	.6	.7	.7	.6	.6
Benefit payments [3]	Billions of dollars [4]	8.4	8.9	8.9	9.3	9.8	10.1	9.9	10.0	10.0
Old-age, Survivors and Disability Insurance:										
Beneficiaries: Total [6]	Millions [5]	30.7	31.1	31.1	31.5	31.9	32.3	32.4	32.6	32.9
Retired workers and dependents	do	19.6	19.8	19.9	20.1	20.3	20.5	20.5	20.6	20.9
Disabled workers and dependents	do	3.9	4.0	4.1	4.2	4.3	4.4	4.5	4.5	4.6
Benefit payments [7]	Billions of dollars [4]	56.8	60.6	63.0	67.1	68.3	69.4	71.4	75.6	76.8
Medicaid:										
Beneficiaries	Millions [5]	8.2	8.8	9.0	8.7	9.0	9.4	9.3	9.1	8.9
Benefit payments	Billions of dollars [4]	11.9	13.4	14.3	13.7	14.6	15.3	15.3	15.8	15.8
Medicare:										
Benefit payments	Billions of dollars [4]	13.7	14.9	15.4	15.5	16.5	17.3	18.3	18.6	19.4
Supplemental Security Income:										
Beneficiaries	Millions [5]	4.0	4.1	4.2	4.3	4.3	4.3	4.3	4.3	4.3
Benefit payments	Billions of dollars [3], [4]	5.5	5.6	5.6	5.9	6.0	6.0	6.0	6.2	6.2

[1] Weekly average.
[2] Federal supplemental benefits (FSB) and special unemployment assistance (SUA).
[3] Includes State as well as Federal payments.
[4] Annual rate.
[5] Monthly average.
[6] Total also includes survivors.
[7] In current payment status.

Sources: Department of Agriculture, Department of Health, Education, and Welfare, and Department of Labor.

did not decline in 1975 despite a decline in real output per capita. Because the number and size of countercyclical programs have increased over time, the extent to which consumer income was maintained was greater in this recession than in past ones. In this recession, per capita real disposable income fell from peak to trough by one-half of 1 percent, compared to a drop of 4 percent in per capita real disposable income net of transfers. By contrast, in the 1958 recession per capita real disposable income fell by 2 percent from peak to trough, while per capita real disposable income net of transfers declined 3 percent.

The extent to which transfer payments replace family earnings lost as a result of unemployment varies with eligibility for the different programs as well as with past earnings. It has been estimated for 1975 that a family of four, headed by an insured unemployed worker who had previously worked at the minimum wage, could be entitled to about 90 percent of previous after-tax earnings through unemployment compensation, public assistance, and food stamps. For a head of family who had earned high wages, however, benefits replace a smaller percentage of after-tax earnings. For example, it has been estimated that an unemployed worker who earned $400 a week before taxes could receive benefits that replace about one-third of his after-tax earnings.

The most important countercyclical program is unemployment compensation, which in the first 10 months of 1975 paid an estimated average weekly benefit of about $70 per worker. As of January 1976, the maximum weekly benefit ranged from $60 in Indiana and Mississippi to $139 in Washington, D.C. As unemployment increased during the recession, the ratio of beneficiaries to persons unemployed rose sharply, from 33 percent in the fourth quarter of 1973 to 69 percent in the second quarter of 1975. This pattern is partly due to changes in the composition of unemployment that usually occur during a downturn and partly to legislated program extensions (FSB and SUA). Largely because of these new programs a larger proportion of the unemployed received benefits in 1975 than in any prior recession. The new programs have therefore more than offset the secular decline in the proportion of the unemployed receiving benefits (estimated to be 40 percent in 1956 and 34 percent in 1973), a decline which is attributable to the disproportionate increase in the share of unemployment caused by entry into the labor force. The proportion of the unemployed receiving benefits was estimated to be 59 percent in 1958 and 66 percent in the first 3 quarters of 1975.

In the second quarter of 1975 there were about 19.2 million food stamp recipients, 54 percent more than in the fourth quarter of 1973. Approximately half the increase is attributable to the recession and half to the extension of the program to areas which had not previously offered food stamps (including Puerto Rico, which added 1.5 million new recipients) and to increases in participation among formerly eligible households. A survey taken by the Bureau of the Census in April 1975 showed that 18 percent of the families in which the head of the household was unemployed were receiving food stamps. Among families with an unemployed head of household and income under $5,000, 35 percent received stamps. The average monthly food stamp bonus (the Federal subsidy), which is not taxed as income, was $84 for families with an unemployed head of household.

TABLE 4–6.—*Proportion of families having transfer income from particular sources, 1970*

Income class [1]	Percent of families in each income class with transfer payments			
	Total	Social security and railroad retirement	Public assistance [2]	Other [3]
All families	38	24	7	15
Under $1,000	41	27	13	3
$1,000–$1,999	77	60	24	8
$2,000–$2,999	72	55	19	17
$3,000–$3,999	60	43	12	17
$4,000–$4,999	50	35	9	17
$5,000–$5,999	42	27	5	19
$6,000–$6,999	35	21	4	16
$7,000–$7,999	30	16	3	17
$8,000–$9,999	29	14	3	17
$10,000–$14,999	26	11	2	17
$15,000–$24,999	24	11	1	16
$25,000 and over	22	12	1	12

[1] Family income is family money income including transfer income in cash.
[2] Public assistance includes AFDC and assistance to the aged, blind, and disabled.
[3] Includes unemployment compensation, workmen's compensation, government employee pensions, veterans' benefits, and unidentified transfer payments.

Source: Department of Health, Education, and Welfare (Social Security Administration).

INCOME DISTRIBUTION EFFECTS
OF MONEY TRANSFER PROGRAMS

The Federal Government's cash income transfer programs affect the money incomes of families. Comparisons between these money transfer payments and the total money income of families show the income redistribution effects of the transfers. How participation in the labor market and family formation are affected by money transfers is an important issue, but too little is known at the present time to quantify what the distribution of family income would be if there were no transfers.

Money Transfers

As the data in Table 4–6 indicate, 38 percent of the families reported receiving some transfer payments in 1970.[5] Social security and railroad retirement benefits were the most common form of transfer and were received by 24 percent of the families. Public assistance went to 7 percent of the families; both unemployment compensation and veterans' benefits were paid to approximately 5 percent of the families. Only 7 percent of money income was derived from transfers. The average

5. 1970 was a year of moderate unemployment (4.9 percent). The data do not include in-kind transfers, including the bonus value of food stamps. [Editors]

transfer per family was $696, of which 56.6 percent was from social security, 13.1 percent from public assistance, and 30.2 percent from other sources.

The higher the income, the smaller the proportion of families receiving a transfer. The percentage of income in each group derived from government transfers was also lower for higher levels of income. For example, those with incomes between $1,000 and $1,999 received an average of 68 percent of their income from transfers, but only 3 percent of the income in the $15,000 to $24,999 range was derived from transfers. Low-income families had approximately twice the dollar value of transfers that high-income families had. Except for the lowest two income groups, however, the mean income from government transfers for those who received transfer income was largely invariant with family income after transfers. High-income families receive a small proportion of their total income from government transfers, not because of a smaller dollar transfer per recipient, but because they have more income from other sources (earnings and property income) and fewer among them receive transfer income.

Public assistance is specifically designed to provide income supplements for those who would otherwise have little income. Since public assistance is heavily concentrated in the lowest income groups and the benefits per recipient are a very large fraction of the income of the poor, public assistance has a strong income redistribution effect. Social security and railroad retirement payments are largely received by aged families and younger families headed by a widow. Although these families tend to have low current income, the benefits are larger for those who had higher earnings in the past.

The target populations for the other forms of transfer payments, that is, the unemployed, those injured on the job, retired Government employees, and veterans, are not necessarily poor. Except for the lowest and highest income groups, approximately 17 percent of the families in each group received funds in 1970 from one or more of these four sources. Again except for the extremes of the distribution, there is virtually no change in dollar benefits per recipient for higher-income groups. The higher the other income of the family, the smaller the proportion of income derived from such benefits. These transfers have a mild income redistribution effect.

Within the category of other payments, unemployment compensation is more important for middle-income families ($4,000 to $15,000) than for the poorest and wealthiest of families. The members of the poorest families ordinarily have too little work experience to qualify for unemployment compensation. The income earners in the highest-income families have lower rates of unemployment.

TABLE 4–7.—*The effect of money transfers on family income inequality, 1970*

Type of income	Income inequality [1]
All income	0. 74
All, excluding "other" transfers [2]	. 77
All, excluding social security	1. 16
All, excluding public assistance [3]	. 85
All, excluding social security and public assistance [3]	1. 45
All, excluding all transfer income	1. 57

[1] Income inequality is measured by the variance in the natural log of income. (See Supplement to this chapter).
[2] "Other" transfers include unemployment benefits, workmen's compensation, government employee pensions, and veterans benefits. The income classes used were: Under $2,000; $2,000–$2,999; $3,000–$3,999; $4,000–$4,999; $5,000–$5,999; $6,000–$6,999; $7,000–$7,999; $8,000–$9,999; $10,000–$14,999; $15,000–$24,999; and $25,000 and over.
[3] Public assistance includes AFDC and assistance to the aged, blind, and disabled.

Sources: Department of Health, Education, and Welfare (Social Security Administration) and Council of Economic Advisers.

Income Inequality Before and After the Transfers

Table 4–7 presents a measure of income inequality, the variance in the natural logarithm of income, for family money income and family money income minus particular transfers (see supplement to Chapter 1). This permits a determination of the extent to which the different types of transfers reduce income inequality. Such an approach implicitly assumes that the transfers do not give rise to labor market or family formation responses by the recipients. The data suggest that social security and public assistance dramatically decreased the measured relative inequality of family income. The combined effect of the other transfers is a small decrease in income inequality.

The Tax Transfer System

The success of the Government's programs for the redistribution of income cannot be judged from any one program or from an examination of taxes or transfers separately. Primarily because of public assistance, social security, medicaid, and food stamps, the transfer system is highly progressive in redistributing income to low-income families. It was shown above (Chapter 1) that the net effect of personal income and payroll taxes on cash and imputed income appears to be progressive. Several studies have examined the effect of the tax system on the distribution of income when accrued capital gains and losses are included in the income concept. These studies suggest that the tax system is roughly proportional over the income intervals in which most families belong, regressive for those with very low incomes, and progressive at the upper end. However, the combined direct effects of the tax and transfer systems clearly appear to be progressive.

Part II

Unemployment

THE EMPLOYMENT ACT OF 1946, which created the Council of Economic Advisers, set forth the goal of maintaining "maximum employment." The extent to which this objective is achieved is usually measured by the unemployment rate, which has come to serve as a measure of the extent of resource underutilization in the economy. For many it is also a measure of economic and social hardship.

Part II examines the various types of unemployment and unemployment rates at different points in time and among demographic groups. It also looks at the welfare implications of unemployment, and at Government measures to ameliorate the difficulties caused by unemployment.

It is important to emphasize, because the point is often misunderstood, that to analyze unemployment is not to provide excuses for it or deny the personal and social problems associated with it. The unemployment of persons who seek work is costly to the workers themselves, their families, and the Nation as a whole. Our goal should be to reduce unemployment whenever this can be done by means which are not more costly than the unemployment itself. It is therefore important to understand the different kinds of unemployment so that the effectiveness of alternative Government policies can be properly evaluated. Part II can be viewed as a guide to the formulation of constructive policies toward unemployment over the long run.

Unemployment is not as simple a concept as is often believed. The meaning of any particular unemployment rate depends on the way unemployment is defined and measured, and on the sources and composition of the unemployment. Although it is generally clear when we are at points of very high unemployment and widespread underutilization of productive capacity, it is much more difficult to determine when we are at "maximum employment." The unemployment rates in 1974 to 1976 clearly represent a substantial departure from maximum employment. At the other extreme, under current definitions, a zero rate of unemployment is impossible to attain, and efforts to do so would have undesirable consequences. Although the period following World

War II was one of rapid economic growth and rising levels of real income, the unemployment rate averaged 4.7 percent from 1947 through 1973. Only during World War II (1944), when 17 percent of the total labor force were in the Armed Forces, did the rate ever fall close to 1 percent. An understanding of the issues related to unemployment is needed to determine the extent to which a particular rate is too high, or when the goal of maximum employment is attained.

[In Chapter 5 unemployment is defined and the sources and nature of unemployment are discussed. This includes a discussion of the Phillips curve trade-off between inflation and unemployment and a comparison of unemployment rates in the United States with those in other developed economies. The distribution of unemployment among demographic groups is the subject of Chapter 6. Unemployment rates are analyzed by age, sex, race, ethnicity, and other characteristics. It concludes with a section on the relation between unemployment and poverty. The unemployment compensation system is described in Chapter 7, with particular emphasis given to the discussion of the incentive effects of the program. Chapter 8 presents a paper prepared by the CEA for the Joint Economic Committee on the effects of specific programs, such as public service employment, public works and an employment tax credit, in reducing unemployment in a recession. The likely effects are compared to that of a reduction in personal and corporate income taxes.]

CHAPTER 5

The Definition and Nature of Unemployment

The major source of information on unemployment is a monthly Government survey of about 47,000 households, the Current Population Survey or CPS. The survey includes detailed questions about the labor force status of household members aged 16 and over, with the object of identifying those who are employed, unemployed, or out of the labor force.

Persons are classified as employed if during the survey week they did any work as a paid employee or in their own enterprise, of if they worked 15 hours or more as an unpaid employee in a family enterprise. Those temporarily absent from jobs because of labor-management disputes, bad weather, vacation, or illness and other personal reasons are counted as employed, regardless of whether they were paid during the week.

Persons are classified as unemployed if they were not employed during the survey week but were available for work and had made a specific effort to find a job at some time within the preceding 4 weeks, or if they were waiting either to report to a new job within 30 days or to be recalled to a job from which they were laid off.

The civilian labor force is the sum of those who are employed (excluding the Armed Forces) and those who are unemployed. The unemployment rate commonly reported is the number of unemployed persons as a percentage of the civilian labor force.

The unemployment rate is, of course, a function of the specific definitions used and the manner in which the questionnaire is administered. For example, in 1967 it was first stipulated that unemployment should include those seeking work at any time during the preceding 4-week period rather than the previously implied 1-week period. This change in definition is believed to have increased the measured unemployment rate of women, because many women are on the margin between being out of the labor force and unemployed. The unemployment rate may also be affected by the expedient of relying on only one adult member of the household to report for all members. The respondent may not be accurately informed about the jobs held or sought by all household members. There is, for example, some evidence from special surveys that teenagers give a different impression of their unemployment and labor force participation when they respond directly to the survey.

SOURCES AND NATURE OF UNEMPLOYMENT

Unemployment has served aspects that shift in relative importance from time to time. Some portion of unemployment is cyclical; that is, it is associated with the business cycle. Other unemployment is primarily a consequence of frictional, structural, and seasonal factors. These components of unemployment are analytical concepts and are difficult to identify empirically. It is nevertheless important to understand their differing nature.

FRICTIONAL UNEMPLOYMENT

The economy always generates a considerable amount of unemployment resulting from the multiplicity of random events that occur in labor markets. Such unemployment arises partly as a by-product of normal economic change—the closing of some firms, a slowdown in others, the opening and expansion of still others, and changing production techniques within firms. Partly in response to these changes, some workers are laid off and others quit or enter or reenter the labor force. Many become unemployed during this process because the matching of workers to the changing job openings is seldom accomplished instantaneously. Unemployment may also arise as a by-product of personal considerations, quite independent of the fortunes of firms. Thus, events such as the completion of school or of service in the Armed Forces and the lessening of household responsibilities often lead to a movement into the labor force. A preference for a different job environment or geographic area also frequently results in job change, as does an employer's dissatisfaction with a worker's performance.

There is substantial turnover among both the employed and the unemployed. Employment in 1973 averaged 84 million persons per month, but about 100 million different persons worked at some time during the year. Similarly, unemployment averaged 4 million persons per month in 1973, while at least 14 million persons experienced some unemployment in the year. About one-fourth of all those holding jobs in January 1973 had begun their job during the preceding 12 months.

Job loss is usually taken to be an involuntary separation, and quitting a voluntary one. During 1974, 43 percent of the unemployed cited job loss as the immediate reason for unemployment; 15 percent said they had quit their jobs; but 42 percent had just entered or reentered the labor force. In 1973, a year of lower unemployment, the percentage citing job loss was smaller, 39 percent; and the percentage citing quits, or labor force entry or reentry, was greater, 16 percent and 46 percent respectively. Thus, while separation from a job accounts for much unemployment, a similar amount is often the by-product of movement into the labor force.

Entering the labor force usually entails search for a job. Since entrants are by definition not working at a paid job (though they may be fully employed in a real sense as students or housewives), they will usually be counted as unemployed, unless they found a job before becoming technically available for work. Starting in the 1950's the composition of the labor force began to change as middle-aged married women increased their participation. Since the 1960's the increasing tendency of younger married women to work, and the increase in the teenage labor force because of the post-World War II "baby boom," resulted in rapid increases in the size of the labor force and in the proportion of the labor force comprised of teenagers and married women aged 20 or over (from 20 percent of the labor force in 1950 to 31 percent in 1974). Both groups have relatively high rates of labor force entry and reentry because of school or home responsibilities. As a result, labor force entrants and reentrants have probably accounted for an increasing proportion of the labor force and of the unemployed during the post-World War II period, and hence for a higher level of frictional unemployment. The unemployment of entrants and reentrants, however, is not always entirely frictional. For example, during a recession one sees a cyclical component in the unemployment of entrants and reentrants that is reflected by longer duration.

In a dynamic economy, wage rates, skill requirements, and other job characteristics are constantly changing. As such changes occur, the information about the labor market that people have acquired depreciates in value. Because it takes time to acquire new and useful information, instantaneous job change is seldom feasible. Individuals looking for more rewarding work and firms looking for more productive employees invest time and other resources in the search process. Thus job mobility and the ensuing frictional unemployment are essential consequences of economic change. To the extent that job mobility increases economic efficiency through a better matching of workers and jobs, it helps promote economic growth.

This is not to say, however, that the actual amount of frictional unemployment necessarily equals the optimal amount required to promote efficient economic growth. That is, it is not known whether labor markets in a private enterprise economy will allocate an optimal amount of resources to the dissemination of job information. Periodic surveys in which workers are asked how they located their current job always show that informal sources of information, such as friends and relatives, are more important than such formal sources as private and public employment agencies. Informal networks seem to provide detail about the tangible and intangible characteristics of job vacancies and of job applicants that workers and firms value highly. Because such detail is much less readily obtained through formal channels, it has been difficult for the Government to devise improvements over the existing system.

STRUCTURAL UNEMPLOYMENT

Even during periods of low unemployment, some groups have persistently high unemployment that tends to be of long duration, occurring either in a single spell or in a sequence of spells. Such unemployment is often referred to as structural, in contrast to frictional unemployment, which tends to be of shorter duration, although there is no hard and fast line between these two classifications.

Structural unemployment represents imperfect labor market adjustment as a result of some barrier to the mobility of resources. For example, the high unemployment in Appalachia during the 1950's and 1960's was initially a consequence of a decline in the demand for coal and of union wages and fringe benefits that were pushed substantially above the competitive level, and thus led to greater mechanization. The resources of the region were not readily adaptable to other industries, and the personal and financial costs of moving to a different area, combined with a chance of obtaining a high-paying job in Appalachia, impeded migration from the region. Since then, the migration out of the region by younger workers, the retirement of older workers, and the improvement of transportation systems which facilitated the development of new industries have dramatically reduced the unemployment rate in Appalachia. As a result, although the unemployment rate in the Appalachian region was 8.6 percent in 1962 compared to the national rate of 5.5 percent, by 1971 it had fallen to 5.9 percent—the same as the national unemployment rate.[1]

The high unemployment rate of teenagers and of workers with little skill may also be partly attributable to structural factors, but of a different sort. In 1974 the unemployment rate of teenagers aged 16 to 19 was 14 percent for white youths and 33 percent for black youths, compared to 3.8 percent for all males aged 20 and over. These higher rates may to some extent result from such artificial barriers to wage rate adjustment as legislated minimum wages; in this sense they can be said to have structural elements. The Federal minimum wage was raised to $2.30 per hour as of January 1976 for workers covered by the legisla-

1. More recently, the increased demand for coal as a substitute for oil, whose price increased sharply since late 1973, has increased employment and income in Appalachia. [Editors]

tion before 1966—mainly construction, manufacturing and transportation workers and employees of large retail firms. For workers who were first covered under the 1966 or subsequent legislation, mainly some agricultural workers, domestics, and employees of small retail chains, the minimum wage is slightly lower.[2] Some employment not covered by the Federal minimum wage is covered by various State and local legislation. In some instances, State and local minimums exceed the Federal level. For example, in 1975 when the Federal minimum wage was $2.10 per hour the minimum wage in the District of Columbia was $2.50 per hour in some industries. Other legislation adds to the minimum cost of employing a low-wage worker by requiring, for example, employers' expenditures for social security, unemployment insurance, and workers' compensation insurance.

Some adults, but more teenagers, do not have the skills to command a wage that equals or exceeds this minimum cost of employment for other than peak periods of demand in the business of a particular firm. The knowledge that some job openings exist at the minimum wage may encourage some to continue searching, thus adding to the number of unemployed. Others may drop out of the labor force altogether. Since the minimum wage reduces wage differentiation among workers, it will generate a greater decline in employment for the less skilled and for those subject to discrimination in the labor market. These effects explain part of the substantially higher unemployment rate for teenagers compared to adults and for black teenagers compared to white teenagers.

SEASONAL UNEMPLOYMENT

Seasonal fluctuations in the demand for and supply of labor cause large flows of persons into unemployment. The seasonal nature inherent in some production processes, such as agriculture and construction, and in some consumption—visiting beach resorts in the summer and ski resorts in the winter—can create seasonal fluctuations in employment and unemployment. For example, the unemployment rate of construction workers in February tends to be 133 percent larger than in August. Changes in technology, such as mechanical harvesting equipment and new methods which permit all-weather construction, may have reduced some seasonal fluctuations in employment. Some industries diversify their product lines or use fluctuations in inventories to reduce the costs associated with seasonal variations in demand.

Seasonal fluctuations can also arise on the labor supply side. The unemployment of young people has a strong seasonal component, re-

2. The Federal minimum wage legislation now covers 85 percent of all private, non-supervisory employees and all non-supervisory Federal Government employees. [Editors]

lated mainly to the search for jobs during school vacations. The school calendar was originally designed to fit seasonal demands for young workers in agriculture, but such employment has declined in relative importance.

If the seasonal pattern is regular from year to year, and if data are available for several years, "seasonal factors" can be computed. Indeed, many of the basic monthly unemployment statistics are "seasonally adjusted" by the Bureau of Labor Statistics to show the month-to-month change in unemployment due to factors other than the change in the season. Adjusting the basic data with the standard statistical technique, however, does not remove the impact of seasonality from the average level of unemployment; rather, it spreads the effects of seasonality uniformly throughout the year. Thus, groups with relatively high seasonal unemployment will, on an annual basis, have a relatively high unemployment rate, other things being the same. For example, the higher annual unemployment rates of blue-collar workers compared to white-collar workers, of Alaska compared to the other States, of teen-age males compared to adult males, are in part attributable to greater seasonality of employment.

CYCLICAL UNEMPLOYMENT

During a downturn in economic activity the rate of plant closings accelerates and the rate of openings or expansions of firms declines. The rise in unemployment accompanying such a general decline in business activity is referred to as cyclical unemployment and is associated with the underutilization of economic resources, both human and physical. The rise in the unemployment rate from 4.7 percent in the fourth quarter of 1973 to 8.7 percent in the second quarter of 1975 is, of course, the most recent example of a cyclical increase in unemployment.

The unemployment resulting from a general business recession differs from unemployment attributable to other causes. As the rate rises during the cycle, there is an increase in the incidence of unemployment, that is, in the proportion of those who are unemployed during some part of the year (Table 5–1). This increase accounts for only part of the increase in unemployment, however. For example, the unemployment rate in 1971 was 69 percent greater than in 1969; but the incidence of unemployment was only 30 percent greater. The total number of weeks of unemployment experienced during the year by the average unemployed person also increases during a recession, and this is an additional factor increasing the unemployment rate. Available data on the unemployment of persons with work experience during the year indicate that for adult males, in the period 1961 to 1973, 28 percent of the annual variation in the unemployment rate can be explained by the duration of unemployment over the year, 24 percent by the incidence of unemployment, and 48 percent by their joint effects. During a recession the greater average duration of unemployment over the year seems to be largely due to more weeks of unemployment per spell, rather than to more frequent spells per unemployed person.

TABLE 5-1.—*Dimensions of unemployment and weekly hours worked: comparison of selected years of high and low unemployment, 1957–75*

	1957	1958	1960	1961	1969	1971	1973	1974	1975
	Percent								
Unemployment rate: [1]									
All civilian workers	4.3	6.8	5.5	6.7	3.5	5.9	4.9	5.6	8.5
Long duration unemployment [2]	.8	2.1	1.4	2.2	.5	1.4	.9	1.0	2.7
Percent unemployed at any time during year [3][4]	14.7	17.9	17.2	18.4	12.5	16.3	14.2	17.6	....
Percent of those with unemployment with two or more spells [4][5]	41.1	41.1	36.6	37.0	32.3	32.5	32.5	33.5	....
Unemployed by reason: [6]									
Total unemployed	....	....	....	....	100.0	100.0	100.0	100.0	100.0
Job losers	....	....	....	....	35.9	46.3	38.7	43.5	55.4
Job leavers	....	....	....	....	15.4	11.8	15.7	14.9	10.4
Reentrants and new entrants	....	....	....	....	48.7	41.9	45.7	41.6	34.2
	Weeks								
Average duration of unemployment:									
Currently unemployed	10.5	13.9	12.8	15.6	7.9	11.3	10.0	9.7	14.1
Completed spells of unemployment [7]	5.7	7.4	6.0	7.2	4.6	6.6	....	....	....
Sum of spells of unemployment during the year [4][5]	13.1	15.6	14.1	14.5	9.8	14.2	12.0	12.2	....
Average hours worked per week	41.0	40.6	40.5	40.5	39.9	39.3	39.3	39.0	38.7

[1] Percent of civilian labor force.
[2] Unemployed for 15 weeks or longer.
[3] Percent of those in the civilian labor force at anytime during the year.
[4] Data from the Work Experience Survey and relate to persons 14 years of age and over for 1957–61 and 16 years and over for other years.
[5] Data relate only to persons with work experience during the year.
[6] Data are not available for 1957–61.
[7] Estimate.

Note.—Data are from the Current Population Survey and relate to persons 16 years of age and over (except as noted). Detail may not add to totals because of rounding.

Source: Department of Labor, Bureau of Labor Statistics.

As unemployment rises during the cycle, layoffs account for a larger proportion of unemployment, while voluntary separation and entry and reentry into the labor force decline in relative importance. Most workers who quit their jobs presumably do not return to them. However, a substantial proportion of those on a layoff do return to their former jobs, rather than take new jobs, and this proportion is greater for layoffs attributable to a recession.

Not all workers are equally likely to experience the effects of cyclical unemployment (Table 5–2). Cyclical fluctuations generally have a small amplitude in the service sectors and a wide amplitude in manu-

TABLE 5-2.—*Unemployment rates by selected demographic and industrial groups: comparison of selected years of high and low unemployment, 1957–1975*

(Percent)

Group	1957	1958	1960	1961	1969	1971	1974	1975
All civilian workers...............	4.3	6.8	5.5	6.7	3.5	5.9	5.6	8.5
RACE								
White...........................	3.8	6.1	4.9	6.0	3.1	5.4	5.0	7 8
Negro and other races..............	7.9	12.6	10.2	12.4	6.4	9.9	9.9	13.9
AGE-SEX								
Men 20 years and over.............	3.6	6.2	4.7	5.7	2.1	4.4	3.8	6.7
Women 20 years and over...........	4.1	6.1	5.1	6.3	3.7	5.7	5.5	8.0
Both sexes 16–19 years.............	11.6	15.9	14.7	16.8	12.2	16.9	16.0	19.9
OCCUPATION								
White-collar workers.............	1.9	3.1	2.7	3.3	2.1	3.5	3.3	4.7
Professional and technical.......	1.2	2.0	1.7	2.0	1.3	2.9	2.3	3.2
Managers and administrators, except farm....................	1.0	1.7	1.4	1.8	.9	1.6	1.8	3.0
Sales workers.................	2.6	4.1	3.8	4.9	2.9	4.3	4.2	5.8
Clerical workers..............	2.8	4.4	3.8	4.6	3.0	4.8	4.6	u 6
Blue-collar workers..............	6.0	10.2	7.8	9.2	3.9	7.4	6.7	11.7
Craft and kindred workers.......	3.8	6.8	5.3	6.3	2.2	4.7	4.4	8
Operatives....................	6.3	11.0	8.0	9.6	4.4	8.3	7.5	13.2
Nonfarm laborers..............	9.4	15.1	12.6	14.7	6.7	10.8	10.1	15.6
Service workers.................	4.7	6.9	5.8	7.2	4.2	6.3	6.3	8.6
Farm workers...................	1.9	3.2	2.7	2.8	1 9	2.6	2.5	3.6
INDUSTRY								
Nonagricultural private wage and salary workers..............	4.9	7.9	6.2	7.5	3 5	6.2	5.7	9.2
Construction.................	10.9	15.3	13.5	15.7	6.0	10.4	10.6	18.1
Manufacturing: Durable goods...........	4.9	10.6	6.4	8.5	3.0	7.0	5.4	11.3
Nondurable goods...........	5.3	7.7	6.1	6.8	3.7	6.5	6.2	10.4
Service industries [2].............	4.2	5.7	5.1	6.2	3.5	5.6	5.1	7.1
Government workers...............	1.9	2.5	2.4	2.5	1.9	2.9	3.0	4.0

[1] Seasonally adjusted.
[2] Quarterly data are for service and finance industries.
Note.—Data relate to persons 16 years of age and over except for 1957 occupation data, which relate to persons 14 years of age and over.

Note.—Updated by editors.

Source: Department of Labor, Bureau of Labor Statistics.

facturing, particularly of durable goods. Within industries, cyclical fluctuations in employment tend to be greater for blue-collar or production workers than for white-collar or supervisory workers. The differences, however, vary from one cycle to another.

To a large extent the demographic characteristics of the unemployed vary over the business cycle because of differences in industry and occupation. Blue-collar workers in goods-producing industries are more likely than white-collar and service industry workers to be adult males and union members and less likely to be college graduates. Groups with these characteristics will therefore generally experience greater fluctuations in unemployment over the business cycle.

Even within an industry-occupation sector, the incidence of unemployment is uneven. Some workers undergo a sharp decline in their weeks or hours of employment during the year, while many others experience little or no decrease. This unequal sharing of unemployment results in greater inequality in the distribution of personal income during a recession.

INFLATION AND UNEMPLOYMENT

It has been suggested that there is a negative relation between the unemployment rate and the rate of increase in wages and prices, and that such a relation exists in the long run as well as over the business cycle.

During a period of cyclical expansion, an increase in aggregate demand leads to a greater demand for labor, which is expressed by increases in wages (or in the rate of increase in wages) or by the hiring of less skilled workers at the same wage. This increase in demand for labor will result ultimately in a reduction in unemployment. Thus, in a cyclical expansion one observes a negative relation between wage-rate increases and unemployment. On the downside of a business cycle, firms with a decreased demand for labor lay off workers and lower the rate of increase in money wages. The unemployment rate will increase, accompanied by a decline in the rate of wage increase.

In the long run, however, there would not appear to be a mechanism linking the rate of unemployment to any one rate of stable wage or price increase. One would expect the unemployment rate to be determined by the magnitude of frictional, structural, and other basic forces which are independent of the particular level of a stable rate of inflation. The rate of unemployment that the economy tends to generate when the rate of inflation has no tendency to accelerate is sometimes referred to as the "natural" rate of unemployment. This is a misnomer, however, since the "natural" rate may vary over long periods in response to changes in the underlying factors which determine its level.

During the 1960's many economists believed that there was a long-run, negative relation between the unemployment rate and the rate of increase in wages or prices, initially described by the "Phillips curve" and later by functions involving additional variables and equations. Empirically, simple charts relating the U.S. rate of increase in prices or wages to the unemployment rate did show a downward-sloping relation for the 1960's, although by the 1970's there was clear evidence that the relation was not stable across decades (Chart 5–1).

One explanation for the instability across decades is that a long-run Phillips curve exists but that the curve has been shifting outwards. Some have suggested that this shift is in response to an increase in

Chart 5–1

Unemployment Rate and Prices, 1948–1974

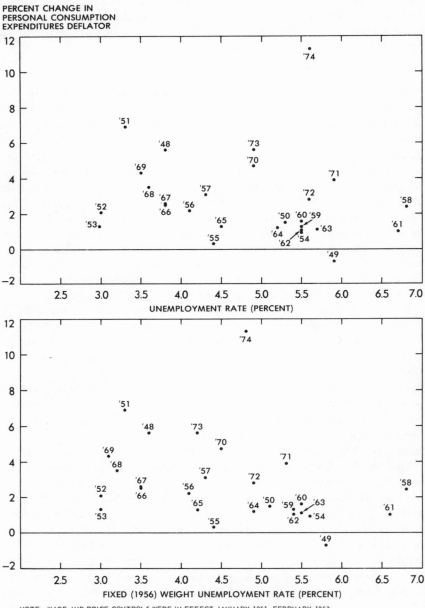

PERCENT CHANGE IN
PERSONAL CONSUMPTION
EXPENDITURES DEFLATOR

UNEMPLOYMENT RATE (PERCENT)

FIXED (1956) WEIGHT UNEMPLOYMENT RATE (PERCENT)

NOTE: WAGE AND PRICE CONTROLS WERE IN EFFECT JANUARY 1951–FEBRUARY 1953
AND AUGUST 1971–APRIL 1974. DURING THESE PERIODS, HOWEVER, THE CONTROLS
VARIED IN COMPREHENSIVENESS.

SOURCES: DEPARTMENT OF COMMERCE, DEPARTMENT OF LABOR, AND COUNCIL OF ECONOMIC ADVISERS.

labor force turnover resulting from the increasing proportion of women and teenagers in the labor force. Even if the tightness of the labor market for each age-sex group were unchanged—that is, if age-sex specific unemployment rates were unchanged—an increase in the proportion of the labor force comprised of adult women and teenagers would increase the measured overall unemployment rate. Hence the same rate of inflation would be associated with a higher level of unemployment.

The lower panel in Chart 5–1 presents data relating the rate of change in a price index to the unemployment rate, adjusted for changes in the age-sex composition of the labor force by the use of 1956 labor force weights. The adjusted unemployment rate has been falling relative to the measured rate. For example, the 1974 unemployment rate of 5.6 percent is reduced to 4.8 percent if the age-sex weights of the 1956 labor force are used. The adjustment reduces but does not eliminate the impression of outward movement of the points during the 1970's; and the pattern of points suggests that the irregularity persists. Despite considerable empirical work allowing for the role of further variables and of lags, it has proved difficult to defend the claim of a long-run Phillips tradeoff between inflation and unemployment.

It should also be noted that a series of shifting, negatively sloped short-run curves relating inflation and unemployment is theoretically consistent with the concept of a "natural" rate of unemployment which is independent of the rate of inflation in the long run. As the short-run curves shift, the observed points on the curves trace out a long-run curve, which becomes more nearly vertical as more time is given to the process. Thus, no stimulus toward lowering unemployment can be derived from a higher inflation rate once the public has adjusted to it. The long-run vertical line originates at a point on the unemployment axis corresponding to the level of the "natural" unemployment rate, a rate which, as noted earlier, depends on the level of frictional and structural unemployment and on other fundamental characteristics of the economy. The changing composition of the labor force would then be one reason to expect an increase in frictional unemployment, and hence a rightward shift of the vertical line in question, that is, a rise in the "natural" rate of unemployment.

Other factors may also have induced a higher natural rate of unemployment over time. The increase in wealth and the accompanying growth of consumer credit have made it easier to maintain consumption during periods of unemployment and may have thereby promoted more job search. Similarly, changes in the welfare program, particularly the availability of food stamps and the program in Aid to Families with Dependent Children (AFDC) for unemployed fathers, available in 23 States and the District of Columbia [28 States by 1976], now provide additional support for unemployed persons from families with few assets and little income from other sources.

Finally, the decline in the proportion of the employed who are self-employed or unpaid family workers, from 21.5 percent in 1948 to 9.6 percent in 1974, would also tend to increase the measured unemployment rate, since both groups typically report very low unemployment, presumably because their earnings are residual and not contractual. For example, in 1974 the unemployment rate for these two groups was 0.9 percent, and the rate for wage and salary workers, 5.3 percent.

Other factors, however, would have tended to decrease the unemployment rate over time. For example, rising wage rates increase the opportunity cost of absence from a job, although this effect may have been neutralized by proportionate increases in unemployment compensation benefits. In addition, the occupational-industrial composition of employment has shifted toward white-collar jobs in the service and government sectors, and these ordinarily have lower rates of unemployment.

In summary, although there does generally appear to be an inverse relation between unemployment and inflation in the short run, the stability of such a long-run relation has been challenged. Much evidence suggests that in the long run the rate of unemployment is consistent with any fully anticipated rate of inflation. Continued research on this topic should eventually provide a more definitive answer.

DURATION OF UNEMPLOYMENT

For the average worker a spell of unemployment lasts only a few weeks. From 1948 through 1969 the average completed spell was estimated at 5.5 weeks, though it tended to be longer during a recession. It was 3.7 weeks in 1953 (unemployment rate, 2.9 percent) and 7.4 weeks in 1958 (unemployment rate, 6.8 percent).

One should note that the duration of unemployment commonly calculated from the CPS refers to a different measure, the number of weeks of unemployment experienced by those who are currently unemployed. Calculated this way, the average duration of unemployment tends to be considerably longer than the average completed spell of unemployment during the year. The difference arises because the probability of leaving unemployment the following week is related to the number of weeks the individual has been unemployed: the longer one has already been unemployed, the greater the probability of remaining unemployed. The proportion with long-term unemployment will, therefore, be greater among the currently unemployed than among those who are completing spells of unemployment. In 1969 about 4.7 percent of the currently unemployed in an average month had been unemployed for 27 weeks or more, while only 1.8 percent of all those who experienced a spell of unemployment at any time during the year were unemployed for 27 weeks or more.

The duration of unemployment can be viewed still a third way. Some persons experience several spells of unemployment in a year, which together add up to a considerable length of time. Indeed those who have completed a spell of unemployment are more likely to become unemployed again than are those who have not been unemployed. In 1973, 13 percent of those working at some time during the year had one or more spells of unemployment, but 32 percent of those with at least one spell had two or more spells, and 52 percent of those with at least two spells had three or more spells. Counting all spells, 11 percent of the experienced workers who had some unemployment reported that they were unemployed for a total of 27 weeks or more in 1973. On the average, workers who had been unemployed at some time reported 12.0 weeks of unemployment during the year. For this group, which excludes persons who were seeking jobs at some time in the year but did not work, the average length of a completed spell was 8.5 weeks and the average number of spells was about 1.7.

Estimates of the duration of unemployment from the work experience survey may be biased upwards because the survey is conducted in March but relates to the previous year and hence must rely on the respondent's memory. Retrospective reporting may be particularly faulty about brief episodes of unemployment and among those who did not receive unemployment insurance. The number of spells may thus be underestimated and their average length overestimated, particularly for women and teenagers. This would explain why the duration of a completed spell obtained from the work experience survey exceeds estimates of the duration of a completed spell based on the data in the monthly CPS.

The duration of a spell of unemployment seems to vary among demographic groups. Among the currently unemployed, the duration of unemployment is somewhat lower for women than for men, and it increases markedly with age for both sexes. In 1973 the group aged 55 and over made up 9 percent of all the unemployed, but 19 percent of those who were unemployed 27 weeks or more.

Older workers usually have longer tenure on the job and greater job security, and thus a low incidence of unemployment. Once they lose a job, however, it is much more difficult for them to find a comparable one. Older workers are likely to have had much training that was useful to their previous employer but would not necessarily be of value to any other; and because their general training was received at an earlier time their general skills may have become obsolete. Firms are reluctant to invest in an older worker whose remaining work life is shorter and whose retirement with pension is more imminent. Fi-

TABLE 5–3.—*Unemployment rates in the United States and seven other developed countries, selected periods, 1969–74*

[Percent; seasonally adjusted]

Country	Adjusted to U.S. concepts [1]				As published [2]			
	1969	1973	1974		1969	1973	1974	
			III	November			III	November
United States_____	3.5	4.9	5.5	6.6	3.5	4.9	5.5	6.6
Canada_____	4.7	5.6	5.4	5.5	4.7	5.6	5.4	5.5
France_____	3.1	3.5	4.1	5.6	1.7	2.1	2.5	3.4
West Germany_____	.8	1.0	2.6	3.1	.9	1.2	3.1	3.7
Great Britain [3]_____	3.0	3.0	3.2	3.1	2.4	2.6	2.7	2.7
Italy_____	3.7	3.8	3.2	[4] 3.5	3.4	3.5	3.0	[4] 3.2
Japan_____	1.1	1.3	1.4	---------	1.1	1.3	1.4	---------
Sweden_____	1.9	2.5	2.1	1.7	1.9	2.5	2.1	1.7

[1] With the exception of Canada, labor force and unemployment data are adjusted where possible to be made more comparable to U.S. definitions and concepts. Age limits roughly approximate the age at which compulsory schooling ends. For the United States and Canada published and adjusted data are identical.

[2] For Great Britain and West Germany, registered unemployed as a percent of employed wage and salary workers plus the unemployed. For others, unemployment as a percent of the civilian or total labor force. With the exception of France, which does not publish an unemployment rate, these are the rates most usually published in the country.

[3] Data as published exclude school leavers and adult students. Including such persons, the unemployment rate was 2.7 in 1973.

[4] October 1974.

Note.—The quarterly and monthly adjusted data are estimates based on annual adjustment factors and should be viewed as approximate indicators of unemployment under U.S. concepts.

Source: Department of Labor, Bureau of Labor Statistics.

nally, geographic mobility is much more costly at older ages. The closing of a firm or a decline in an industry or an area may thus result in severe problems for older workers.

INTERNATIONAL COMPARISONS

Generally the United States and Canada have higher measured rates of unemployment than most other developed countries with market economies (Table 5–3). The sources of unemployment, its duration, and the hardship associated with it differ greatly from country to country, and an understanding of these factors is needed to interpret the differences.

The definition of unemployment also varies among countries, and this can cause differences in the measured unemployment rate. In some countries measured unemployment represents the number of persons registered with government unemployment exchanges; such a procedure usually produces lower rates than the one used in the United States. The U.S. Department of Labor has adjusted the unemployment rates of major developed countries to conform more closely to U.S. concepts. However, although the greatest care is taken in making these difficult adjustments, it is probably impossible to achieve full comparability.

The adjustments must depend on labor force surveys which differ in the wording and sequence of questions, and the true effect of these differences cannot be determined. Moreover, the vast institutional differences among countries would raise serious questions about the comparability of data even if the questionnaires were identical.

The Labor Department adjustments (Table 5–3) bring the unemployment rates of some countries closer to the U.S. level, although for West Germany the differential widens. Significant differentials still remain. Although international data on duration of unemployment are less comparable, the United States appears to have more short-term frictional unemployment, but a relatively low rate of long duration unemployment compared to several other countries (Table 5–4). It is not known to what extent differences in the proportion of those unemployed for long periods can be attributed to differences in the duration

TABLE 5–4.—*Long-term unemployment in the United States and six other developed countries, selected periods, 1970–74*

Country and period	Unemployment rate [1]		Percent of unemployed who have been seeking work for: [1]		Long-term unemployment rate (percent) [1,2]	
	Percent	Relative to average 1968–1973	3 months or more [3]	6 months or more [4]	3 months or more	6 months or more
United States:						
1970	4.9	1.04	16.2	5.7	0.8	0.3
1973	4.9	1.04	18.9	7.8	.9	.4
1974: III	5.5	1.17	19.0	7.6	1.0	.4
Canada:						
1970	5.9	1.05	33.1	15.6	2.0	.9
1973	5.6	1.00	35.4	15.6	2.0	.9
France:						
1970: March	2.2	.85	56.3	40.6	1.2	.9
West Germany:						
1970: April	.5	.63	69.9	50.5	.2	.2
1972: April	.9	1.06	63.4	41.4	.6	.4
Great Britain:						
1971	3.3	1.18		28.2		.9
1973	2.6	.93		41.6		1.1
1974: July	2.7	.93	47.0	33.7	1.2	.9
Italy:						
1970	3.1	1.09	73.0	42.8	2.4	1.4
Sweden:						
1970	1.5	.68	21.8	9.8	.3	.1
1973	2.5	1.14	36.7	18.7	.9	.5

[1] Data for Canada, France, West Germany, Italy and Sweden are based on labor force surveys and are fairly comparable to U.S. data However, they have not been adjusted to U.S. concepts. Data for Great Britain are from the series on registered unemployed and are not comparable to the United States.

[2] Percent of civilian or total labor force, except in Great Britain where it is a percent of registered unemployed plus employed wage and salary workers.

[3] Fifteen weeks or more in the United States, 4 months or more in Canada, and 13 weeks or more in Great Britain and Sweden.

[4] Twenty-six weeks or more in the United States, 7 months or more in Canada, 26 weeks or more in Great Britain, and 27 weeks or more in Sweden.

Sources: Department of Labor (Bureau of Labor Statistics) and Council of Economic Advisers.

of unemployment benefits or in other provisions of unemployment compensation systems.

One reason for the greater frictional unemployment in the United States and Canada, compared to many countries in Western Europe, may be the rapid rate of growth in the labor force and in employment, primarily because of their more rapidly growing populations. From 1962 to 1972, the civilian labor force increased at annual rates of 2.1 percent in the United States and 3.0 percent in Canada; but the civilian labor force (adjusted to U.S. concepts) increased only 1.3 percent in Japan, 1.0 percent in France, and 0.7 percent in Sweden; and it declined by 0.1 percent in West Germany and by 0.7 percent in Italy. A more rapidly growing labor force may imply a larger proportion of recent entrants who have a high incidence of unemployment, though often of short duration. In addition, employers may be less reluctant to lay off workers when there is a steady flow of new workers into the market.

The relatively high level of frictional unemployment in the United States is also reflected in comparatively high rates of job turnover. For example, turnover rates in manufacturing, measured as the number of separations (quits and layoffs) per 100 employees per year, were 55 and 65 respectively in the United States and Canada in the 1960's—from 70 percent to more than 100 percent higher than in countries such as West Germany, Great Britain, or Italy, even in years of very low unemployment. Institutional and cultural factors may account for these differences in turnover. In many Western European and Asian countries worker-employer relationships discourage layoffs and quits. A distinctive characteristic of Japanese labor markets is the system of "lifetime employment," in which many workers are felt to be committed to employment by a single firm throughout their careers. The firms with such arrangements are usually large, and intrafirm job mobility replaces interfirm mobility. Available data indicate very low rates of job change in Japan, even for young workers. Among young graduates of manpower training programs in 1968, only 28 percent changed employers during the next 3 years. Among U.S. youths aged 15 to 20 who had left school and entered the labor force, however, about 53 percent of whites and 66 percent of blacks changed employers between 1966 and 1967, according to the National Longitudinal Survey. It is difficult to evaluate the efficiency of intercountry differences in job mobility, but the variation in behavior is striking.

Another factor in the differing measured unemployment among some countries is the extent of self-employment. Self-employed persons and unpaid workers in family enterprises, mainly farms, are seldom reported as unemployed. In the United States, about 10 percent of the employed are self-employed or unpaid family workers. Although in Sweden the proportion is similar to that in the United States, it is considerably higher in several other countries: 32 percent in Japan, 29 percent in Italy, 21 percent in France, and 16 percent in West Germany. Thus, relative to the United States, unemployment appears lower in these countries than it would be if only wage and salary workers were considered.

Finally, government actions can influence the extent to which measured unemployment varies over the business cycle. In Sweden, for example, extensive expenditures on training and public employment programs during recessions reduce the cyclical increase in measured unemployment. During 1973, a year of cyclical downturn in Sweden, an annual monthly average of 79,000 persons were in training or public employment programs and hence were counted as employed or out of the labor force. Since this group is large compared to the monthly number of persons reported unemployed, about 98,000, it is clear that without the programs, or if persons in the programs were counted as unemployed, the measured rate would have been substantially higher than the reported rate.

In West Germany, some adjustment to the business cycle has been made through the migration of foreign workers who now comprise about 10 percent of the civilian labor force. During slack times the foreign workers, who are more prone to layoff, usually returned to their home countries. In 1974, however, this pattern seems to have changed, perhaps partly because of recent restrictions on new migrant labor; and fewer unemployed foreign workers left the country. Thus, in October 1974 foreign workers made up 13 percent of the registered unemployed, compared to 6 percent in March 1973. In January 1975 renewed government efforts were made in West Germany to encourage the emigration of unemployed migrant workers.

UNEMPLOYMENT IN THE 1974–1975 RECESSION

The unemployment rate averaged 8.5 percent in 1975, sharply above the 5.6 percent rate in 1974 and the previous post-World War II high of 6.8 percent in 1958. The unemployment rate increased rapidly, from 5.6 percent in the third quarter of 1974 to 8.1 percent in the first quarter of 1975, and reached a peak of 8.7 percent in the second quarter. By the fourth quarter the rate had declined to 8.5 percent.

As in past recessions, the sharp rise in unemployment was widespread among major demographic groups (Table 5–2).[3] The rate for married men, who typically have the lowest unemployment rate, increased from 2.7 percent in 1974 to 5.1 percent in 1975. Most other demographic

3. Demographic group differences in unemployment are discussed in depth in Chapter 6. [Editors]

groups experienced a similar or slightly larger percentage point increase in unemployment rates, but a substantially smaller relative increase.

The increase in the unemployment rate was largely a consequence of unemployment arising from the loss of a job, particularly among adult men and women (Table 5–5). The unemployment rate for job leavers

TABLE 5–5.—*Unemployment rates by reason for unemployment, age, and sex, 1973–75*

[Percent of civilian labor force]

Reason for unemployment	Men 20 years and over			Women 20 years and over			Both sexes 16 to 19 years		
	1973	1974	1975	1973	1974	1975	1973	1974	1975
Total unemployment rate_____	3.2	3.8	6.7	4.8	5.5	8.0	14.5	16.0	19.9
Job separation_____	2.4	3.0	5.6	2.5	3.1	5.1	4.1	5.0	6.8
Job losers_____	1.9	2.5	5.1	1.6	2.1	4.0	2.4	3.1	5.1
Job leavers_____	.5	.5	.6	.9	1.0	1.1	1.7	2.0	1.7
Previously out of labor force	.8	.8	1.1	2.3	2.4	2.9	10.3	10.9	13.1
Reentrants_____	.7	.7	1.0	2.0	2.1	2.6	4.3	4.9	6.0
New entrants_____	.1	.1	.1	.3	.3	.3	6.0	6.0	7.1

Note.—Detail may not add to totals because of rounding.

Source: Department of Labor, Bureau of Labor Statistics.

(unemployed persons who quit their jobs, expressed as a percentage of the labor force) was essentially unchanged from 1974. Unemployed new entrants and reentrants increased as a percentage of the labor force in 1975. The increase in the unemployment rate among labor force entrants likely reflected a greater difficulty in finding a job, that is, a longer duration of unemployment rather than a greater influx of entrants, since the new-hire rate declined and the labor force participation rate did not change from 1974 to 1975.

There was a large increase in the number of persons unemployed 15 weeks or longer as a percentage of the labor force. The long-duration unemployment rate increased from 1.0 percent in 1974 to 2.7 percent in 1975, a much higher level than the previous postwar peak of 2.2 percent in 1961. This sharp increase compared to past recessions was due partly to the severity and duration of the most recent recession and partly to wider coverage and longer duration of unemployment compensation benefits than in the past.

Under legislation enacted in December 1974 and amended in March 1975, the maximum duration of unemployment compensation benefits for workers covered under the regular Federal and State programs was increased from 39 weeks to 65 weeks by adding a 26-week program called Federal supplemental benefits (FSB). This program is now scheduled to expire at the end of 1977. Another temporary program, special unemployment assistance (SUA), was also enacted in December 1974 to provide unemployment compensation coverage for an estimated 12 million wage and salary workers employed in industries not covered by the regular Federal and State programs. These are largely State and local government workers, farm workers, domestics, and employees of small nonprofit organizations. In June the duration of benefits under SUA was extended from 26 to 39 weeks.

There is now considerable research suggesting that a longer maximum duration of unemployment benefits tends to lengthen the duration of actual unemployment by discouraging some from withdrawing from the labor force and some from accepting reemployment in a less attractive job. While the exact magnitude of any increase in measured unemployment is unclear, these studies suggest that interpretation of unemployment statistics has become more complex.[4]

4. The U.S. unemployment compensation system is discussed in detail in Chapter 7. [Editors]

CHAPTER 6

The Distribution of Unemployment Among Demographic Groups

The U.S. data show a wide disparity in unemployment among demographic groups. The unemployment rate is higher for teenagers than for adults, for women than for men, for blacks than for whites, and for unskilled workers than for the skilled. These differentials have endured in U.S. labor markets for a long time. Even in 1969, a year of extremely tight labor markets, when the unemployment rate for adult men was 2.1 percent, the unemployment rate was 3.7 percent for adult women, 6.4 percent for blacks, and 12.2 percent for teenagers. The development of efficient public policy requires an understanding of the nature and causes of these unemployment differentials.

DIFFERENTIALS DUE TO LABOR FORCE TURNOVER

Labor force turnover seems to explain much of the unemployment of women and teenagers. Some teenagers and more women have a continuous attachment to the labor force; others are just beginning such an attachment; and still others enter and leave the labor force, sometimes more than once during the year. For example, although more than half the women and teenagers were in the labor force at some time in 1973, only 31 percent and 22 percent respectively were in the labor force for 50–52 weeks. Of all males aged 25 to 54, however, 87 percent were in the labor force for the entire year.

As noted above, high rates of labor force turnover generally have the effect of increasing measured unemployment, while job-to-job mobility does not always have such an effect. In our unemployment statistics, persons with a job are not classified as unemployed, even though they may be searching for another. During the recession year of 1961 less than half the persons who changed jobs for any reason, including job loss, experienced unemployment as it is defined here. In a year of normal unemployment the proportion is likely to be still lower. Entry and reentry into the labor force, on the other hand, is subject to a more direct translation into measured unemployment, since search by those working as students or in the home is counted as unemployment. Not surprisingly, a large amount of unemployment among teenagers and women is accounted for by labor force entrants and reentrants (Table 6–1).

In 1974, 44 percent of the unemployed adult women and 68 percent of the unemployed teenagers had been out of the labor force before becoming unemployed, compared to only 21 percent of unemployed adult men. We can exclude both new entrants and reentrants from the unemployed and from the civilian labor force to compute an unemployment rate referring only to persons who are unemployed because they lost or quit their jobs. The resulting unemployment rate for adult women declines almost to that for adult males, and the differential between adults and teenagers is substantially narrowed (Table 6–2).

Labor force turnover has another side, exits from the labor force; and some suggest that many of those who leave the labor force are discouraged workers who cannot find jobs. The flows of women and teenagers out of the labor force are large; quantitatively they can be expressed as the percentage of those in the labor force who withdrew. Withdrawals represented 33 percent of the teenage labor force in 1973; 21 percent of the labor force for women aged 20 to 24 and 13 percent for women aged 25 to 59; and 1.8 percent for men aged 25 to 59. Only a small proportion cited economic factors as the reason for leaving the labor force, however; and among this group still fewer cited "slack work" as opposed to what would seem to be a planned short-term job— "seasonal or temporary job" (Table 6–3).

"Discouraged workers" are often defined more broadly to include all persons outside the labor force who would like a job but think it is useless to seek one. Some of the people so classified in 1973, about 14 percent, have never worked. Most, about 77 percent, intend to seek work within a year, and about 40 percent had looked for a job at some time but could not find one. One can calculate an unemployment rate in which those who are out of the labor force because they believe they cannot find a job are added to the unemployed and to the labor force. This change increases the unemployment rate for adult men by 0.3 percentage point and for adult women by 1.1 to 1.5 percentage points, and hence increases the male-female unemployment differential (Table 6–2).

When discouraged workers are included in the unemployment data, the increment in the unemployment rate fluctuates somewhat with the business cycle for adult women (by 0.3 percentage point from 1969 to 1971), but not for adult males. It is thus not the business cycle but

Unemployment

TABLE 6–1.—*Distribution of unemployed by reason for unemployment, by age, and sex, 1973–74*

[Percent]

Reason	Men 20 years and over		Women 20 years and over		Both sexes 16 to 19 years	
	1973	1974	1973	1974	1973	1974
Total unemployed_____	100.0	100.0	100.0	100.0	100.0	100.0
Job separations_____	75.0	79.4	53.2	56.5	29.0	31.9
Job losers_____	59.1	65.4	34.6	38.6	17.2	19.7
Job leavers_____	15.9	14.1	18.6	18.0	11.8	12.2
Previously out of labor force__	25.0	20.5	46.8	43.5	71.1	68.1
Reentrants_____	21.6	18.2	41.5	37.9	29.5	30.6
New entrants_____	3.4	2.4	5.3	5.6	41.5	37.4
Unemployment rate [1]_____	3.2	3.8	4.8	5.5	14.5	16.0

[1] Unemployment as percent of civilian labor force.

Note.—Detail may not add to totals because of rounding.

Source: Department of Labor, Bureau of Labor Statistics.

TABLE 6–2.—*Civilian unemployment rates by age and sex, under alternative definitions, 1969–76*

[Percent]

Sex, age, and year	Unemployment rate			
	All unemployed [1]	Job losers and job leavers [2]	Job losers [3]	Unemployed plus discouraged workers [4]
Men 20 years and over:				
1969	2.1	1.6	1.2	2.4
1970	3.5	2.7	2.3	3.8
1971	4.4	3.4	2.9	4.7
1972	4.0	3.0	2.5	4.3
1973	3.2	2.4	1.9	3.5
1974	3.8	3.0	2.5	4.1
1975	6.7	5.7	5.1	7.2
1976 [5]	5.9	4.8	4.2	6.3
Women 20 years and over:				
1969	3.7	1.9	1.3	4.9
1970	4.8	2.7	2.0	6.0
1971	5.7	3.3	2.5	7.2
1972	5.4	3.1	2.2	6.9
1973	4.8	2.6	1.7	6.0
1974	5.5	3.2	2.2	6.6
1975	8.0	5.3	4.2	9.8
1976 [5]	7.6	4.6	3.4	8.9
Both sexes 16 to 19 years:				
1969	12.2	3.6	2.0	13.4
1970	15.3	5.0	3.2	16.6
1971	16.9	5.3	3.6	18.4
1972	16.2	5.3	3.5	17.6
1973	14.5	4.7	2.8	15.8
1974	16.0	5.7	3.6	17.2
1975	19.9	7.8	6.0	21.5
1976 [5]	19.0	6.8	5.0	20.3

[1] Percent of civilian labor force.
[2] Percent of civilian labor force excluding new entrants and reentrants.
[3] Percent of civilian labor force excluding new entrants, reentrants, and job leavers.
[4] Percent of civilian labor force plus discouraged workers. Discouraged workers are defined here as those not in the labor force because they believe they cannot find a job.
[5] Eleven month average.

Sources: Department of Labor (Bureau of Labor Statistics) and Council of Economic Advisers.

TABLE 6-3.—*Reason for separation from last job for persons not in the labor force but who worked during the previous 12 months, by age and sex, 1973*

Reason for separation	Total	Age in years			
		16 to 19	20 to 24	25 to 59	60 and over
MEN					
Number (thousands)	3,714	1,427	776	660	849
Percent distribution by reason:					
Total	100.0	100.0	100.0	100.0	100.0
School, home responsibilities	41.6	61.8	64.0	21.2	2.8
Ill health, disability	12.0	1.6	2.3	34.0	21.1
Retirement, old age	14.4	(1)	(1)	9.5	55.4
Economic reasons	16.2	19.0	13.9	15.0	14.3
End of seasonal or temporary job	11.8	15.1	9.9	8.5	10.7
Slack work	4.3	3.9	4.0	6.5	3.5
All other reasons	15.9	17.6	19.7	20.3	6.5
WOMEN					
Number (thousands)	6,329	1,360	1,348	2,994	626
Percent distribution by reason:					
Total	100.0	100.0	100.0	100.0	100.0
School, home responsibilities	51.4	63.9	68.8	46.1	12.3
Ill health, disability	7.9	1.8	3.0	10.9	18.0
Retirement, old age	4.4	(1)	(1)	1.3	38.4
Economic reasons	18.9	16.5	12.8	22.8	18.5
End of seasonal or temporary job	14.4	13.8	9.7	17.2	13.5
Slack work	4.4	2.7	3.1	5.7	4.9
All other reasons	17.4	17.9	15.4	18.9	12.9

[1] Not applicable.

Note.—Detail may not add to totals because of rounding.

Source: Department of Labor, Bureau of Labor Statistics.

rather demographic or structural economic factors, such as age, skill, and region, that account for most of the "discouraged worker" phenomenon.[1]

THE MALE-FEMALE DIFFERENTIAL
FOR EXPERIENCED WORKERS

When entrants are excluded from the data, as in Table 6–2, the sex differential in unemployment becomes very small. When the comparison is confined only to those among the unemployed who lost their jobs, the unemployment rate for women is about that of men during times of low unemployment; but it is lower than the rate for men during times of higher unemployment.

In principle, women would be more vulnerable to layoffs than men, because on average they do not have as many years of work experience as men of the same age. They are therefore likely to have accumulated fewer seniority rights and to have received less training or other invest-

1. The number of "discouraged workers" did increase sharply with the severe 1974–75 recession; from 679,000 in 1973 to 686,000 in 1974 to 1,082,000 in 1975. [Editors]

ment in skills specific to the firm. In addition—and it is difficult to separate this factor from the preceding one—employers may discriminate against married women when reducing the firm's payroll. On the other hand, a smaller proportion of employed women are in occupations and industries with sharp cyclical fluctuations. Women are more likely to be employed in white-collar jobs—62 percent of women and 40 percent of men were in such jobs in 1974—and in service industries like government where unemployment fluctuates less over the business cycle. The industrial-occupational mix factor seems to dominate, since during recessions the unemployment differential by sex narrows for experienced workers. In addition, the slower rate of entry of women into the labor force during a recession narrows the sex differential in the overall unemployment rate (including labor force entrants).

Another factor that tends to increase the unemployment rate of married women is the migration of families, who generally move where the husband's job opportunities are better. Although in some cases this migration may also improve the wife's job opportunities, it more often results initially in her unemployment in a new labor market. Thus in 1970, married women aged 25 to 34 who had moved to a different county within the year had an unemployment rate of 11 percent, compared to 5 percent for nonmigrants; among married men of the same age the rates for migrants and nonmigrants were 4.8 percent and 2.1 percent respectively. This effect diminishes, however, in the course of time.

Women differ from men in the way they search for jobs. Among married women, this difference may well be a function of their dual responsibilities in the labor market and at home. In 1973, a sample of workers who had taken their current jobs within the year responded to a survey about job search methods. Men spent more time in search: 40 percent of the men and 29 percent of the women usually spent 6 or more hours per week looking for work. Men searched over a wider area: 67 percent of the men and 45 percent of the women reported that they had traveled 11 or more miles from home in search of a job. Men also used more methods of search than women. [For a more detailed analysis of unemployment and labor force participation differentials between men and women, see Chapter 10.]

STUDENT AND NONSTUDENT TEENAGERS

The unemployment of teenagers who have ended their schooling is quite different from that of students seeking part-time or summer jobs often unrelated to their eventual careers.

The proportion of teenagers aged 16 to 19 who are enrolled in school in October has increased from 58 percent in 1956 to 66 percent in 1973. The proportion of students who participate in the labor force during the school year has also been increasing—from 32 percent in October 1956 to 41 percent in October 1973. As a result, 52 percent of the teenage labor force were enrolled in school in 1973 compared to only 39 percent in 1956.

Every June brings a large increase, usually a 30–40 percent increase, in the teenage labor force, which currently averages 8.1 million youths during the school months. The economy manages to absorb most of this influx. In 1969, as many as four out of five teenage students were reported in the labor force at some time during the summer; all but 11 percent eventually found jobs. About one-third of the unsuccessful jobseekers searched only 2 weeks or less, and 68 percent searched 4 weeks or less. During the summer the teenage unemployment rate rises sharply, thereby increasing the average annual rate of teenage unemployment.

In the second half of the 1960's the unemployment rate among teenage students increased in relation to the rate for nonstudents and responded little to the expansion in the economy. Because of students' increased participation in the labor force, however, employment ratios of students (employed students as a percentage of the population) also increased in comparison with those of nonstudents. Thus unemployment rates should be evaluated in conjunction with employment ratios or labor force participation rates for teenagers or any other group whose participation rate is substantially below 100 percent.

Since the middle 1950's the labor force participation rate of nonstudents aged 16 to 19 has been around 70 percent. Many of these young people are interested in full-time jobs and remain in the labor force all year. Since they are learning about the labor market, more of their unemployment arises from changing jobs than from the movement into the labor force that characterizes student unemployment.

Although youths out of school have above average layoff and quit rates, the resulting job changes may have beneficial consequences. New or relatively new members of the labor force search extensively for desirable conditions of employment, experimenting among different occupations and employers. Moreover, since young workers do not have a work history, employers have less information about teenagers than they have about older workers, and this makes the hiring process more difficult. Information from a survey of out-of-school male youths between 1966 and 1968 suggests that job changing may be a good investment. Those who changed employers generally obtained larger pay gains over the period than those who did not: and among black youths the pay increases during the period rose consistently with the number of changes.

The unemployment rate of all teenagers has risen sharply relative to the rate of adult men since the late 1950's. This rise is due partly to the increase in school enrollment and to the changing participation pattern of students, both of which result in higher turnover. Part of this relative rise in teenage unemployment may stem from the extension of minimum wage coverage and from the growth of social legislation that raises the cost to the firm of teenage compared to adult labor.

The minimum wage may also have a more insidious long-run effect on the careers of youths, particularly teenagers out of school. Traditionally, on-the-job training has done much to improve skills. Such job training may be unprofitable for employers if they must pay higher minimum wage rates. The youths who suffer most would be precisely those who might need the most help—youths with little schooling and greater learning difficulties and those subject to discrimination.

VETERANS AND NONVETERANS

The higher unemployment rate of male veterans of the Vietnam era compared to nonveterans has been a matter of public concern. When the rate is disaggregated by age, however, it is clear that only veterans aged 20 to 24 have significantly higher rates of unemployment than nonveterans (Table 6–4). The relative and absolute difference in unem-

TABLE 6–4.—*Unemployment rates for male Vietnam era veterans and nonveterans 20 to 34 years, by age, 1970–74*

[Percent [1]]

Age and veteran status	1970	1971	1972	1973	1974
20 to 34 years:					
Veterans	6.7	8.3	6.7	4.9	5.3
Nonveterans	5.3	6.3	5.7	4.9	6.0
Ratio [2]	1.26	1.32	1.18	1.00	.88
20 to 24 years:					
Veterans	9.5	12.3	10.6	8.8	10.9
Nonveterans	8.1	9.5	8.7	6.8	8.2
Ratio [3]	1.17	1.29	1.22	1.29	1.33
25 to 29 years:					
Veterans	4.5	5.8	4.9	3.7	4.3
Nonveterans	3.9	4.7	4.2	4.3	4.9
Ratio [2]	1.15	1.23	1.17	.86	.88
30 to 34 years:					
Veterans	3.2	3.5	3.0	2.6	2.7
Nonveterans	3.1	3.7	3.0	2.4	3.4
Ratio [2]	1.03	.95	1.00	1.08	.79

[1] Except as noted.
[2] Ratio of rate for veterans to that for nonveterans.

Note.—Vietnam era veterans are those who served after August 4, 1964. In 1973, of the Vietnam era veterans of all ages, 91 percent were 20 to 34 years of age.

Source: Department of Labor, Bureau of Labor Statistics.

ployment declines with age and disappears for those aged 30 to 34. The relative unemployment rate of veterans aged 20 to 34 has fallen since 1971, largely because of a decline in discharges and the consequent increasing average age of veterans compared to nonveterans.

Since young veterans include most of those recently discharged from the Armed Forces, they are likely to be new entrants or reentrants to the civilian labor force. As discussed above, entry is generally associated with higher unemployment. Veterans may also be less informed about the current civilian labor market than other entrants whose activities have been largely centered in the home and school. After being away for a number of years, veterans may find that previously acquired information about the labor market has become obsolete, and new information is difficult to acquire because of weakened ties with friends and home. This drawback disappears as the veterans acquire information relevant to job search in the civilian sector.

Under the federally financed program of Unemployment Compensation for Ex-Servicemen (UCX), newly discharged veterans with at least 90 days of continuous active service and a discharge other than dishonorable are eligible for unemployment compensation in any State where they wish to file a claim, under the conditions and benefits prevailing in that State. In fiscal 1974 there were 527,000 military separations and 342,000 initial claims for UCX, a claim rate of 65 percent. The average weekly benefit was $66, and benefits were received for an average of 13.6 weeks in a benefit year, about the same as for all insured unemployed.

The UCX program may encourage unemployed veterans to spend more time searching for a job; and among veterans who become students it may encourage a period of unemployment rather than withdrawal from the labor force. Most young nonveterans, on the other hand, have too little work experience to qualify for substantial unemployment insurance benefits, if any. Again, as the cohort ages, the veterans exhaust their eligibility for UCX, nonveterans acquire more job experience, and the gap in eligibility for unemployment benefits narrows. These developments also narrow the unemployment differential.

UNEMPLOYMENT DIFFERENTIALS BY EDUCATION

A pronounced inverse relation exists between education and unemployment (Table 6–5). The differential varies among demographic groups and over time. For example, the differential narrowed perceptibly in the last decade for males aged 35 to 54.

There is a presumption that firms would be most reluctant to lose, through a layoff or a quit, those workers in whom they had made the largest investments. Among such investments are hiring costs (such as the cost of evaluating prospective employees), and the cost of training that is specific to the particular firm (that is, training useful almost exclusively in the firm where it is acquired). Workers with more education tend to be less homogeneous, and the less homogeneous the class of workers, the greater the resources devoted by the firm to acquiring

TABLE 6–5.—*Unemployment rates by education, sex, and age, 1962 and 1972*

[Percent]

Sex and years of school completed	Age					
	20 years and over		20 to 34 years		35 to 54 years	
	1962	1972	1962	1972	1962	1972
Men: Total_____	5.7	4.9	7.1	6.8	4.8	3.4
8 years_____	7.3	5.8	11.4	10.0	7.3	6.2
9 to 11 years_____	7.3	6.4	11.2	11.0	5.7	4.0
12 years_____	4.3	4.8	5.7	6.9	3.0	3.0
16 years or more_____	1.5	2.2	1.9	2.9	.9	1.7
Women: Total_____	5.6	5.4	8.0	7.2	4.9	4.7
8 years_____	6.2	5.5	13.6	8.7	6.4	5.6
9 to 11 years_____	8.3	7.5	13.0	14.4	7.0	5.4
12 years_____	5.2	5.1	7.2	6.6	4.0	4.3
16 years or more_____	1.5	3.0	1.9	4.0	1.6	2.4

Note.—Data relate to March of each year.

Source: Department of Labor, Bureau of Labor Statistics.

information about the characteristics of particular individuals. More educated workers also appear to receive more training on the job, because their prior education facilitates further training and because they are more likely to have characteristics such as ability, steadfastness, and good health which firms find desirable in their trainees. Thus one expects a lower incidence of turnover (layoffs plus quits) among more educated workers. Related to these points is the different occupational and industrial distribution of those with more schooling: a greater concentration in white-collar jobs and in the service sector. As indicated above, these occupational and industrial characteristics are associated with a reduced amplitude of cyclical fluctuations in unemployment.

Workers with more education are more likely to change jobs without undergoing unemployment. It may be easier for them to search for a new job while employed because their more cerebral and portable work permits more flexible work schedules, or because prospective employers can evaluate their qualifications initially without their presence. Moreover, unemployment is more expensive for those with higher levels of schooling: as a result of their higher wages, unemployment benefits replace a lower proportion of their lost wages.

Data on job mobility which are available for 1961 by occupation but not by education support these hypotheses. Job turnover was generally much lower in the highly skilled occupations associated with more education. Thus, only 1.7 percent of male nonfarm managers and 8.5 percent of male professionals changed jobs in 1961. The rate of job change increased considerably for those with less skill, reaching 16.4

percent for laborers. When the number of changes made by those who changed jobs is also considered, the differentials in total turnover become even more pronounced: the job changers with lower skills were more likely to have made more than one change (40 percent for laborers), while a smaller proportion of the highly skilled had changed jobs more than once (22 percent for professionals). The proportion of males who changed jobs without any unemployment was 55 percent for professionals, 37 percent for operatives, and 32 percent for laborers.

It has been suggested that the increase in education over the past three decades may have reduced overall unemployment. The reasons why unemployment differs among education groups, however, need not apply to unemployment over time. For example, the amount of training specific to the firm would not necessarily respond proportionately to increases in the education of the population, although at a given moment training and education may be strongly linked. In addition, increases in education over time result in increases in schooling levels within occupations, as well as an increase in the proportion of the labor force in more skilled occupations. If unemployment is more strongly associated with occupation than with education, secular increases in the level of education would result in less than proportionate declines in the unemployment rate. For a rising level of education to have no effect on the overall unemployment rate would require an increase in unemployment rates within at least some education groups. It is not possible to test this hypothesis adequately since unemployment rates by education, controlling for demographic characteristics, are not available for the years before 1962, and hence there are not enough data points to separate cyclical from longer-term effects.

UNEMPLOYMENT DIFFERENCES BY RACE

The rate of unemployment among blacks has been about double that of whites in the post-World War II period. From 1948 through 1973 the unemployment rate averaged 8.6 percent for blacks and 4.3 percent for whites. Although the black-white differential in earnings has narrowed over the past 20 years, no such narrowing is as evident in the unemployment differential.

The race difference in unemployment may be attributed to differences in demographic and socioeconomic characteristics, as well as to current discrimination in the labor market. Some demographic and socioeconomic differences, however, may themselves be consequences of past discrimination. Among whites, unemployment rates vary across groups with different characteristics; for example, rates are higher for teenagers than for adults, for high school dropouts than for college graduates, for laborers than for professionals; and they are higher in the West than in the South. Because these characteristics differ by race, unemployment rates for blacks and whites with the same characteristics could be the same although their overall rates differed. The younger average age and lower levels of schooling and occupation of blacks would imply higher black unemployment rates. The greater residential concentration of blacks in the South would, on the other hand, imply lower black unemployment rates.

The extent to which racial differences in unemployment can be attributed to various measurable factors has been computed for March 1970 from data collected in the 1970 Census of Population. As reported in the census, the unemployment rate for persons aged 16 and over was 6.3 percent for black men and 3.6 percent for white men: 7.7 percent for black women and 4.8 percent for white women (Table 6–6).

TABLE 6–6.—*Unemployment rates by race, Spanish heritage, and sex, March 1970*

[Percent]

Item	Comparison of blacks and whites		Comparison of persons of Spanish heritage and whites not of Spanish heritage	
	Men	Women	Men	Women
Persons 16 years of age and over:				
White or white not of Spanish heritage	3.6	4.8	3.5	4.7
Black or Spanish heritage	6.3	7.7	5.8	8.1
Persons 25 to 64 years of age who worked in 1969:				
White or white not of Spanish heritage	2.5	3.1	2.4	3.0
Black or Spanish heritage	3.5	5.2	3.7	5.4
Predicted black or Spanish heritage rate if blacks or persons of Spanish heritage had the white or white not of Spanish heritage distribution of:[1]				
Age	3.4	4.7	3.7	4.6
Plus: Region	3.8	4.9	3.1	3.9
Plus: Schooling	3.3	4.2	2.5	2.5
Plus: Marital status	3.0	4.1	2.6	2.5
Plus: Occupation	2.6	3.9	2.5	2.1

[1] Using micro-data from the 1/1,000 sample of the 1970 Census of Population, the dichotomous variable unemployed-employed in the survey week in March 1970 was regressed for each group on the control variables. The mean values of the control variables for whites or whites not of Spanish heritage of the same sex were inserted into the regression for blacks or persons of Spanish heritage to obtain the predicted value for blacks or persons of Spanish heritage.

Note.—The unemployment status refers to the week prior to Census Day, April 1, 1970. For those who returned the forms late, the data may refer to April. The data, therefore, are not strictly comparable to unemployment rates obtained from the Current Population Survey and reported by the Bureau of Labor Statistics. Data relate to persons living in the 50 States and the District of Columbia.

Sources: Department of Commerce (Bureau of the Census) and Council of Economic Advisers.

The computations were performed separately for the more restricted group of men and women aged 25 to 64 who were experienced workers, that is, who had worked at some time during 1969. For this group the civilian unemployment rate for men was 3.5 percent for blacks and 2.5 percent for whites. By excluding young persons, those aged 65 and older, and those who had been out of the labor force the preceding year, the unemployment rate is reduced, and more so for blacks. The race differential is thereby reduced, especially for men. It is primarily the exclusion of young workers which accounts for this effect.

The remaining race differential in unemployment rates of 1.0 percentage point for March 1970 among males aged 25 to 64 who worked in 1969 would be increased to 1.3 percentage points if adult blacks had the same distribution of age and region of residence as whites (Table 6–6). This arises primarily because blacks are more concentrated in the South, where unemployment is lower. When control for the race difference in schooling is added, the differential is reduced to 0.8 percentage point: and 20 percent of the original differential is explained. A substantial reduction in the differential is obtained, however, only when marital status and occupation (10 broad categories), are introduced. With these five variables, one can account for 90 percent of the differential in unemployment. Under the same stepwise procedure as for men, 62 percent of the larger race differential for women is accounted for by the five control variables. Among women, however, age, region, and schooling have a larger effect on the differential than among men.

These results cannot easily be used to determine the extent to which the racial differences in unemployment are due to current discrimination in the labor market. Race differences in some of the control variables, such as marital status and occupation, may themselves be partly attributed to the effects of current discrimination. For example, unemployment and low income due to discrimination in employment could lead to higher rates of marital separation; employers may bar some persons from particular occupations on the grounds of race. However, other relevant variables which were not measured—such as the quality of schooling and the extent of training on the job—could also have important effects and help to explain race differences in unemployment.

Differences between blacks and whites in their basic education and other skills may also have arisen indirectly through discrimination. Labor market discrimination can lower or make more uncertain the monetary return from schooling and consequently lower the incentive for additional schooling. Perhaps more important, past discrimination, unrelated to the current labor market, clearly lowered the quantity and quality of schooling for blacks. Several decades ago when the older workers in today's labor market were of school age, the quality of schooling for blacks was vastly inferior by almost any measure. There has been considerable progress in this area, so that today available measures of schooling resources, such as expenditures per pupil, have been brought to approximate equality.

Even if discrimination in the labor market were widespread, it could result in lower wages instead of higher unemployment for blacks relative to whites with the same skill and other relevant characteristics. If there were no equal opportunity legislation or other restrictions on wages, and if employers discriminated against blacks, blacks might work for less pay than similarly qualified whites; this would provide an incentive for employers to hire them, although the incentive might not always be sufficient. If white employees were to refuse to have a black supervisor, employers might hire blacks for jobs below their skill level or maintain segregated work forces. If, because of racial tension, it were too costly to employ black and white workers of similar skill levels in an integrated work force, segregated work forces may also develop. In each case, discrimination could take the form of reduced compensation, inferior jobs, or segregation, rather than higher unemployment.

Discrimination is more likely to lead to unemployment differentials when employers are prevented from paying different wages for equal work, because of legal, union, or social pressure. Discrimination may then to a greater extent take the form of restricted job openings for blacks, because it is sometimes more difficult to prove discrimination in hiring or promotion than in overt pay differences. Such a development could increase the difficulty of finding and maintaining employment, and hence increase the unemployment rate for blacks. Moreover, the prospect of equal pay may encourage blacks to quit jobs with low pay and search longer for more promising positions.

Empirical studies have estimated the extent to which differences in State laws requiring "equal pay for equal work" (prior to the national Civil Rights Act of 1964) affect race differences in income and unemployment, when other economic variables are held constant. The results indicate that State equal pay laws reduced the gap between the wage rates of equally skilled blacks and whites but increased the difference in unemployment. The wage effect was greater than the unemployment effect, however, and annual earnings differentials between blacks and whites consequently narrowed.

The ambiguity of the relation between discrimination and unemployment is further illustrated by a comparison of the unemployment differential between the urban South and the urban non-South during the decennial census years 1940 through 1970 (Table 6–7). The unemployment differential between white and black men tends to be larger in the non-South, particularly in 1950 and 1960. Since the black-white difference in education has been larger in the South than in the non-South, unemployment rate differentials adjusted for education would show an even more exaggerated tendency for the South to display a smaller race differential in unemployment. On the other hand, broadly considered, economic opportunities have generally been greater for blacks outside the South both absolutely and relative to whites; this is

TABLE 6–7.—*Unemployment rates for males in the urban South and urban non-South, by race and age, selected years, 1940–70*

Age group and year	North and West (percent)		South (percent)		Difference between black and white rates (percentage points)		Ratio of black to white rate	
	Black	White	Black	White	North and West	South	North and West	South
Males 14 to 24 years:								
1940_____	34.7	22.6	23.1	14.7	12.1	8.4	1.54	1.57
1950_____	22.9	10.7	14.0	8.0	12.2	6.0	2.14	1.75
1960_____	18.5	9.0	13.4	7.7	9.5	5.7	2.06	1.74
1970_____	16.7	8.6	12.4	6.7	8.1	5.7	1.94	1.85
Males 25 years and over:								
1940_____	16.5	9.4	11.6	6.4	7.1	5.2	1.76	1.81
1950_____	10.6	4.7	7.0	3.4	5.9	3.6	2.26	2.06
1960_____	9.8	3.9	7.0	3.3	5.9	3.7	2.51	2.12
1970_____	5.5	2.9	3.5	1.9	2.6	1.6	1.90	1.84

Note.—In 1940 black includes Negro and other nonwhite races; in 1950, 1960, and 1970 Negro only. In 1970 white includes some races other than Negro and American Indian usually classified as nonwhite. These other races made up 0.6 percent of the combined group "white and other" in the South and 1.8 percent in the North and West.

Source: Department of Commerce, Bureau of the Census.

reflected in the much smaller differences in earnings in the non-South between blacks and whites of the same education.

By 1950 eight States had passed enforceable fair employment laws, and by 1960 eight more had such legislation. All were outside the South. Perhaps for this reason the unemployment differential by race became much more pronounced in the non-South than in the South in 1950 and 1960. By 1970, however, the national Civil Rights Act (1964) prohibited discrimination in all States, and the regional difference in the unemployment differential became much smaller.

Factors other than equal opportunity legislation may also have influenced the regional pattern of unemployment by race. A large proportion of black workers in the North and West migrated from the South as young adults. As relative newcomers, they had less access to information about job opportunities than whites, who were more likely to have an established network of information among friends and relatives. Among blacks new to an area, information about where to expect discrimination would be gained primarily by experimentation. In the South, although many blacks migrated to urban areas, the available opportunities were probably much better known to the black community.

The persistence of a differential in unemployment between blacks and whites, after adjustment for skill and other factors, is therefore not easily explained. In part, the direct influence of discrimination may be greater on unemployment but less on wage rates now than in previous periods because of nationwide equal employment legislation. Moreover, ending all forms of current labor market discrimination would not necessarily affect unemployment in the short run. It could increase unemployment for a time as blacks found it worthwhile to search more widely for new and unfamiliar, but potentially highly rewarding, opportunities. On the other hand, groups that have been discriminated against for a long time may not immediately believe that a change has taken place, and therefore only gradually respond to the new opportunities. One would not, of course, expect substantial new investments or changes in occupation by older blacks in response to a decrease in current labor market discrimination, because they have already made investments specific to their job or occupation, and the length of their future work life is shorter.

UNEMPLOYMENT OF PERSONS OF SPANISH ORIGIN

Another group which has been subject to discrimination in the United States is made up of persons of Spanish descent who comprise about 5 percent of the population and of whom about 95 percent are white. In 1974 the unemployment rate for men classified as of Spanish origin was 7.3 percent, compared to 4.8 percent for all white men. For women, the comparison was 9.4 percent and 6.7 percent respectively.

Persons of Spanish origin differ from whites as a whole in characteristics that are likely to influence their unemployment rates. For example, among men aged 25 and over in 1974, the median years of school completed by men of Spanish origin was 9.7 years, compared to 12.4 years for all white men. Difficulties in communicating in English may affect employment opportunities, although this factor interacts with level of schooling. About 16 percent of persons classified as of Spanish heritage in the 1970 Census of Population were foreign-born, compared to 5 percent for all whites. Persons of Spanish origin are also more likely to be young and to live in the western regions of the country, two categories associated with higher unemployment. For example, about 30 percent of all persons of Spanish origin in the United States live in California, compared to about 10 percent for all whites in the United States; and the unemployment rate for California tends to be higher than the national average—44 percent higher in the period 1969 through 1973.

To determine the extent to which particular demographic and economic characteristics account for the difference in unemployment between those of Spanish heritage and whites not of Spanish heritage, an analysis similar to that for the black-white comparison was made on the basis of data from the 1970 Census of Population (Table 6–6). Although in the census (March 1970), men of Spanish heritage aged 16 and over had substantially higher unemployment rates than other white men, the differential of 2.3 percentage points is nearly halved when the data are restricted to men aged 25 to 64 who worked in 1969. The decline in the differential is largely due to the exclusion of youths aged 16 to 24, who make up a greater proportion of the Spanish heritage labor force than of the white labor force. Of the 1.3 percentage point differential in unemployment rates for adult men who worked in 1969, 0.6 percentage point, or nearly half, is attributable to region, that is, to the greater relative concentration of men of Spanish heritage in the West, where unemployment is high. Nearly all (92 percent) of the differential in unemployment rates of adult men is explained by the three variables: age, region, and schooling.

In March 1970 women of Spanish heritage aged 25 to 64 who worked in 1969 had higher unemployment rates than white women not of Spanish heritage, although 63 percent of the differential is due to differences in age and region (Table 6–6). After adjusting for differences in schooling, as well as in age and region, one finds that women of Spanish heritage actually have lower unemployment rates than other white women with the same characteristics—2.5 percent compared to 3.0 percent.

The analysis of unemployment differences between persons of Spanish heritage and other whites suggests that the significantly higher unemployment rate of the former is due to differences in age, region, and schooling. The extent to which these differences in characteristics are attributable to historical discrimination in the United States is not known, but it would seem that differences in unemployment rates are not a consequence of current labor market discrimination. This analysis does not, however, shed light on the magnitude of discrimination against persons of Spanish origin in other phases of their economic and social life.

UNEMPLOYMENT, INCOME, AND POVERTY

Assistance to the unemployed has been widely accepted on grounds of equity and economic efficiency as an appropriate Government function since the Great Depression of the 1930's. Greater equity can be achieved by increasing the income of the unemployed through transfers which spread the cost of unemployment among the public. In addition, the transfers may stimulate the employment of otherwise idle resources by increasing the aggregate demand for goods and services. Two major Government programs of the last four decades to provide income support for the unemployed are the unemployment insurance system and public service employment. These programs are discussed in the following chapters. This section considers the relation between unemployment and income, with particular emphasis on the issue of poverty.

A cyclical downturn in business activity is associated with lower employment and a shorter average workweek for the employed. The effect of a downturn is to change the level and distribution of aggregate earnings. Because approximately 95 percent of the labor force is employed, however, even a sharp rise in the unemployment rate means a relatively small decline in employment and therefore in earnings. For example, from 1969 to 1971 the unemployment rate increased from 3.5 to 5.9 percent, with little change in the rate of labor force participation; employment as a percentage of the labor force decreased from 96.5 percent to 94.1 percent, or by 2.5 percent. The average length of the workweek decreased by 0.6 hour (1.5 percent) to 39.3 hours. Thus, aggregate hours worked per member of the labor force decreased by approximately 4 percent.

This decrease in the hours of employment during a cyclical downturn is not shared equally throughout the labor force. Rather, for most workers little or no decline occurs in their hours of work, while for others the decrease is large. The result is more inequality in the distribution of income from employment. Empirical studies of income inequality among families and adult males in the post-World War II period demonstrate that inequality increases in recessions and decreases during cyclical expansions, but there has been no secular trend.

Because many unemployed individuals are eligible for income transfers, the decline in income for those who become unemployed is smaller than might be suggested by the decline in hours of work or in labor market earnings. In 1974 experienced workers who became unemployed because of layoffs (and in some cases because they quit their jobs) generally received unemployment insurance benefits for up to 26 or 39 weeks; and if income were sufficiently low, they qualified for income maintenance programs. Those who remained employed, though their hours of work fell, and those who were unemployed but ineligible for unemployment benefits could have received assistance from other income maintenance programs if their incomes were sufficiently low. Temporary legislation enacted in December 1974 increased the proportion of workers covered by unemployment compensation and, with amendments in 1975, increased the duration of benefits up to a maximum of 65 weeks during this period of high unemployment.

Recent studies based on 1971 survey data have estimated the extent to which transfer programs replace income losses associated with rising overall unemployment. The transfer programs include unemployment insurance, Aid to Families with Dependent Children, food stamps, and social security. Among households headed by a person aged 65 or under and at the poverty level before receiving the transfers, the programs were estimated to replace 31 percent of the lost earnings of male-headed households and 56 percent of the lost earnings of female-headed households. The replacement ratios were lower for higher-income families.

One study also calculated the average family income loss, after taking account of transfer benefits and changes in work participation of other family members, arising from unemployment of the family head. Among households experiencing some unemployment and headed by a man aged 65 or under, the average annual family income loss (net of transfers) associated with a 1 percentage point higher unemployment rate was estimated to be 5.7 percent for those at the poverty level. At five times the poverty level, the loss was 4.9 percent of the family income. Among households headed by a woman aged 65 or under, the estimated loss was approximately 3 percent for all income levels. There was, of course, considerable variation in income loss within these groups.

These estimates of income loss may be biased upward for several reasons. In surveys there is much more underreporting of transfer income than of earned income. Moreover, the appropriate comparison is with income after deduction of payroll and income taxes and of work-related expenses; and, although transfers are not subject to payroll and income taxation, the estimates were made for pretax earnings. In addition, no estimate was made of the value of extra home productivity or leisure arising from the reduced work time, a value that may not be negligible during brief spells of unemployment. The study is especially likely to underestimate replacement of lost earnings by transfers when the increased unemployment results from the business cycle, because the estimates were based on differences in income and unemployment between households at a moment in time. Cyclical increases in unemployment involve a larger proportion of workers eligible for unemployment compensation, because the unemployment is more heavily weighted toward layoffs than quits or labor force entry, and toward the covered sector of the work force. In addition, the maximum number of weeks for which benefits are available generally increases in a recession. For example, 64 percent of the unemployed received benefits in the high unemployment year of 1961, compared to 39 percent in the low unemployment year of 1966. On the other hand, additional factors may lead to a downward bias. The study could not account for the loss of employees' fringe benefits when they are unemployed, or for the adverse psychological and other effects due to the greater uncertainty among both the employed and the unemployed when unemployment rises. However, it would appear that the transfer programs may replace a substantial proportion of the loss in after-tax earnings, particularly during cyclical increases in unemployment.

Even during times of relatively low unemployment, more weeks of unemployment and lower incomes are associated with each other. Contrary to common belief, however, unemployment is no longer a major cause of poverty. Although during the Great Depression the relation between unemployment and poverty was undoubtedly strong, in the postwar period the relation weakened. Table 6–8 shows data on the

TABLE 6–8.—*Work experience of family heads below the low-income level, by sex, 1959 and 1972*

Work experience of head	Total		Male head		Female head	
	1959	1972	1959	1972	1959	1972
Total families (thousands)_____	8,320	5,075	6,404	2,917	1,916	2,158
Total families (percent)_____	100.0	100.0	100.0	100.0	100.0	100.0
Did not work full year_____	61.5	76.0	54.7	65.4	84.2	90.4
Unemployment a main reason for not working a full year_____	15.6	13.2	18.4	16.8	6.4	8.4
Worked 1–49 weeks_____	14.4	11.1	17.3	14.9	4.9	5.8
Did not work, unable to find a job_____	1.2	2.2	1.0	1.9	1.5	2.6
Unemployment not a main reason for not working a full year_____	45.9	62.7	36.3	48.5	77.9	82.0
Worked 1–49 weeks_____	16.5	19.1	14.8	16.4	22.3	22.7
Did not work and did not seek a job_____	29.4	43.7	21.5	32.2	55.6	59.3
Keeping house_____	10.9	19.0	(1)	(1)	47.5	44.7
Ill, disabled_____	9.5	14.6	10.8	17.1	5.4	11.3
Retired, going to school, and other reasons_	8.9	10.1	10.7	15.1	2.7	3.3
Worked a full year (50–52 weeks) [2]_____	38.5	24.0	45.3	34.6	15.8	9.6

[1] Not applicable.
[2] Includes head in Armed Forces.

Note.—Persons below the low-income level are those falling below the poverty index adopted by the Federal Inter-agency Committee in 1969.
Data for 1959 and 1972 are not exactly comparable because of changes in definition and methodology.
Detail may not add to totals because of rounding.

Sources: Department of Commerce (Bureau of the Census) and Council of Economic Advisers.

work experience of persons who headed poverty households in 1959 and 1972, years with roughly the same level of unemployment (5.5 percent) although the number and percentage of the population in poverty declined considerably over the period.

Although failure to work a full year was strongly associated with poverty in both years, only a minority of the heads of households in poverty cited inability to find work as the reason for working less than a full year. In 1959, only 15.6 percent of the heads of poverty households worked less than a full year because they could not find work, and by 1972 this percentage had decreased to 13.2 percent.

An increasing proportion of poor families are headed by someone who works only part of the year, or more often, who does not work at all—because of ill health, old age, or home responsibilities, not from inability to find a job. Low wage rates, however, remain an important cause of poverty.

The long-term decline in the relative importance of unemployment as a reason for poverty is primarily related to rising real wage rates during periods of employment and to increased real income supplements for the unemployed. In addition, for the same overall unemployment rate, the proportion of male heads of households experiencing unemployment has been declining.

CHAPTER 7

Unemployment Compensation Programs

The recession of 1974–75 has again demonstrated that the unemployment compensation system is one of our most effective countercyclical tools. As workers are placed on a layoff, benefits begin immediately, thereby providing financial assistance to those families most severely hurt by the fall in employment. This provision of purchasing power to the unemployed is of substantial importance in promoting economic recovery and in more equitably distributing the economic hardships of a recession. As the unemployment rate increased from the second quarter of 1973 to the second quarter of 1975, for example, the average weekly number of beneficiaries under all unemployment compensation programs increased from 1.5 million to 5.4 million. As the recovery continues, the size of the unemployment compensation programs will decrease when persons receiving benefits gain employment.

This section reviews the main features of the unemployment compensation system and considers some of its implications for income maintenance and efficiency in the long run.

PROGRAM CHARACTERISTICS

The nationwide unemployment compensation system had its origins in the 1935 Social Security Act. It is a joint program administered by the States within Federal guidelines. In addition, direct Federal unemployment programs cover four special groups: railroad workers, recently discharged members of the Armed Forces, Federal civilian employees, and those unemployed as a consequence of imports. A temporary federally funded program, special unemployment assistance (SUA), was introduced in January 1975 to provide benefits for wage and salary workers not covered by a regular Federal or State program. In addition, temporary Federal programs to extend the duration of benefits have been in effect in all recessions since 1958.

The legal rules and administrative practices of the unemployment compensation system vary substantially from State to State. There are, however, certain basic features. Generally, to be eligible for benefits a person must have had sufficient work experience and earnings in covered employment in a recent 1-year period prior to the onset of unemployment. As a result of the work experience requirement, new entrants and most reentrants to the labor force do not qualify for benefits. Nearly all workers on a job layoff but with work experience in a covered industry can qualify, so that total expenditures for unemployment benefits are highly sensitive to cyclical movements in the economy.

Eligibility also depends on the cause of unemployment. In all States persons unemployed because of a job layoff are eligible for benefits. Persons who voluntarily quit without "good cause" are subject to disqualification; however, the definition of good cause varies substantially among the States. For example, mandatory retirement, loss of transportation to work, or a change in location because a spouse changes jobs constitute good cause in some States, but not in others. Unemployment without good cause can still lead to compensation under the program in 31 States, but only after a disqualification period, and the length of the period varies widely. Strikers can receive unemployment benefits in New York and Rhode Island after a disqualification period. Thirteen States reduce or deny benefits to persons receiving social security retirement benefits.

As a further condition, to receive benefits the unemployed claimant must be able to work, be available for and actively seeking employment, and cannot reject a "suitable" job offer. The administration of the work test varies among the States. It also varies over the business cycle. The work test is harder to administer during a recession than when jobs are plentiful. Some States require weekly or biweekly visits to the local unemployment office to file a claim and collect benefits, and the claimant must present specific proof of job search. Other States require periodic interviews, ask for little or no documented proof of job search, and permit the mailing of benefit checks to the claimant's home.

In 43 States the duration of benefit entitlement under the regular program increases with the amount of work experience during the base period, generally up to a 26-week ceiling. Weekly benefits for these States are about one-half of the worker's pretax wage, up to a ceiling that varies among the States from $60 in Indiana to $139 per week in the District of Columbia as of January 1976. The other seven States have a fixed-duration program in which all eligible persons receive benefits for the same number of weeks, but the weekly benefit is itself determined by work experience and weekly earnings prior to unemployment. States where the maximum is $90 a week or more contain 70 percent of covered workers. Twelve States supplement the benefit check with a small dependency allowance for a spouse or dependent children who are not working.

Benefits have increased at about the same rate as wages in covered employment.[1] There has, however, been an increase over time in the extent to which income maintenance benefits from other programs, particularly food stamps, are available to supplement unemployment compensation. Some unemployed fathers in low-income families will receive larger benefits because of the June 1975 court decision which allows them to accept AFDC–UF benefits instead of unemployment compensation.

From the worker's point of view, the fact that unemployment insurance benefits are not subject to payroll or income taxes (as they are in some other industrial countries such as Canada and the United Kingdom) increases their value. For household heads earning $150 per week, unemployment benefits replace about 60 percent of wages (net of taxes) and fringe benefits lost because of unemployment, while for those earning $400 per week the replacement rate is about one-third. The replacement rate can be very high (close to 100 percent) for low-wage workers in high-income families: for example, where the wife has low earnings and the husband has high income and they are in a high marginal tax bracket.

Benefits under the State unemployment insurance system are funded by taxes levied on employers in proportion to workers' base wages, equal in most States to the first $4,200. In principle, the tax rate varies according to employers' experience ratings, which are based on the extent to which their workers draw benefits from the system. However, because the variation in tax rates is usually within narrow margins, many firms with very high or very low unemployment experience relative to their industry often realize no change in their tax rates as a result of changes in their unemployment experience. Because the unemployment insurance funds in many States have been seriously depleted by the recent recession, the Administration has proposed increases in the taxable earnings base and in the Federal component of the tax rate.

Potential coverage of workers has been extended under the regular programs, from 59 percent of all workers in 1950 to 81 percent in 1974,

---

1. As indicated in Table 7–1, in the 1970s the average weekly unemployment insurance benefit has been about 36 percent of average weekly wages in covered employment (a slight increase over the 33 percent ratio that prevailed in the 1950s). However, these ratios are underestimates of the amount of earnings replaced by unemployment compensation for those who are actually unemployed. As noted above, benefits are generally one-half of former earnings (before taxes) up to the state maximum. The unemployed receiving benefits tend to be workers with lower earnings, with a larger proportion below the state maximum than is the case for those who are employed at any time. Moreover, benefits are not subject to either payroll or income taxes, although earnings are. The ratio of benefits to past earnings after taxes for those who are collecting benefits is estimated to be about 50 to 60 percent. [Editors]

because industrial coverage was made broader in 1954 and 1972 and because of a decline in the proportion of the labor force in the major remaining sectors not covered: agriculture, self-employment, and unpaid employment in a family business. As a result of special unemployment assistance, coverage was extended to the approximately 12 million wage and salary workers not covered by a regular program, primarily State and local government, farm, and domestic workers.[2] Legislation enacted in 1976 requires that the states bring under coverage about 9 million of the 12 million wage and salary workers now covered by SUA so that their employers will contribute to the unemployment insurance trust fund. Those still not included are primarily employees of small farms and domestics working few hours in a calendar quarter. The 8 million self-employed and unpaid workers in family businesses are not covered by a regular or temporary program.

In spite of the increased coverage there has been a decline over the past 20 years in the proportion of the unemployed receiving benefits under the regular State programs (Table 7–1). This is probably due to the change in the composition of the labor force. Because of the eligibility requirements, many unemployed youths and women with weak labor market attachment do not have sufficient work experience to qualify for benefits. As these groups have increased in relative importance both in the labor force and among the unemployed, the proportion of the unemployed receiving benefits declined. Among the group with a more stable labor force attachment, men aged 25 and over, there has been a secular increase in the proportion of the unemployed claiming benefits. For example, this proportion declined from 54 percent in 1960 to 41 percent in 1973 for all unemployed persons, but for men aged 25 and over it increased from 63 percent to 72 percent.

Temporary programs to extend the duration of benefit entitlements in a recession have become more common. Prior to 1970 benefits were temporarily extended to 39 weeks in 1958 and 1961–62. A 1970 law permanently authorized an extension of benefits to 39 weeks in times of high State or national unemployment. In 1975, there was an unprecedented temporary extension of benefits in all States to a maximum duration of 65 weeks through the 26 weeks of federal funded benefits provided under Federal supplemental benefits (FSB). Under current legislation, FSB benefits are scheduled to terminate in March 1977, or earlier if there is a sufficiently low State or nationwide unemployment rate. The purpose of this phasing out is that unemployment compensa-

2. Farm and domestic workers had generally been excluded from coverage under the regular State programs because of the substantial administrative difficulties in the verification of previous employment and wages, availability for work and experience rating of employers. [Editors]

TABLE 7–1.—*Insured unemployment as percent of total unemployment and unemployment benefits as percent of average weekly earnings, 1948–73*

Year	Insured unemployment as percent of total unemployment						Average weekly State unemployment benefits as percent of average weekly earnings in covered employment
	Total insured [1]	State insured [2]					
		Total 16 years and over	Men		Women		
			16 to 24 years	25 years and over	16 to 24 years	25 years and over	
1948	63.5	43.1					34.1
1949	68.0	54.2					36.0
1950	48.8	46.0					34.4
1951	48.7	47.2					32.2
1952	56.8	55.4					33.0
1953	58.2	54.0					32.3
1954	58.1	52.9					33.5
1955	49.1	44.4					32.1
1956	48.1	44.2					33.3
1957	54.9	50.6					33.5
1958	71.0	54.9					35.3
1959	56.1	45.0					33.4
1960	53.8	49.5	24.0	63.3	19.2	63.9	35.2
1961	63.5	48.6	25.3	62.8	19.2	58.6	35.4
1962	49.8	45.6	20.9	60.3	17.1	58.3	34.9
1963 [3]	48.5	44.4	19.5	59.4	16.7	58.6	34.6
1964	46.3	42.4	16.8	60.9	14.8	56.5	33.8
1965	43.1	39.5	14.6	59.9	12.3	54.6	33.8
1966	39.3	36.9	11.9	61.0	9.8	53.3	34.7
1967	42.7	40.5	13.6	72.4	11.8	53.2	34.7
1968	42.1	39.4	11.7	74.0	9.8	56.9	34.3
1969	41.6	38.9	10.7	76.6	9.3	57.3	34.4
1970	50.6	44.2	16.0	76.9	12.8	65.1	35.7
1971	46.3	43.1	17.6	74.2	13.4	58.6	36.5
1972	45.1	38.2	15.7	70.6	11.2	52.6	35.9
1973	41.4	37.8	15.7	71.7	11.2	53.8	36.0

[1] Includes persons covered under the following unemployment compensation programs: State, Federal employee, Railroad Retirement Board, and veterans. Also includes Federal and State extended benefit programs.
[2] Includes only persons covered under the State programs and excludes all other programs as well as Federal and State extended benefit programs.
[3] Totals include Puerto Rican sugar cane workers beginning July 1963; but they are excluded from data by sex and age

Note.—State insured unemployment data are not available by age and sex prior to 1960.

Source: Department of Labor, Manpower Administration.

tion should not discourage workers from actively seeking employment when job possibilities improve. During 1976 FSB benefits were reduced in states with low unemployment rates.

Some union contracts have provisions for private supplements to State unemployment compensation. For example, United Auto Workers' contracts have established Supplemental Unemployment Benefit Funds (SUB Funds) to which the employer contributes. A worker with at least 3 years' experience could receive a stipend from the fund for up to 52 weeks which would make his total State plus SUB Fund compensation approximately 95 percent of his regular take-home earnings, less $7.50. In January 1975 the average weekly SUB Fund benefit was approximately $100 for a worker receiving State unemployment insurance benefits and $185 for a worker who had exhausted the State benefits. SUB Fund benefits are subject to income taxation. Many of these private funds were eventually depleted during the very high unemployment in 1975.

Some Effects of the Program

In recent years there has been considerable research on how the availability, potential duration, and size of unemployment benefits affect the measured unemployment rate. Although their estimates must be interpreted with caution, the studies are suggestive of the general impact of the program.

Several studies have used individual data to examine the effect on unemployment of the potential duration and level of benefits. The quantitative findings vary from study to study, in part because they differ in methodology, data, and time period. However, they all tend to indicate that the duration of actual unemployment is greater the higher the benefit level and the longer the potential duration of benefits. There is evidence, moreover, that the duration of benefit entitlement may be even more important than the level of benefits in explaining unemployment duration.

One study examined the effect of covering agricultural wage and salary workers (who had previously been covered in only two States) with the introduction of special unemployment assistance in January 1975. The study developed equations to predict agricultural unemployment rates and employment on the basis of cyclical and other factors. Seasonally adjusted data were used to compare the observed and predicted values before and after the introduction of SUA. After SUA, seasonally adjusted employment was lower during the off-season, presumably because of the availability of unemployment compensation. The seasonally adjusted unemployment rate increased by about 20 percent (2 percentage points) in the off-season, but did not change in the on-season. Apparently because of the SUA benefits, in 1975 the annual unemployment rate of agricultural wage and salary workers seems to have been about 10 percent greater than that predicted on the basis of cyclical and other factors. However, one year's experience may not be sufficient to estimate the long-term magnitude of these effects.

The extent to which States engage in eligibility screening can affect the amount of observed unemployment. The proportion of claims for unemployment compensation under the State programs that are rejected on the basis of individual State administrative decisions regarding eligibility can be called a "denial rate". Using State data for 1971, one recent study found that this denial rate had a significant impact on the State unemployment rate. It was estimated, for example, that at the margin a 10 percent increase in the national denial rate from the observed 25 per 1,000 claimant contacts would lower the national unemployment rate by 0.14 percentage point. It appears that a higher denial rate may not only decrease the period of unemployment among those denied benefits but many have an even larger impact by discouraging unemployment among others. Eligibility screening is subject to administrative control. Greater administrative expenditures and more time devoted to eligibility screening appear to result in a higher denial rate, particularly for reasons related to unavailability for work and the rejection of suitable employment. These effects are likely to be weaker during a period of high unemployment when job vacancies are more scarce. And, beyond some point, additional expenditures would have much smaller effects.

Certain categories of workers are more strongly affected by benefits than others. Those who have home responsibilities or are approaching retirement are more likely to remain unemployed until they exhaust their benefit entitlements. A study of the unemployment insurance system in Nevada in 1971–72, for example, found that a substantially larger proportion of exhaustees were either aged 55 or over or women, compared to those who stopped collecting benefits prior to exhausting their entitlement. Although greater difficulty in finding jobs may explain part of the differential, it cannot explain all of it. In this study, for example, 2 months after benefit exhaustion, 30 percent were employed, and another 30 percent had withdrawn from the labor force, primarily because of ill health, retirement, or family responsibilities. Similar findings emerge from other studies.

For most persons, however, the income support provided by the unemployment compensation system is a means of financing the search for a job. For these persons, if a longer period of unemployment facilitates job search and leads to a job with higher wages and better fringe benefits, more pleasant working conditions, or a longer expected job tenure, it may represent a worthwhile investment. Thus far, however, studies of the effect of the additional job search stimulated by unemployment compensation have been inconclusive.

The unemployment insurance system also affects employers' behavior through the operation of the payroll tax. The tax levied on a particular employer does not depend strongly on the actual unemployment experience of his workers. Because of the weak experience rating the cost of a layoff is reduced. Partly because of the unemployment compensation benefits, workers would be less likely to seek other jobs during these periods of unemployment, particularly if unemployment is widespread. Thus the payroll tax subsidizes seasonal, cyclical, and casual unemployment relative to stable employment. This greater frequency of unemployment thereby leads to an increase in the unemployment rate. Data from a variety of sources indicate that much of the unemployment arising from job layoffs is temporary and does not involve a change in employer. For example, since 1960, manufacturing establishments had an average of 1.5 layoffs per 100 employees per month. During this period their rehire rate was 1.3 workers per 100 employees per month. Thus, on average, 85 percent of layoffs resulted in reemployment by the same establishment.

Results of various studies of the effects of unemployment compensation indicate that it is our most efficient tool for quickly providing financial help to those who lose a job. However, and to a large extent unavoidably, the existence of this automatic aid makes it easier for employers to lay off workers and for workers to prolong their period of unemployment. One implication is that the unemployment rate is affected by the amount and duration of unemployment compensation benefits.

CHAPTER 8

Policies to Increase Employment

[The sharp rise in unemployment in 1974 and 1975, combined with forecasts that it will be several years before the unemployment rate is reduced to the 1973 level (4.9 percent), spurred renewed interest in Federal Government policies to reduce unemployment. The two basic issues under debate were the size of the budget deficit and the form of the Federal program. Larger deficits were called for by those who wanted to reduce unemployment more rapidly. However, larger deficits were cautioned against by those who feared that a too rapid increase in spending would re-ignite the excessive inflation of 1974.

Some wanted the government fiscal stimulus in the form of reductions in personal and corporate income taxes to promote output and employment in the private sector. Others favored a more direct job creation program through expanded public service employment (PSE) and public works programs. An employment tax credit was also suggested as a means of stimulating the private sector's demand for labor.

After a brief review of the recent history of public service employment in the United States, this chapter presents a paper prepared by the CEA for the Joint Economic Committee as a supplement to the 1976 Economic Report. The paper analyzes the relative merits of direct policies (PSE, public works, employment tax credit) compared to indirect policies (neutral tax cuts) to stimulate employment.]

PUBLIC SERVICE EMPLOYMENT—HISTORY

Federal public service employment programs are a means of increasing employment opportunities, particularly during periods of high unemployment. It is intended that Federal revenues will be used to employ persons who would otherwise be jobless, in government jobs that would not otherwise exist.

The Emergency Employment Act of 1971 (EEA) provided the first large-scale public employment program broadly applicable to the unemployed population since the Works Progress Administration (WPA) of the 1930s. Special types of public employment programs for particular target groups, however, have been funded on a more limited scale since the 1960s, for example, the summer employment of youths in the Neighborhood Youth Corps and the subsidized employment of the elderly in Operation Mainstream. In contrast to the WPA, which was administered by separate Federal agencies created for the task, the Public Employment Program (PEP) under EEA was essentially a form of revenue sharing, with the Federal Government supplying the funds and State and local governments actually administering the program. PEP was conceived as a counter-cyclical program to provide "transitional" jobs at a time when the unemployment rate was about 6 percent. In fiscal 1973, when the program was in full operation, an estimated 150,000 man-years of employment were funded by the PEP program.

The Comprehensive Employment and Training Act (CETA), which became operative in 1974, provides public employment funds to States and localities which act as prime sponsors. Under Title I, bloc grants for manpower programs allocated to the sponsor may at the sponsor's discretion be applied to public service employment or to any other activity related to manpower. Title II is labeled Public Employment Programs, but the funds can be used for either public service employment or traditional manpower programs, such as on-the-job training. Title II funding is to be provided only to areas where the unemployment rate has averaged 6.5 percent or higher for 3 consecutive months. In practice, Title I funding is almost entirely for manpower training and Title II is almost entirely PSE. Titles III and IV of CETA are relatively small programs that provide training for Indians, migrant workers, and some others, and provide funding for the Jobs Corps. Title VI of CETA is a temporary program created in December 1974 (Emergency Jobs and Unemployment Assistance Act) to provide additional PSE slots. About 310,000 PSE slots were funded under all CETA titles in fiscal years 1975 and 1976. Compensation and administrative costs per man-year were about $9,000 for PSE jobs.

POLICIES TO INCREASE EMPLOYMENT

The Council of Economic Advisers has examined a number of policy proposals to increase employment. The main issues are: (1) for a given increase in fiscal stimulus, can employment be increased more with a selective policy rather than with a neutral policy such as a tax cut? and (2) the extent to which selective policies and measures contain defects that pose other problems which are not inherent in the use of general fiscal measures.

The conclusion of our analyses is that selective policies such as public service employment, private employment tax credits, or public works construction may temporarily add more employment than a neutral tax cut (though only after a long lag in the case of both the tax credit and public works program). However, at the same time, resources are mis-allocated and, on balance, we may therefore get less economic growth and less employment with selective policies than with a neutral cut of personal and business income taxes. In addition, selective policies are more difficult to control in amount, in timing and in termination.

A tax cut has the great virtue of assisting the normal forces at work in the economy to stimulate growth and employment. If relative prices are not distorted it is reasonable to assume that expansion will be greatest in those activities with the highest economic payoff, and that capital and labor will be used in the most efficient—i.e., least cost—way.

The three selective policies which have attracted the most attention as ways of getting a greater increase in employment than a tax reduction, with a similar cost to the Federal Government, are public service employment, an employment tax credit, and public works.

Public Service Employment

Public service employment (PSE) programs are a special form of grant that aims to encourage a temporary expansion of state and local employment. A general Federal tax cut could also result in an increase in public sector employment. However, to do so, State and local governments would be required to divert the reduction in Federal revenues to their own use by raising their taxes; if taxpayers preferred private goods to public goods, this would be a difficult task.

Proponents of public employment programs argue that it is a less expensive and a surer way to guarantee that a given amount of Federal outlay or tax reduction will result in increases in employment. However, there is no easy way of distinguishing a worker filling a PSE slot from a worker who would, in the ordinary course of events, be hired by a state or local government.[1] Furthermore, State and local governments now have more experience with, and can plan for, PSE slots. Hence, they may now be more effective in using PSE monies for job slots that they would otherwise fund from their own resources. On the basis of experience with the Public Employment Program (PEP) of 1971–1973, it has been estimated that a PSE program does initially create more jobs than an income tax reduction. However, the effect diminishes over time, becoming negligible after two years, as State and local governments substitute Federal funds for their own funds.

A $1 billion PSE program for example could pay for approximately 110,000 job slots at $9,000 per job (wages and the 10 percent allowance for other costs). Based on research of previous programs, however, State

1. State and local government employment increased by 570,000 jobs (4.7 percent) in 1975, more than twice the increase in PSE slots.

TABLE 8–1.—*Jobs paid for and jobs created under a $1 billion public service employment program.*
(Jobs in thousands)

Start of Spending	Jobs	By End of Quarter							
		1	2	3	4	5	6	7	8
Initial quarter	Paid for [1]	55	55	55	55	55	55	55	55
	Created [2]	41.3	33.0	27.5	22.0	13.7	5.5	5.5	5.5
Second quarter	Paid for [1]	0	55	55	55	55	55	55	55
	Created [2]	0	41.3	33.0	27.5	22.0	13.7	5.5	5.5
All Spending	Total jobs paid for [1]	55	110	110	110	110	110	110	110
	Totals jobs created [2]	41.3	74.3	60.5	47.5	25.7	19.2	11.0	11.0

[1] Number of persons in PSE slots.
[2] Incremental jobs created compared to a $1 billion reduction in personal income taxes.

Source: Council of Economic Advisers.

Assumptions for Table 8–1:

(1) **Total Spending:** $1 billion annual spending.

(2) **Cost per Worker:** $9,000. (To cover wages and salaries and the 10 percent allowance for other costs.)

(3) **Maximum Jobs Funded:** From (1) and (2)—The maximum funding is 110,000 jobs.

(4) **Time Path of Jobs Funded:** Based on past experience, the time path for the initiation of spending is assumed to be:

By end of:
1st quarter—50 percent
2nd quarter—100 percent

Hence, 55,000 jobs are funded by the end of the first quarter and 110,000 by the end of the second quarter.

(5) **Displacement effect:**

Based on previous research,[1] the displacement effects are assumed to be:

1st quarter—25 percent
2nd quarter—40 percent
3rd quarter—50 percent
4th quarter—60 percent
5th quarter—75 percent
6th quarter—and thereafter 90 percent

While the Federal Government has an incentive to reduce the replacement effect, prime sponsors have an incentive to increase it. The estimates are mainly based on the PEP program which was the first of its type in the postwar period. The experience gained with the PEP and CETA programs will probably operate to increase replacement ratios in future programs.

(6) **Marginal Propensities to Consume:** It is assumed that the families of the recipients of the jobs created by PSE have the same marginal propensity to consume as the beneficiaries of a tax cut.

(7) **State and Local Budgets:** Because of the replacement effect, some of the Federal grant (e.g., 25 percent in the first quarter under assumption (5)) can be used for other purposes:

(a) to reduce the size of the state and local government annual deficit (or increase the surplus).

(b) to keep taxes lower than otherwise.

(c) to purchase goods from the private sector.

Dollars allocated under (a) are likely to have a smaller aggregate stimulus than an equal dollar of a Federal tax cut, while dollars allocated under (c) are likely to have a larger aggregate stimulus. No large difference in stimulus would be expected from a tax cut at the Federal rather than the State and local level. In the long run the dollars freed by the replacement effect are likely to appear primarily as lower taxes, but the short-run allocation is ambiguous. In the absence of more specific information it is assumed that the net stimulus from the dollars freed by the replacement effect is the same as an equal dollar amount of a Federal tax cut.

(8) **Time Path of Spending:** The lag in the initiation of spending under a tax cut is likely to be shorter than under PSE. Then, the procedure adopted would result in an upward bias in the short run in the number of jobs created by PSE compared to a tax cut.

[1] See Alan Fechter, **Public Employment Programs** (Washington, American Enterprise Institute 1975), and George Johnson and James Tomola, "An Impact Evaluation of Public Employment Programs," Technical Analysis Paper, A.S.P.E.R., Department of Labor, 1974, mimeo. and the references therein.

and local government displacement of the funds is estimated to be about 40 percent after two quarters, 60 percent after one year and 90 percent after two or three years. There are, however, also lags in program spending. It is estimated that, compared to a personal income tax reduction of a similar magnitude, the impact of a $1 billion PSE program after two quarters would result in about 74,000 jobs created, after one year 48,000 jobs and after two years about 11,000 (see Table 8–1). After two years, nearly $100 million of the $1 billion program would be spent to create new jobs and nearly $900 million would in effect be supporting jobs that States and localities would otherwise have financed themselves.

The foregoing estimates might vary somewhat for a massive PSE program i.e., a program which attempts to "create" jobs far in excess of the normal State and local government job needs. However, the spending of funds for such a program would be much slower. It takes time to "create" jobs, and State and local governments would be reluctant to hire a large number of workers who would have to be either discharged when the temporary Federal program ended or funded out of State and local sources.

The difficulty in discharging workers under PSE-type programs leads to the strong likelihood that a massive program would mean a permanent increase in relatively non-productive public employment. Several European countries have inadvertently created too large a ratio of public to private employment, with significant adverse consequences on economic growth and standards of living.

Other drawbacks of PSE programs in general should be noted. State and local governments are presumably now doing the tasks they, and their taxpayers, view as most important. Although workers undertaking tasks with only marginal value will appear as employed in the labor force data, in an economic sense they are really unemployed. However, they are receiving a higher level of income through the PSE program than would have been received through unemployment compensation. This is not to say that it is better to receive unemployment compensation or welfare than to work. Rather, it necessitates more consideration of the type of work that can be done in a temporary program, the cost per individual of this kind of program, and of the alternatives available.

The workers hired under PSE are usually those with a better than average chance to get unsubsidized jobs (Table 8–2). While the statutes often contain preferences for the long-term unemployed, the programs are not able to target those out of work who have the most difficulty finding regular employment.

Persons in public service jobs (whether essential or marginal) have less time available and less of a financial incentive to search for, and accept, private sector employment. During a period of expanding pri-

TABLE 8–2.—*Comparison of selected characteristics of participants in fiscal 1974 categorical programs, CETA Titles I, II and VI in fiscal 1975 and the U.S. unemployed population, July 1, 1974 through June 30, 1975.*

Characteristic	Fiscal 1974 Categorical programs	CETA—Fiscal 1975 Title I	CETA—Fiscal 1975 Title II	CETA—Fiscal 1975 Title VI	U.S. Unemployment Population
Total:					
Percent....................	100.0	100.0	100.0	100.0	100.0
Sex:					
Male........................	57.7	54.4	65.8	70.2	54.9
Female.....................	42.3	45.6	34.2	29.8	45.1
Age:					
Under 22 years...........	63.1	61.7	23.7	21.4	34.8
22 to 44 years............	30.5	32.1	62.9	64.8	46.0
45 years and over........	6.2	6.1	13.4	13.8	19.1
Education:					
8 years or less...........	15.1	13.3	9.4	8.4	15.1
9 to 11 years..............	51.1	47.6	18.3	18.2	28.9
12 years and over.........	33.6	39.1	72.3	73.3	56.0
Economically disadvantaged...........	86.7	77.3	48.3	43.6	(¹)
Ethnic Group					
White.......................	54.9	54.6	65.1	71.1	81.1
Black........................	37.0	38.5	21.8	22.9	
American Indian...........	3.5	1.3	1.0	1.1	18.9
Other........................	4.6	5.6	12.1	4.9	
					6.5
Spanish-speaking..........	15.4	12.5	16.1	12.9	
Limited English-speaking ability......	(¹)	4.1	8.0	4.6	(¹)
Veterans:					
Special Vietnam Era................	15.3	5.2	11.3	12.5	7.5
Other........................	(¹)	4.4	12.6	14.6	9.3

¹ Not available.

Note:Detail may not add to total due to rounding.

Source: Employment and Training Administration, Department of Labor.

vate sector employment opportunities it would be more appropriate to be encouraging workers to seek and accept regular, productive private sector jobs.

For a public employment program to be counter-cyclical, a mechanism is needed to phase out the program as unemployment falls. The jobs provided must be such that they can be both established quickly and readily "detriggered" as job opportunities in the private sector increase. In part, this will occur if workers voluntarily leave public sector employment for higher paying regular jobs. However, the more attractive public service employment is in terms of current and expected future wages, the more difficult it is to reduce the program. And the more essential the services performed, the greater will be the pressure from State and local governments to maintain Federal funding.

PSE jobs that are truly temporary, in many cases are likely to be filled by persons who would otherwise be out of the labor force rather than by the unemployed who are already receiving benefits, and for whom a temporary job may be a deterrent to more permanent public or private sector re-employment. To provide jobs for those who are most needy a public employment program must create jobs, requiring a very short training period, which can be filled by persons of diverse prior training, employment experience and age. It is extremely difficult to design a program which meets all of these criteria.

There is a tendency for PSE legislation to urge that the jobs be of the type to lead to permanent careers. But the more closely the jobs resemble the ordinary occupational structure of the sponsoring government, and the more career-oriented they are, the more likely it is that the displacement effect will be large. Thus, to insure that jobs are net additions to the economy it may be necessary for States and localities to try to create distinct tasks for these subsidized workers, in separate job categories created for the purpose. This may increase the difficulty of creating programs that provide productive employment.

It should also be noted that State and local government employment is only 16 percent of non-farm payroll employment. This sector by itself could not be a major factor in generating enough useful jobs to substantially reduce the unemployment rate, without dramatically increasing the proportion of output devoted to publicly-produced services at the expense of privately-produced goods and services.

In summary, a moderate PSE program, whether temporary or permanent, suffers from a high replacement rate, and generates only a small, temporary increase in employment compared to a tax cut of a similar magnitude. If a PSE program is permanent it is likely to become, in effect, a permanent increase in Federal grants to State and local governments, without however a corresponding permanent increase in the number of jobs. A massive temporary PSE program is not likely to substantially increase useful employment within a year or two. In the short run, many of the additional jobs would be marginal, and they would soon compete with the expanded opportunities for private sector employment. If the PSE programs were to work over longer periods of time, moreover, they would represent a permanent addition to the size of the public sector relative to the private sector, unless offset by program reductions elsewhere. The long-term costs of funding public jobs programs, to produce public goods and services not now produced, would fall upon a relatively smaller private sector.

Employment Tax Credit

A private employment tax credit subsidizes the wages of additional workers in order to encourage more labor-intensive methods of production while stimulating output. One version of an employment tax credit would give employers a credit of a fixed number of dollars per month for each full-time equivalent worker on the payroll in excess of, for example, 1975 employment levels. Another version would provide a credit proportional to the increase in the wage bill above the 1975 level.

In either case, it is difficult to estimate the outcome and the final budget cost. Because there is no way of identifying for each firm the increases in employment induced solely by the tax credit, a large component of the Federal expenditure would be for employment increases which would have taken place in any event. Thus, much of the tax credit would simply provide a windfall to private firms. Although the proponents of an employment tax credit have suggested that the Federal cost per net job created would be very low—lower in fact than for public service employment jobs—this windfall effect is likely to raise the cost per job actually created far above the figures usually cited.

As we approach full employment, the problem will arise of either maintaining the credit and perpetuating what was intended to be a counter-cyclical program or removing the credit and perhaps inducing layoffs and unemployment. A gradual reduction of the credit would reduce or eliminate this disemployment but would extend its life and the program cost several years into the future. Unless the credit is removed, however, the subsidy to the use of labor relative to other factors of production would retard growth by maintaining a less efficient allocation of resources.

Furthermore, it is not easy to design an "equitable" employment tax credit. An employment tax credit would tend to provide larger subsidies to rapidly growing industries, those that have greater short-term flexibility in employment patterns, and to cyclically sensitive industries during periods of business expansion. Stable, slow growing industries which would incur large costs in adjusting temporarily to a higher ratio of labor to capital might not receive any subsidy. The pressures to broaden the scope of the program to prevent inequities would be difficult to resist. It is worth recalling that the investment tax credit was originally proposed as a credit for increases in investment. But equity problems quickly dictated giving credit for all investment, not just increases. It is likely that similar pressures could cause an employment tax credit to be converted to a general wage subsidy.

Theoretically, an employment tax credit that is a fixed amount per worker, rather than a percent of the wage bill, would have a greater effect on the number of workers, as there would be a substitution toward unskilled workers and the industries that employ them, and away from higher-paid skilled workers and the industries in which they are employed in substantial numbers. Although possibly desirable in the short run, such a substitution would adversely effect the long-term growth of the economy.

A tax credit tied to the total wage bill is neutral with respect to the skill level of the workers. It may, however, make it more difficult for employers to resist large salary increases that inflate the wage bill.

Once the precedent is set for an employment tax credit, employers may expect it to reappear in the future. On the basis of this expectation they would have less of an incentive to engage in labor "hoarding" (reducing employment by less than the fall in output) in future recessions. It is interesting to note that one major difference between this recession and the most comparable previous recession—that of 1957–58—is the smaller percentage point decline in employment for each percentage point fall in output. If one and a half years ago, employers had expected an employment tax credit during the recovery, the fall in employment and the rise in the unemployment rate would presumably have been much sharper.

Because of a concern with the high youth unemployment rate, some have suggested an employment tax credit for youths. Minimum wage and mandated social insurance taxes may have raised the minimum employment cost of labor above the productivity of many young workers, thereby decreasing their employment opportunities. An employment tax credit for youths applied only to increments in employment above the 1975 level in a particular firm would encourage a substantial shifting of employment. Some firms would decrease youth employment while others would increase it to qualify for the credit, with the net increase in youth employment perhaps being small. To reduce this socially inefficient shift of labor would require providing the credit for all employed youths. This, of course, would create a substantial windfall for youth-intensive industries—e.g., fast food chains.

From experience with other programs it is known that firms will respond to an employment tax credit program in such a way as to have the subsidy apply to an even larger proportion of workers who would be employed in any case. Because we have not had experience with an employment tax credit, the likely magnitude of this effect cannot be estimated. This problem however would be more severe for a program that focuses on a particular demographic group (e.g., youths).

Countercyclical Public Works Programs

Large-scale public works programs as a method of reducing unemployment are subject to several significant drawbacks. Analyses of past efforts to use public work construction projects as a countercyclical fiscal measure do not support the idea that such programs will quickly provide for the unemployed. Large-scale public works programs require long lead times before the projects get under way and even longer lead times before they are completed. Past experience suggests that only 10 percent of the funds are actually spent in the first year in which

Part III

Economic Issues Concerning the Aged and Women

[CERTAIN ISSUES HAVE particular social and economic importance, and over the past decade the CEA Reports have included more detailed discussion of several of these issues. The social security system, once the least controversial of Government programs, has recently become a subject of growing concern. Current deficits and the prospect of serious long-range financing problems have contributed to the concern. Furthermore many have begun to challenge the equity of the income transfers created by social security and to question the effects of the program on work incentives and savings. The social security system is the subject of Chapter 9.

Chapter 10 looks at women's role in the economy, which has changed so significantly over the past 20 years. The chapter stresses the factors behind the shift from work in the home to work in the market and the consequences of women's past role in the home on their current experiences in the labor market. The earnings, occupational, and unemployment differentials between men and women are analyzed and there is a discussion of discrimination as a factor in causing differentials. Additional topics covered in the chapter are, the female-headed household, the equity of the income tax structure as it affects the working wife, child care, and the role of Government action.]

CHAPTER 9

Social Security and the Aged

The old-age, survivors, and disability insurance program, generally referred to as social security, is the largest income transfer program, in terms of both funds and number of recipients. In 1975, 32 million persons received cash benefits of $67 billion, which was 19 percent of the Federal budget and 4.5 percent of GNP (Table 9–1). Growth in the program has been extraordinary during the past 5 years. The number of recipients increased by 22 percent, and after adjusting for the increase in prices over this period, the average monthly benefit for retired workers increased by 26 percent.

TABLE 9–1.—*Beneficiaries and cash benefits in the old-age, survivors, and disability insurance program (OASDI), selected years, 1950–75*

Beneficiary or benefit	1950	1960	1965	1970	1974	1975
Number of beneficiaries (millions) [1]:						
Total_____	3.5	14.8	20.9	26.2	30.9	31.9
Retired workers, dependents, and survivors_____	3.5	14.2	19.1	23.6	26.9	27.6
Retired workers only_____	1.8	8.1	11.1	13.3	16.0	16.5
Disabled workers and dependents_____	--------	.7	1.7	2.7	3.9	4.3
Annual cash benefits (billions of dollars)_____	1.0	11.3	18.3	31.9	58.5	67.1
Average monthly benefits (dollars):						
All retired workers [1]_____	44	74	84	118	188	206
Maximum to men retiring at age 65 [2]_____	45	119	132	190	[3] 305	[3] 342
Maximum to women retiring at age 65 [2]_____	45	119	136	196	[3] 316	[3] 360
Minimum to persons retiring at age 65 [2]_____	10	33	44	64	[3] 94	[3] 101

[1] As of December of each year.
[2] Assumes retirement at beginning of year.
[3] As of June.

Source: Department of Health, Education, and Welfare.

The social security system has been successful in raising the income levels of a large proportion of the elderly who otherwise would have been impoverished. However, because of the sheer size of the program, there is a need to evaluate recent developments in the pattern of expenditures and of the taxes required to fund them.

PROGRAM CHARACTERISTICS

The first social security legislation of 1935 intended that the program operate on a self-financed and actuarially sound basis. Contributions from the payroll tax were to exceed benefits in the early years so that a substantial trust fund relative to annual benefit outlays could be accumulated. Individual benefits were to be closely related to each individual's prior earnings except for preferential treatment at the base (minimum) amount. The amendments of 1939 changed the character of the program by stipulating that individuals retiring early in the life of the program would receive benefits greater than the actuarial value of taxes paid, and that dependents of retired workers would also receive benefits without any additional tax payments required. The 1950 amendments moved still farther away from a fully funded trust to the "pay-as-you-go" system which prevails today, under which those currently working essentially pay for the benefits of those who are retired.

As of January 1976, OASDI benefits are funded from a tax of 9.9 percent levied on the first $15,300 of wages, the maximum taxable earnings, with the payments shared equally by employer and employees. The self-employed pay a tax of 7 percent. (An additional tax of 1.8 percent for wage and salary workers and 0.9 percent for the self-employed is for medicare hospital insurance.) Tax payments are paid into separate trust funds, one for retirement and survivors, and one for disability. About 90 percent of all wage and salary earners and the self-employed are covered by the program and subject to mandatory contributions. The major exclusions are Federal civilian employees, who are under a separate Federal retirement program, and some State and local employees. In the past, increases in benefits and taxes have been legislated by the Congress periodically. Starting in 1975, on the basis of the 1972 amendments, benefit levels were "indexed" or linked to the consumer price index so that they rise automatically depending on increases in prices. Similarly, the maximum taxable earnings base was roughly indexed to changes in average covered wages, and hence it also increases automatically over time.

Social security is designed as a replacement for earnings lost because of a worker's retirement, disability, or death. Eligibility for benefits depends on work in covered employment for a minimum period as well as on age, disability, or survivor status. Although there are no restrictions on the amount of income that may be received from property, other pensions, or any sources other than work, individual benefits may be reduced if the beneficiary has earnings from employment and is less than 72 years of age. In 1976 beneficiaries can earn $2,760 without any reduction in benefits, but for each $2 in earnings above $2,760, benefits are reduced by $1. The amount of a worker's basic monthly benefit (before any reductions) depends on the worker's record of covered earnings, averaged over a specified number of years (at present 20 years for retirement benefits). Dependents and dependent survivors receive payments tied to the benefit level of the primary beneficiary. Workers choosing to retire between ages 62 and 65 receive a permanently reduced benefit. Disabled workers under the age of 65 have been eligible for benefits since 1957.

Table 9–2 shows the relation between the size of the benefit awarded and preretirement earnings for hypothetical male workers at different earnings levels, as calculated by one study. Examples are given for men retiring at age 65 and age 62, for single men, and for married men whose wives did not work in covered employment. The social security formula for determining benefits is scaled progressively so that benefits as a proportion of earnings fall as the benefit base rises. The benefit base, in turn, is calculated from prior earnings. For example, a male worker with a low-wage history culminating in $4,000 in annual earnings in the year before retirement would receive 55 percent of his preretirement earnings in benefits if he is single, 82 percent if he is married. But a male worker making $12,000 before retirement would receive only 30 percent of such earnings if single and 46 percent if married. Because benefits are tax free and taxes are relatively more important at higher earnings levels, however, the decline in after-tax replacement rates as earnings rise is somewhat less than indicated here.

TABLE 9–2.—*Social security benefits for single men and for married men with a dependent wife retiring at age 65 years and age 62 years, 1974*

1973 earnings before taxes and marital status	Men retiring at age 65 years		Men retiring at age 62 years	
	Amount of tax free benefit (dollars)	Benefit as percent of 1973 earnings before taxes	Amount of tax free benefit (dollars)	Benefit as percent of 1973 earnings before taxes
$4,000:				
Single	2,197	54.9	1,758	43.9
Married	3,296	82.4	2,582	64.5
$8,000:				
Single	3,349	41.9	2,679	33.5
Married	5,024	62.8	3,935	49.2
$12,000:				
Single	3,644	30.4	2,916	24.3
Married	5,467	45.6	4,282	35.7

Note.—Benefits are based on average amount of a worker's wages over a 19-year period. Wage histories for each category of wage earners were simulated by assuming that their wages grew at the same rate as that of the average wages of non-supervisory personnel. The wife is assumed to be same age as worker and to have no covered earnings.

Source: Department of Health, Education, and Welfare (Office of Income Security Policy).

SOCIAL SECURITY AND THE NON-WORKING WIFE

[One issue that has received growing attention is the equity of benefits to non-working wives under the social security system. Present law stipulates that a retiring male worker with a wife of retirement age automatically receives 150 percent of the benefit to which he is entitled. No additional taxes are paid, however, by the married male worker. A retiring female worker can also receive a benefit for her spouse, but only if her husband can prove he was dependent on his wife for at least half his support.[1] In practice, the spouse benefit goes mainly to the male workers with a dependent wife. When a working wife reaches retirement age she is in effect entitled to her own earned benefit or the dependent wife's benefit (50 percent of her husband's) and would receive the higher of the two.

As a result of this situation, total benefits can be smaller for couples where both work than for couples where only the husband worked, even though both couples had the same total earnings. For example, as indicated in Table 9–2, for the hypothetical couples retiring at age 65 years a husband and wife each earning $4,000 a year, would each receive benefits of $2,197 for a total of $4,392 a year (55 percent of former earnings). However, the couple where the husband alone earned $8,000, and had paid the same total taxes, would receive benefits of $5,024 (63 percent of former earnings). In addition, if one considers that the couple where the husband is the sole earner has the benefit of the goods and services produced by the wife in the home (tax free), the real income of the one-earner couple is actually greater than that of the working couple.

The case where the working couple actually receives less in benefits than the one-earner couple with the same combined earnings and tax record occurs only in certain ranges of earnings. However, even when benefits are greater for the working couple, they never are high enough to bring an equivalent return on the tax dollar paid. Thus, a study comparing the present value of lifetime social security benefits with the value of accumulated payroll tax payments finds that couples where the wife does not work receive about twice the amount of social security benefits per dollar of tax contributions as couples where the wife works.

In the world of 1939, when the social security system was starting to

1. This provision has been successfully challenged in the lower courts and is working its way up to the Supreme Court. The Supreme Court has already ruled against male-female distinctions in the social security law in the case of Weisenfeld v. Secretary of Health, Education, and Welfare, in which it was held unconstitutional for social security benefits to be denied to a father who has in his care a child of his deceased wife when a mother in the same situation would receive benefits.

pay out benefits, most married women did not work and were entirely dependent on their husband's earnings. The wife's benefit was perhaps not a major source of inequity. This is not the situation in the mid-1970s when a significant proportion of wives do work, although in varying amounts over their lifetime. Moreover, couples in which the wife does not work are not necessarily poor. In fact, the wives of higher income men are less likely to work. So an income transfer from working couples to couples with a non-working wife cannot be easily justified on social welfare grounds.

Although the issue of equity among couples has become a source of concern, the situation is not easily remedied. Solutions that increase the benefits going to two-earner couples, without any offsetting reduction in the spouse benefit for one-earner couples, create greater disparities between unmarried and married workers. In addition, the higher benefit payments would necessitate increased tax payments from workers during a time when taxes must rise just to pay for presently legislated benefits. On the other hand, solutions which reduce the spouse benefit are difficult to achieve. Some proposals involve the averaging of the earnings of the husband and wife for purposes of determining the benefit, even if one spouse has no earnings. Such proposals can be structured to maintain the same total benefits to couples as would be the case under present law, but provide somewhat lower benefits for spouses without earnings and higher benefits for working couples. Other proposals stress individual equity and advocate a major restructuring of the social security system whereby individual benefits would be related to individual lifetime tax contributions. Those who do not work in jobs covered by social security could receive benefits, but only if they had paid contributions.]

INCOME OF THE AGED

Social security is an important source of income for the aged. Largely because earnings decline with age, and because women are less likely to work than men, and earn less if they do, social security increases in relative importance with age and is relatively more important for households headed by a widowed woman (often single-person households). In 1973, among households headed by a widow aged 70 or older, the average annual income was $2,819, of which social security accounted for 57 percent. By contrast, among households headed by a married man aged 65 to 69, the total mean income was $9,691; social security on the average accounted for 25 percent of income, and wages and self-employment earnings accounted for 46 percent. In 1974, 23 percent of all persons 65 years old and over were women living alone, while 60 percent were married and living with a spouse.

The rapid increases in social security benefits of recent years have made a substantial contribution in improving the income status of the elderly. In 1966, 28.5 percent of those aged 65 and over were below the poverty level compared to 14.2 percent for all persons; in 1974, 15.7 percent of the elderly were in poverty compared to 11.6 percent of all persons. In addition to cash income, many of the elderly have imputed income from owner-occupied homes for which they are no longer making mortgage payments (70 percent of elderly households own their own homes). Virtually all of those aged 65 and over receive medicare or medicaid benefits, and many also finance some of their consumption out of their assets. These additional sources raise the relative level of consumption of the aged.

WORK INCENTIVES

Social security has created incentives for the aged and disabled to reduce their work during the year. The availability of the pension itself is an inducement to work less and take more leisure. In addition, the earnings test which applies up to age 72 restricts the amount that can be earned without forfeiting any benefits.

Between 1940 and 1950 only about a third of men aged 65 and over were eligible for social security benefits (Table 9-3), and benefits were low and declining in real value. After 1950 there was a sharp increase in the percentage eligible for social security—to 81 percent in 1960 and 93 percent in 1975. Benefit amounts also increased sharply, even after adjusting for inflation. After remaining stable from 1940 to 1950 the labor force participation of men at 65 years of age and over declined sharply. Hours worked per week for men 65 years of age and over also fell, from 42 in 1950 to 34 in 1970.

The same relation between benefits and retirement behavior is evident for the group aged 62–64, who became eligible for retirement at reduced benefits in 1961. Although their labor force participation rate had been fairly stable until 1960, it declined markedly after benefits became available. One recent study finds that for every 10 percent increase in social security benefits relative to average wages, the number of male beneficiaries aged 62–64 increases by 2.8 percent in the first quarter after the increase, and by 6.0 percent after 5 quarters.

Persons eligible for social security have also been found to adjust their work behavior to avoid losing benefits under the earnings test. Thus, following a liberalization in the earnings test during 1966, over 10 percent of the working beneficiaries raised their earnings from $1,200 to $1,500, the new ceiling. The earnings test does not apply to those aged 72 and over, who may earn any amount without forfeiting benefits. For this reason many of those with high earnings wait until age 72 to start collecting benefits.

TABLE 9–3.—*Labor force participation rates and social security benefits for men 60 years of age and older, selected years, 1940–75*

Age group	1940	1950	1960	1970	1970	1975
Percent of men in labor force [1]:						
60–64 years	79.0	79.4	77.8	73.2	75.0	65.7
60–61 years	81.7	81.8	82.0	80.3	78.7	75.2
62–64 years	77.0	77.7	74.7	67.9	69.8	58.8
65–69 years	59.4	59.7	44.0	39.3	41.6	31.7
70 years and over	28.4	28.3	21.9	16.6	17.7	15.1
70–74 years	38.4	38.7	28.7	22.5	25.2	21.2
75 years and over	18.2	18.7	15.6	12.1	12.0	10.2
Percent of men eligible for social security benefits [2]:						
62–64 years	(3)	(3)	(3)	93.8	----------	96.4
65 years and over	[4] 10.9	32.4	80.7	91.0	----------	92.5
Average monthly primary social insurance benefit for men filing for benefits in given year:						
Current dollars	23.26	31.88	92.03	146.99	----------	263.53
1975 dollars [5]	89.81	71.80	168.24	205.12	----------	263.53

[1] Data in the first four columns are from the "Census of Population." Data in the last two columns are from the "Current Population Survey"; they exclude institutional population and are for April.
[2] Based on number of persons eligible at beginning of year.
[3] Not eligible for social security benefits.
[4] Data are for 1941.
[5] Deflated by the consumer price index.
Sources: Department of Commerce (Bureau of the Census), Department of Labor (Bureau of Labor Statistics), and Department of Health, Education, and Welfare.

Although social security appears to have been an important factor in the decline in employment among those of retirement age, other factors were operating as well. Increases in earnings and income over time enabled workers to save more in order to enjoy more years of leisure at older ages, and a larger proportion of the elderly now have asset holdings and private pensions. The decline in self-employment on the farm and in nonfarm industries also contributed to declining work at older ages, since the self-employed retire at a later age than employees. Studies indicate that in years of relatively high unemployment retirement is accelerated. Compulsory retirement practices may also have had an effect. However, the spread of compulsory retirement may itself have been stimulated by the availability of social security and the development of private pension systems.

There were additional incentives for the elderly to work longer, however, which have probably served to prevent labor force participation at older ages from falling even faster. Most notable may be the increase in the availability of white-collar employment, which tends to make less demand on physical strength. Increases in part-time employment opportunities have made work more feasible for those wishing a limited schedule, although the increase in part-time jobs may itself have been partly stimulated by the supply of older workers.

SHORT-RUN AND LONG-RUN FINANCING PROBLEMS

Issues have arisen with respect to both the short-run and long-run financial situation of the social security system. The Administration is proposing measures to deal with both of these problems.

Legislation has resulted in increases in benefit awards as a percentage of preretirement earnings, from 32 percent in 1965 to 43 percent in 1975 for the median wage earner aged 65 years and over. Other liberalizations in benefits have occurred, such as the increase in the dependent widow's pension from 82.5 percent to 100 percent of the husband's benefit if neither claimed benefits before age 65. Increases in early retirements have also contributed to rising outlays. Despite increases in the payroll tax rate (from 8.4 percent in 1969 to 9.9 percent in 1975) and in the maximum of earnings to be taxed (from $7,800 in 1969 to $15,300 in 1976) receipts have not risen as rapidly as benefits.

The tax shortfall has been exacerbated by the high levels of unemployment and the relatively slow growth of earnings in the past few years. Preliminary figures for 1975 indicate that expenditures exceeded payroll tax receipts by $2.6 billion, or 4.2 percent of tax receipts. Total expenditures, including administrative costs, exceeded total receipts, including interest on assets, by $1.6 billion, or 2.4 percent. The cyclical component of the problem will eventually diminish with the economic recovery, although a $4.4-billion deficit is forecast for 1976, and the trust fund will be permanently reduced. In response to the decline in the trust fund the Administration is proposing to increase the combined social security tax rate paid by employers and employees by 0.6 percentage point as of 1977. This increase will enable the trust fund to be maintained at a level of at least one-third of outgo for at least the next 5 years.

Projections of the social security system indicate that program costs relative to payroll receipts, under present law, are likely to escalate considerably. The size of the projected shortfall depends on assumptions about the birth rate, the rate of inflation, and the growth rate of real wages. Under commonly used assumptions (births per woman of 2.1, a 4 percent rate of inflation, and a 2 percent growth rate in real wages), expenditures would rise to 22 percent of taxable payroll by the year 2030, an amount which, if benefits were to be matched by tax receipts, would imply a social security tax rate about double today's level. However, with a lower fertility rate (1.7) and more pessimistic assumptions about inflation (5 percent) and real wage growth (1.5 percent), social security expenditures would require taxes of 32 percent of payrolls by the year 2030. Optimistic economic assumptions, on the other hand, combined with a projected increase in the fertility rate to 2.5, lead to payroll taxes of 15 percent of the total payroll by 2030.

Even this would represent a 50 percent increase in the present tax rate.

One reason the long-run social security projections described above are so high is that 1972 legislation provided for the double-indexing of social security benefits. Under the legislation, once a person starts getting benefits the amount is kept constant in real terms through automatic adjustments tied to increases in the CPI. However, the legislation inadvertently provided for a second effect of inflation on future benefits for those who are now working, since the schedule that relates retirement benefits to past earnings was also tied to the CPI. In this way replacement rates, the ratio of retirement benefits to average wages in the year before retirement, can automatically rise as a result of inflation. It has been estimated that, under current law, if nominal wages increase at 6 percent and the CPI at 4 percent per year, replacement rates for the median wage earner at age 65 would increase from 43 percent in 1976 to 59 percent in 2030. For low-wage workers, the increase would be from 63 percent to 99 percent over the same period and would exceed 100 percent by the year 2040. This rise in replacement rates for those retiring in the future is estimated to add about 26 percent to program costs by the year 2030, compared to a system in which replacement rates remain at the 1975 level.

"DECOUPLING": SOLUTIONS TO DOUBLE INDEXING

[The problem of the double indexing or "coupling" of social security benefits discussed above has led to concern as pessimistic forecasts have been made about its implications for long-run costs. Two major proposals for dealing with the issue have been put forth. Before discussing these proposals, however, it is necessary to understand the complex issue of double indexing.

Social security benefits are determined when an individual reaches retirement age by a procedure whereby monthly earnings are averaged over a specified number of years.[2] These average monthly earnings (AME) are then applied to a formula which relates the AME to benefits. For example, during the period June 1974 to June 1975 the formula roughly provided a monthly benefit (termed the "primary insurance amount") of 120 percent of the first $110 of AME, 44 percent of the next $290, with declining percentages of each additional dollar of AME down to 20 percent. Thus the social security benefit structure replaces a lower percentage of pre-retirement earnings the higher the level of these earnings. This is referred to as a progressive benefit structure.

2. At present, the 20 highest years of earnings are averaged and the law provides that this period is to increase by one year, each year, until a total of 35 years of earnings are to be included in the average.

The double-indexing or coupling provision automatically changes this benefit formula in the following way. Each year, if the rate of increase in the consumer price index (CPI) is 3 percent or more, the percentages in the benefit formula are increased by the same percent increase in the CPI. Thus if the CPI were to rise by 10 percent, the formula given above would provide 132 percent [120 + (.10) (120)] of the first $110 of AME, 48 percent [44 + (.10) (44)] of the next $290, and so on. If the CPI increases by less than 3 percent in the year there is no adjustment. It is clear that if inflation continued at high rates over a number of years, many retirees could receive monthly benefits that exceeded their prior monthly earnings.[3]

Note, however, that inflation alone would have raised benefits since inflation increases the nominal wages of workers and benefits rise with wages. In order to insure that wage increases would be reflected in higher benefits, a provision was also made in the 1972 amendments for automatically raising the maximum wage covered by social security by the rate of increase of average money wages. Thus, inflation has a double effect on benefits. It raises wages, which moves workers higher up in the benefit schedule, and adjusts the schedule so that each step is associated with a higher dollar benefit.[3]

The major proposals for "decoupling", that is, remedying the double-indexing provision, involve the indexing of benefits and earnings. The aim is to provide for a system for determining real benefits that would not vary capriciously because of changes in the rate of inflation. One proposal for decoupling was presented to Congress in 1976 by the Panel on Social Security Financing headed by William C. L. Hsiao and appointed by the U.S. Senate Committee on Finance in 1974. The Hsiao proposal would first index the earnings of workers by the CPI so that earnings and the AME would be expressed in dollars of constant purchasing power. The benefit formula would also be expressed in real dollars. (For example, if the price index used to deflate earnings related to 1976 dollars, the benefit formula would also be expressed in 1976 dollars.)

Under the Hsiao proposal, cohorts of workers retiring in future years would always receive the same real benefit if they had the same earnings history (after accounting for inflation). For example, a hypothetical unmarried worker retiring in 1976 with earnings of $8,600 in the year before retirement could receive benefits of $3,612 a year ($5,418 if married). Under the Hsiao proposal a worker with the same real earnings history but retiring in the year 2050 would receive the same

3. Moving up the schedule, however, does not have as great an impact on benefits as the adjustment in the formula because of the progressive nature of the benefit formula.

benefit in real terms as such a worker would in 1976. However, by the year 2050 fewer workers would have earnings of $8,600 (expressed in 1976 dollars) because economic growth is likely to move workers into higher real earnings brackets. As noted above, under the social security formula benefits do not rise as fast as earnings. Thus, as a result of their higher real earnings, by the year 2050 more workers will be in brackets where benefits replace a smaller proportion of past earnings. Under the Hsiao proposal, benefits awarded to the retiring population will rise for the average worker, but not as fast as average pre-retirement earnings. In other words, as average real earnings rise over time, average replacement rates will fall.

Another proposal for decoupling was outlined in the report of the 1974 Quadrennial Advisory Council on Social Security, a group appointed by the President every four years. Under this proposal the social security benefit formula would be adjusted each year to account for increases in real earnings. The purpose of the adjustment would be to counter the decline in average replacement rates that would naturally occur as average real earnings rise. Thus, as real earnings rise over time the benefit schedule would be raised in *real* terms in order that the average benefit would increase as rapidly as average earnings. However, this adjustment would result in workers at a given level of real earnings receiving increasingly higher real benefits over time. Let us take as an example the hypothetical earner considered above who earned $8,600 in the year before his retirement. Under the Advisory Council's proposal, if real average earnings were to increase by 2 percent a year, a worker with that real earnings level retiring in the year 2050 would receive annual benefits of $8,600 in real dollars if single ($12,900 if married), whereas with that level of earnings the worker retiring in 1976 would have received benefits of $3,612 ($5,418 if married).

Because it provides for higher benefits than the Hsiao proposal, the Advisory Council's proposal would entail much higher expenditures in the future. It is estimated that under the assumptions of a 2 percent average annual rate of growth in real wages and an average of 2.1 births per married woman, the Advisory Council plan would require social security taxes reaching a peak of 17 percent of taxable payroll by the year 2030, compared to 22 percent under the present coupled system, and 11 percent under the Hsiao proposal, which is close to today's level.

Implicit in the Advisory Council proposal is the view that even if the real pre-retirement income of the average worker should double, his social security benefit should double in real dollars. That is, society must assume that the average worker in 2050 will be just as dependent on the social security system as he is today, relative to his pre-retirement earnings. If the social security pension replaces 45 percent of earnings today, so should it in 2050.

Implicit in the Hsiao proposal is the view that the logic that made the social security benefit structure progressive for workers retiring today should pertain to workers as they become richer over time. The expectation is that workers with a lifetime history of high earnings are likely to have private pensions and savings so that at retirement they will be relatively less dependent on social security benefits. Over time, as the average income of workers rises, pensions and other private savings are also likely to increase.[4] Moreover, by maintaining lower payroll tax rates, private savings would be encouraged. Thus the average worker retiring in the year 2050 can be expected to be less dependent on public transfers, relative to pre-retirement earnings, than is the case today.

If a decoupling proposal such as that outlined by the Advisory Council were to be chosen, an increasingly severe burden would be placed on the working population in the coming decades, unless fertility rates were suddenly to rise sharply. This could become a socially divisive issue for future generations. The burden could be eased by a combination of one or more measures, none of which would be without opposition. For example, age of retirement could be increased; social security benefits in excess of the value of employee contributions could be subject to income taxation; or dependents' benefits could be reduced. Although general revenues could be used to finance increasing social security benefits, this merely changes the form of taxation. It does not alter the fundamental issue: what percent of the nation's GNP is to be transferred from the working population to the aged? The complex social security financing problem is likely to become a subject of intensive public debate for several decades.]

4. The Pension Reform Act of 1975 and related legislation, as well as Treasury Department regulations have gone far to insure that private pensions and retirement funds are a reliable source of income upon retirement.

CHAPTER 10

Women and the Economy

One of the most important changes in the American economy in this century has been the increase in the proportion of women who work outside the home. This increase is the most striking aspect of the expansion of the role of women in the economy.

The addition of millions of women to the labor force has contributed substantially to the increase of total output. This is most obvious if we focus attention on the output that is measured and included in the gross national product (GNP). But even if we subtract from the contribution of working women to the GNP the value of the work they would have done at home, there has been an addition to total output. Most of the benefits of this additional output accrue to the women who produce it, and to their families. There are, however, also direct benefits to the society at large, including the taxes paid on the women's earnings.

Concern is sometimes expressed that the increase in women in the labor force will reduce the employment opportunities for men and raise their unemployment. There is no reason to think that would happen and there is no sign that it has happened. The work to be done is not a fixed total. As more women enter employment and earn incomes they or their families buy more goods and services which men and women are employed to produce. A sudden surge of entrants into the labor force might cause difficulties of adjustment and, consequently, unemployment, but the entry of women into the labor force has not been of that character.

Women work outside the home for the same reasons as men. The basic reason is to get the income that can be earned by working. Whether—for either men or women—work is done out of necessity or by choice is a question of definition. If working out of necessity means working in order to sustain biologically necessary conditions of life, probably a small proportion of all the hours of work done in the United States, by men or women, is necessary. If working out of necessity means working in order to obtain a standard of living which is felt by the worker to be desirable, probably almost all of the work done by both men and women is necessary.

The Employment Act of 1946 sets forth a goal of "maximum employment." We understand that to mean employment of those who want to work, without regard to whether their employment is, by some definition, necessary. This goal applies equally to men and to women. The Act also sets forth a goal of "maximum production." We understand the meaning of that goal which is relevant to the present context to be that people should be able to work in the employments in which they will be most productive. That also applies equally to men and women.

Although the goals apply equally to men and women, some of the obstacles to their achievement apply especially to women. Women have gained much more access to market employment than they used to have, but they have not gained full equality within the market in the choice of jobs, opportunities for advancement, and other matters related to employment and compensation. To some extent the cause of this discrepancy is direct discrimination. But it is also the result of more subtle and complex factors originating in cultural patterns that have grown up in most societies through the centuries. In either case, because the possibilities open to women are restricted, they are not always free to contribute a full measure of earnings to their families, to develop their talents fully, or to help achieve the national goal of "maximum production."

The roles played by women and men have been sharply differentiated. It is obvious that only women are capable of childbearing. But along with this biologically determined role, women have by tradition come to assume primary responsibility for child care and home management, while men have primary responsibility for the family's financial support. Until very recently this division of labor within the family has had such general acceptance as to impose limitations on women's work outside the home. The way in which the economic role of women evolves thus hinges on the most fundamental societal patterns, and the extent to which social action can and should influence further change in these patterns will be one of the most difficult and important questions.

By way of an introduction to the problem, this chapter looks at job-related aspects of the economic role of women.

PARTICIPATION IN THE LABOR FORCE

In 1900 about 20 percent of all women were in the work force (Table 10–1). In the succeeding decades this percentage hardly increased, reaching about 25 percent by 1940. With World War II, however, the movement rapidly accelerated, and by 1972 the percentage of women 16 years and older in the work force had risen to 43.8 [46.4 percent in 1975].

Single women and women widowed, divorced, or separated, have always had higher labor force participation rates than married women living with their husbands. By 1950, the participation of women in the two former groups had already reached levels close to those of today. Thus, the upward trend in labor force participation since World War II has been due almost entirely to the changed behavior of married women (Table 10–2). The first to respond were the more mature married women beyond the usual childbearing years. More recently there has also been a sharp upturn in the labor force participation of younger married women.

TABLE 10–1.—*Women in the labor force, selected years, 1900–75*

Year	Women in labor force (thousands)	Women in labor force as percent of	
		Total labor force	All women of working age
1900	5,114	18.1	20.4
1910	7,889	20.9	25.2
1920	8,430	20.4	23.3
1930	10,679	22.0	24.3
1940	12,845	24.3	25.4
1945	19,270	29.6	35.7
1950	18,412	28.8	33.9
1955	20,584	30.2	35.7
1960	23,272	32.3	37.8
1965	26,232	34.0	39.3
1970	31,560	36.7	43.4
1972	33,320	37.4	43.8
1975	37,037	39.1	46.4

Note.—Data for 1900 to 1940 are from decennial censuses and refer to a single date; beginning 1945 data are annual averages.

For 1900 to 1945 data include women 14 years of age and over; beginning 1950 data include women 16 years of age and over.

Labor force data for 1900 to 1930 refer to gainfully employed workers.

Data for 1972 and 1975 reflect adjustments to 1970 Census benchmarks.

Note.—Updated by Editors.

Sources: Department of Commerce, Bureau of the Census, and Department of Labor, Bureau of Labor Statistics.

The record for men has tended to run in the opposite direction. A secular reduction in time spent in paid work over most men's lifetimes has taken place: A man spends more years at school and enters the labor force later than formerly; he retires earlier, works fewer hours a week, and has longer vacations. Of course these changes have also affected women, but for them the increase in years worked has far outweighed the other work-reducing factors.

In one very important respect, however, the working life patterns of men and women have not merged. The typical man can expect to be in the labor force continuously, for an unbroken block of some 40 years between leaving school and retirement. Of men in the 25–54 year age group, 95.2 percent were in the labor force in 1972. For most women, this continuity in participation is the exception rather than the rule.

TABLE 10–2.—*Labor force participation rates of women by marital status and age, 1950, 1960, 1972 and 1975.*

[Percent [1]]

Marital status and year	Total	Age					
		Under 20 years	20–24 years	25–34 years	35–44 years	45–64 years	65 years and over
Single:							
1950	50.5	26.3	74.9	84.6	83.6	70.6	23.8
1960	44.1	25.3	73.4	79.9	79.7	75.1	21.6
1972	54.9	41.9	69.9	84.7	71.5	71.0	19.0
1975	56.7	45.3	69.3	80.0	76.4	68.3	16.1
Married, husband present:							
1950	23.8	24.0	28.5	23.8	28.5	21.8	6.4
1960	30.5	25.3	30.0	27.7	36.2	34.2	5.9
1972	41.5	39.0	48.5	41.3	48.6	44.2	7.3
1975	44.4	45.6	57.1	48.3	52.1	44.1	7.2
Widowed, divorced, or separated:							
1950	37.8	([2])	45.5	62.3	65.4	50.2	8.8
1960	40.0	37.3	54.6	55.5	67.4	58.3	11.0
1972	40.1	44.6	57.6	62.1	71.7	61.1	9.8
1975	40.7	41.4	67.6	67.4	69.1	60.5	8.1

[1] Labor force as percent of noninstitutional population in group specified.
[2] Not available.

Note.—Data relate to March of each year.
Data for 1950 and 1960 are for women 14 years of age and over; data for 1972 and 1975 are for women 16 years of age and over.
Note.—Updated by Editors.

Source: Department of Labor, Bureau of Labor Statistics.

THE HISTORICAL PATTERN

What are the causal factors that induced women to enter the labor force? One might have expected that the strong increases in husbands' real incomes which occurred during the period would have provided an incentive to women not to enter the labor force. This seeming puzzle is resolved, however, when one considers that by entering the labor force women did not leave a life of leisure for work, but rather changed from one kind of work, work at home, to another kind of work, work in the market. The incentive for women to make this dramatic occupational change came from several developments which made paid work outside the home the increasingly more profitable alternative.

Rapidly rising earnings and expanded job opportunities for women gave a strong impetus to the change. The expansion of job opportunities for women was undoubtedly influenced by the expansion of the service sector of the economy, where employment increased by 77 percent from 1950 to 1970, compared to the increase of 26 percent in the goods-producing industrial sector over the same period. Women have always been more heavily represented in services than in industry, since the service sector offers more white-collar employment and provides opportunities for part-time work, an especially important feature for women with small children. On the other hand, the increasing supply of women workers perhaps itself contributed to the rapid expansion in the service sector.

The increase in women's educational attainments has also helped to raise the amount they can earn by working. Education may make women more productive in the home, that is, more efficient housekeepers, consumers, and mothers, but education appears to increase still more their productivity in work outside the home. Women with more education earn more, and they are more likely than less educated women to seek work in the market.

Because life expectancy has increased considerably over the century (and more for women than for men), and because most women complete their childbearing at a younger age, women can look forward with more certainty to a longer uninterrupted span of years in the labor force. This lengthening of a woman's expected working life is significant because it increases her return on her investment in training and education: the greater the number of years in which to collect the return the greater is the return.

These increases in the income a woman could potentially earn meant essentially that time spent producing goods and services at home was coming at a higher and higher cost in terms of the income foregone by not working in the market. It made sense then to buy available capital equipment (such as washing machines) which would substitute for some of the housewife's time and free her to go to work. And changes in technology which lowered the cost and increased the array of time-saving devices facilitated the substitution.

The most difficult home responsibility to find a good substitute for is child care; and, although the labor force participation of married women with children under 6 years has increased from 12 percent in 1950 to 30 percent in 1971, to 37 percent in 1975 child-rearing is probably the major factor causing some women to interrupt, and others to curtail, their careers.

The long-term decline in the average number of children in the family has undoubtedly had a strong influence on the proportion of women entering the labor force. Advances in birth control techniques permit parents not only to reduce the number of births but also to control their timing to suit a mother's working career. Declines in infant and child mortality may also have encouraged a reduction in births by increasing the parents' expectation that all their children would survive to adulthood. On the other hand, reductions in family size may themselves be influenced by the desire of women to work.

Childbearing has a very noticeable effect on the patterns of women's labor force participation by age. Based on census data, Chart 10–1

Chart 10-1

Labor Force Participation Over a Working
Life of Cohorts of Women Born in Selected
Time Intervals, 1886-1955

PARTICIPATION RATE (PERCENT)*

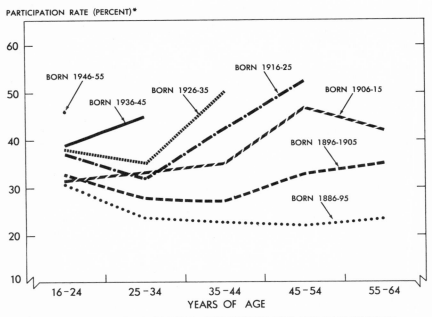

*TOTAL LABOR FORCE AS PERCENT OF TOTAL NONINSTITUTIONAL POPULATION IN GROUP SPECIFIED.
NOTE: FOR WOMEN BORN BETWEEN 1886 AND 1915, THE FIRST AGE PLOTTED IS 14-24 YEARS. COHORTS
REACH EACH AGE INTERVAL ACCORDING TO THE MIDPOINT OF THEIR BIRTH YEARS. THUS, THE
COHORT BORN 1886-95 REACHED AGES 25-34 IN 1920 AND AGES 55-64 IN 1950; THE COHORT BORN 1916-25
REACHED AGES 25-34 IN 1950 AND AGES 45-54 IN 1970.
SOURCE: DEPARTMENT OF COMMERCE.

traces the lifetime changes in labor force participation by groups of
women born at different times, the earliest group consisting of women
born between 1886 and 1895. The chart therefore simulates the actual
work history of particular cohorts of women followed longitudinally.
According to this chart, the various forces in the economy that have
induced women to work have generally had a more powerful effect
on women beyond the childbearing ages than on younger groups.
Those increases in labor force participation that have occurred for
groups of women reaching the childbearing ages of 20–34 years have
been closely associated with declining fertility rates. Thus labor force
participation for the group reaching 25–34 years increased substantially
from 1930 to 1940, and again between 1960 and 1970, while there was
a decline between 1940 and 1950 in the participation of those reaching

this age group—the baby boom mothers. Whether the young women now in their twenties have simply postponed having children and will later drop out of the labor force or whether many will continue to work, choosing to have small families or remain childless is, of course, a question of great interest.

THE WORKING WOMAN TODAY

Although the decisions of individual women to work outside the home are undoubtedly based on many different factors, there are some economic factors which seem to be of overriding importance. The necessity to support oneself or others is one obvious reason and, not surprisingly, adult single women and women who have been separated from husbands or widowed are highly likely to work.

The increase in earnings opportunities, which proved to be such a powerful factor influencing the secular growth of women's participation in the labor force, is a similarly powerful factor influencing the pattern of women's participation at any given time. Thus, education and other training which affect the amount a woman can earn are strongly related to women's work patterns. The importance of education is such that, whether a woman is single, married or separated, the more education she has, the more likely she is to work. One striking exception to this pattern is that, among mothers of children under 6 years old, there is scarcely any relation between education and labor force participation. Thus, the rearing of children of preschool age causes all women, regardless of education, to curtail their work outside the home. However, the drop in participation during this childrearing period is most pronounced for highly educated women who in other circumstances have much higher participation rates.

Although for most women the childbearing period has been reduced, childbearing still means an interruption of outside work. A longitudinal survey of the lifelong work experience of women indicates that among all women who were 30–44 years old in 1967, only 7 percent had worked at least 6 months out of every year since leaving school. Among married women with children the proportion was still lower, dropping to 3 percent. By contrast, 30 percent of childless married women in the same group had worked at least 6 months out of every year. Information on job tenure collected by the Bureau of Labor Statistics illustrates much the same phenomenon. As of January 1968, continuous employment in their current job came to 2.4 years (the median) for women and 4.8 years for men. Job tenure increases with age for both men and women. At ages 45 and over the median was 12.7 years for men and 6.6 years for women. Since women tend to change jobs less frequently than men, their shorter time spent on any given job is the result of a higher propensity to leave the labor force at least temporarily. In 1964 a survey of women who had dropped out of the labor force in 1962 or 1963 and had not yet reentered was undertaken by the Labor Department in an effort to find out why they had left. Pregnancy was most frequently cited as the primary reason —by 74 percent of the 18- to 24-year-olds and 56 percent of the 25- to 34-year-olds.

Among married women, husband's income does not have a very pronounced effect on work patterns. The median annual income of husbands with working wives was $8,070 in 1971 compared to $8,330 for husbands of wives not in the labor force. The ratio was 0.97. Since then it has widened. The incomes were $10,936 and $11,886 respectively in 1974 for a ratio of 0.92. Only when husbands' incomes reach the $10,000-and-over category does wives' participation decline to any noticeable extent. However, many other things vary with husbands' incomes, such as wives' education and age as well as family size. These other factors are sufficiently important to obscure the simple relation between husband's income and a wife's tendency to work. It should be noted, however, that during a time of hardship, such as when a husband experiences a prolonged spell of unemployment, wives who usually do not work may be compelled to do so. Thus, the labor force participation of women with unemployed husbands is generally above that of women with employed husbands.

Although the probability that a black woman will work seems to vary with education and presence of children in much the same way as it does for all women, there is one very striking difference: the labor force participation of black women is higher. Particularly pronounced differences are observed when the comparison of labor force participation is confined to married women living with their husbands. In March 1971, about 53 percent of black wives were in the labor force compared to 40 percent of white wives. In March 1975, the percentages were 53 percent and 44 percent respectively. One important reason why this difference prevails may be that the earnings of black wives are closer to their husbands' than is the case among white married couples. In 1971 black married women who worked year-round, full-time earned 73 percent as much as black married men who worked year-round, full-time. Among whites the percentage was only 51 percent. In 1974, they were 69 percent and 49 percent respectively. Behind these relationships is the fact that black men earn considerably less than white men, while black women's earnings are much closer to those of white women.

[The economic concepts of substitution and income effects are useful in understanding changes in the labor force participation of married women and men. The traditional economic analysis of labor force participation viewed the choice between work and leisure time as the outcome of the strength of a substitution effect (the substitution between psychic income from leisure time and money income from work) and an income effect. The presumption was that leisure was a "normal" good so that as income increased, other things being the same, workers would choose more leisure and less work. However, as income increases, other things are not necessarily the same, since earnings are the major source of income. As hourly wage rates rise, the "price" of leisure increases. There are then two influences with opposite effects when wage rates rise. The income effect would induce a reduction in work (and increase leisure) while the substitution effect, reacting to the higher price of leisure, would induce an increase in work.

For men, the net outcome of the two effects has been a reduction in work, reflecting an income effect dominating a substitution effect. The reduction is particularly apparent when considering work over the lifetime; that is, reductions in work have been most pronounced at older ages although there have been some reductions in hours worked during the week (largely during the first half of the century) and increases in vacation time. The pattern of a shortening of the work life through early retirements was undoubtedly encouraged by increasing social security benefits (see Chapter 9).

The increasing labor force participation of women appears contrary to the pattern for men. However, the choice for women is not just between leisure and work in the labor market, since work in the home is a third important alternative. The increase in women's labor force participation mainly reflects the substitution of work in the market for work in the home. (The factors increasing the relative attractiveness of work in the market were discussed earlier in this chapter.) There is little historical information about the division of time in the home between work and leisure. One suspects that women along with men have increased their leisure time as income has increased, although the lifetime pattern of their leisure may not be the same as men's.]

UNEMPLOYMENT

Women have generally experienced more unemployment than men and this differential has been more pronounced in recent years (Table 10–3). However, the source of women's unemployment differs from that of men's, and this makes a comparison of unemployment differences more complex than might appear.

Some of the difference arises from the way people are classified in our unemployment statistics. A person with a job is not classified as unemployed even though he or she may be searching for another job. However, work at home is not counted as a job. Thus, a woman who may in a real sense be clearly employed in the home while she searches

TABLE 10–3.—*Unemployment rates by sex and age, selected years, 1956–75.*

[Percent [1]]

Sex and age	1956	1961	1965	1969	1972	1973	1975
All workers	4.1	6.7	4.5	3.5	5.6		8.5
Men	3.8	6.4	4.0	2.8	4.9	4.1	7.9
16–19 years	11.1	17.1	14.1	11.4	15.9	13.9	20.1
20–24 years	6.9	10.8	6.4	5.1	9.2	7.3	14.3
25–54 years	3.0	5.1	2.7	1.6	3.1	2.5	5.7
55 years and over	3.5	5.7	3.3	1.9	3.3	2.6	4.5
Women	4.9	7.2	5.5	4.7	6.6	6.0	9.3
16–19 years	11.2	16.3	15.7	13.3	16.7	15.2	19.7
20–24 years	6.3	9.8	7.3	6.3	9.3	8.4	12.7
25–54 years	4.1	6.2	4.3	3.5	4.9	4.4	7.5
55 years and over	3.3	4.4	2.8	2.2	3.4	2.8	5.1

[1] Unemployment as percent of civilian labor force in group specified.

Note.—Updated by Editors.

Source: Department of Labor, Bureau of Labor Statistics.

for a job, will be counted as unemployed, unlike the man who searches while on his job.

Most adult men are continuously in the labor force and therefore become unemployed because they have either quit or lost their jobs (Table 10–4). For women, the picture is different: labor force participation is frequently interrupted, sometimes for several years, but sometimes just for several weeks during the year. Thus, although 59.8 percent of the women 24–54 years old were in the labor force at one time or another during 1971, only 38.2 percent were in the labor force for 50–52 weeks during the year. This high rate of labor force turnover generates unemployment, and it is not surprising to find that in both the tight labor market of 1973 and the looser labor market of 1975 a considerable portion of unemployed women were labor force entrants (Table 10–4). People entering or reentering the labor force tend, how-

TABLE 10–4.—*Distribution of unemployment of adult men and women by reason for unemployment, 1973 and 1975.*

[Percent]

Reason for unemployment	Men 20 years and over		Women 20 years and over	
	1973	1975	1973	1975
Total unemployment	100.0	100.0	100.0	100.0
Separated from a job	75.0	83.5	53.2	63.9
Job losers	59.1	75.0	34.6	50.0
Job leavers	15.9	8.5	18.6	13.9
Labor force entrants	25.0	16.6	46.8	36.1
Reentrants	21.6	14.5	41.5	31.9
New entrants	3.4	2.1	5.3	4.2
Unemployment rate	3.2	6.7	4.8	8.0

Note.—Detail may not add to totals because of rounding.
Note.—Updated by Editors.

Source: Department of Labor, Bureau of Labor Statistics.

TABLE 10-5.—*Unemployment of adult men and women by duration and reason, 1972*

Sex, age, and reason	Total unemployment (thousands)	Percent of total unemployment	
		Unemployment of less than 5 weeks	Unemployment of 15 weeks and over
Men 20 years and over	1,928	37.0	31.6
Lost last job	1,207	33.6	35.3
Left last job	245	44.9	24.9
Reentered labor force	416	41.7	25.4
Never worked before	59	39.0	28.8
Women 20 years and over	1,610	48.4	22.8
Lost last job	635	35.6	33.4
Left last job	262	50.0	19.2
Reentered labor force	635	59.8	14.4
Never worked before	79	55.7	16.5

Note.—Detail may not add to totals because of rounding.

Source: Department of Labor, Bureau of Labor Statistics.

ever, to be unemployed for relatively short periods, and this is one of the reasons why the duration of unemployment is in general shorter for women than for men (Table 10–5).

In order to know what significance to attach to the observation that the greater unemployment of women appears to be related to their greater labor force turnover, it is of course necessary to know more about the causes of the turnover. Some have stressed that excessive labor force turnover indicates a poor job market. According to this view, women drop out of the labor market because lack of opportunities has discouraged them from continuing the search. Evidence for this point of view is cited from Labor Department surveys, which indicate that some of those women out of the labor force are there because they do not believe they could find work. In 1972, 525,000 women or 1.2 percent of those out of the labor force were reported in this category. In 1975, a recession year, the proportion was 1.7 percent. (See Chapter 6 for a more detailed discussion of "discouraged workers".)

Another school of thought, however, stresses that the labor force turnover of women and the unemployment it generates is largely induced by factors external to the current labor market, such as the uneven pressures of home responsibilities. Several kinds of evidence support this point of view. Unemployment among women appears to be related to the nature of home responsibilities. For example, in 1971 the unemployment rate for married women with children under 3 years was 11.7 percent, compared to the rate of 4.5 percent for married women with no children under 18 years. In 1974, these rates were 9.8 percent, and 3.7 percent, respectively. Moreover, on numerous surveys women cite pregnancy, home responsibilities, or husband's relocation as primary reasons for leaving the job or the labor force.

It would of course be interesting to know more about the unemployment experience of women who do remain continuously in the labor force. Some evidence from the Labor Department's longitudinal survey indicates that women who were in the labor force in both 1967 and 1969 had considerably lower unemployment in 1969 than those who were in the labor force in 1969 but not in 1967. The unemployment rate in 1969 for the group who were also in the labor force 2 years previously was 2.9 percent, compared to the rate of 6.9 percent for the women who were in the labor force only in 1969. However, this was still above the rate of 2.1 percent for men 20 years old and over in 1969, as measured by the household survey.

Although movement in and out of the labor force is probably the most important factor leading to higher unemployment for women compared to men, two other factors seem to be important. Women with less time on a job and in whom the employer had made negligible training investments are more vulnerable to layoffs. Finally, one additional factor which doubtless contributes to unemployment of married women is the difficulty in maximizing employment opportunities for both the husband and the wife. A wife seldom is free to migrate to wherever her own prospects are best.

It is important to emphasize, because the point is often misunderstood, that to explain the unemployment of women is not to excuse it or belittle it or to place blame on the women who are unemployed. The unemployment of women who seek work is costly to themselves, their families, and the Nation. Our goal should be to reduce this unemployment wherever that can be done by means which are not themselves more costly. Some unemployment entails more loss for the workers involved and to the economy as a whole than other; some is more amenable to correction by the persons directly affected than other unemployment. But these distinctions do not run along sex lines.

THE WIDENING IN THE REPORTED MALE-FEMALE UNEMPLOYMENT DIFFERENTIAL

During the 1960's the differential in reported unemployment between women and men widened. Two factors may help to explain the change. The first has to do with changes in the unemployment survey questionnaire introduced in 1967.

Persons are classified as unemployed if they have not worked during the survey week, were available to work during the survey week, and had made specific efforts to find a job such as looking in the "want-ads" section of the newspaper or going to an employment agency. Prior to 1967 the period of jobseeking efforts was not specified, and it is believed that many respondents interpreted the question narrowly to mean that one had to have looked for a job in the week just prior to the survey. In 1967 the unemployment question was changed by specifying 4 weeks preceding the survey as the point of reference. Data from samples taken on both the old and new basis are available for 1966. In that year the unemployment rate for women aged 20 years or older was 0.4 percentage points higher on the new basis than on the old. This increase in the rate for women as a result of the change in the questionnaire has been interpreted as reflecting the likelihood that the jobseeking activities of women are more intermittent. As a result of lengthening the reference period to 4 weeks, persons who had briefly looked for work but who were not actively seeking work by the time of the survey week would be added to the unemployed under the new definition.[1]

Although the reported unemployment of some men may also have been increased as a result of the effective lengthening of the unemployment reference period, other changes in the questionnaire in 1967, which were evidently unimportant for women, seemed to reduce the reported unemployment of men. Indeed these changes were of sufficient importance that the net effect was to lower the unemployment rate for men 20 years old and over by 0.3 percentage points. The unemployment rate for men was evidently lowered for two reasons: By a reclassification from unemployed to employed of persons absent from work because of a vacation or a labor dispute but at the same time looking for work; and by the fact that persons stating that they had given up the search for work were no longer counted as unemployed.

The 1966 samples indicate that as a result of the changes in the unemployment questionnaire, which increased the rate for women and lowered the rate for men, the reported male-female unemployment differential, comparing men and women 20 years old and over, increased from 1.3 percentage points to 2.0 percentage points. We cannot, of course, be sure that effects of the same precise magnitude have persisted ever since the new definitions were substituted in 1967. However, the definitional change has undoubtedly contributed to a wider unemployment differential since the late 1960's.

Another factor contributing to the widening of the unemployment differential may be the rapid increase in the labor force participation of women during the 1960's, since its effect was to increase the proportion of women entering or reentering the labor force, with an accompanying increase in unemployment.

1. A similar situation occurred in Canada when the Canadian government changed their household survey to include a question about job seeking in the past week. Under the new questionnaire the unemployment rate was 8.6 percent for women compared to 6.6 percent based on a matched sample taken at the same time (1975) but using the old questionnaire. [Editors]

EDUCATION AND THE
OCCUPATIONAL DISTRIBUTION

Some of the hesitancy of women to enter or to stay in the labor force is undoubtedly the result of societally determined factors that restrict the possibilities open to them. The low representation of women in positions of responsibility is striking. Despite gradual gains, progress has not been sufficient to alter the picture significantly (Table 10–6).

TABLE 10.6—*Women as a percent of persons in several professional and managerial occupations, 1910–70*

[Percent]

Occupational group	1910	1920	1930	1940	1950	1960	1970
Clergymen	0.6	1.4	2.2	2.4	4.0	2.3	2.9
College presidents, professors, and instructors [1]	18.9	30.2	31.9	26.5	23.2	24.2	28.2
Dentists	3.1	3.3	1.9	1.5	2.7	2.3	3.5
Editors and reporters	12.2	16.8	24.0	25.0	32.0	36.6	40.6
Engineers	(2)	(2)	(2)	.4	1.2	.8	1.6
Lawyers and judges	.5	1.4	2.1	2.5	3.5	3.5	4.9
Managers, manufacturing industries	1.7	3.1	3.2	4.3	6.4	7.1	6.3
Physicians	6.0	5.0	4.4	4.7	6.1	6.9	9.3

[1] Data for 1920 and 1930 probably include some teachers in schools below collegiate rank. The Office of Education estimates the 1930 figure closer to 28 percent.
[2] Less than one tenth of 1 percent.

Note.—Data are from the decennial censuses. Data for 1910 and 1920 include persons 10 years of age and over; data for 1930 to 1970 include persons 14 years of age and over.

Source: Department of Commerce, Bureau of the Census.

Exactly how much of this situation has been imposed on women because of prejudice and how much of it derives from a voluntary adjustment to a life divided between home responsibilities and work remains obscure. The existence of discriminatory barriers may discourage women from seeking the training or adopting the life style it would take to achieve a responsible and highly demanding job. On the other hand, women who expect to marry and have children and who also put their role at home first are subject to considerable uncertainty about their future attachment to the labor force. In the latter case, incentives to train extensively for a career would be few; and, once such women started working, the restrictions imposed by home responsibilities could limit their ability to take a job requiring long hours or the intensive commitment that most high-status positions demand. At the same time, changes in the accepted social roles of men and women would alter current patterns if they changed women's expectations about their future in the labor force.

For whatever reasons, from school onward the career orientation of women differs strikingly from that of men. Most women do not have as strong a vocational emphasis in their schooling; and for those who do, the preparation is usually for a stereotyped "female" occupation.

Although the probability of graduating from high school has been somewhat greater for women than for men, it is less probable that a woman will complete college, and still less that she will enter graduate school. The representation of women consequently declines as they move upward through the stages of education beyond high school. In 1971, 50 percent of all high school graduates were women and 45 percent of first-year college students were women. During 1971 women earned 44 percent of the bachelor's degrees granted, 40 percent of the master's degrees, and 14 percent of the doctorates. Since then, women have increased their relative attainment. In 1973–74 women were 51 percent of the high school graduates and were 48 percent of first time college students in the following year. In 1973–74 women earned 44 percent of the B.A.'s, 43 percent of the M.A.'s and 19 percent of the Ph.D's.

Even more striking are the differences in the courses taken. At both the undergraduate and advanced levels, women are heavily represented in English, languages, and fine arts—the more general cultural fields. They are poorly represented in disciplines having a strong vocational emphasis and promising a high pecuniary return. In 1970, 9.3 percent of the baccalaureates in business and 3.9 percent of the master's in business went to women. In the biological sciences, women had a larger share, taking about 30 percent of the bachelor's and master's degrees and 16 percent of the doctorates. But only 8.5 percent of the M.D.'s and 5.6 percent of the law degrees went to women. Most of these percentages, low as they are, represent large gains from the preceding year. The representation of women in these areas appears to be still on the rise. In 1974, women received almost 10 percent of the degrees in the professions (mainly business and law) compared to 6.3 percent in 1971.

The situation is quite different in the so-called women's occupations. In 1971 women received 74 percent of the B.A.'s and 56 percent of the M.A.'s given in education. In library science, which is even more firmly dominated by women, they received 82 percent of all degrees in 1971. And in nursing, 98 percent of all the degrees went to women.

It is not surprising, then, to find that women do not have anything like the same occupational distribution as men. Even within an educational level, significant differences remain in the distribution across broad occupational categories (Table 10–7). Although 77 percent of women college graduates in 1970 were in the professions, mostly as teachers, only 4.8 percent, compared to 20 percent for men, were classified as managers. At high school levels, the proportion of women working as skilled craftsmen is minuscule, although a substantial proportion of women are blue-collar workers in the lower paying operative categories.

The supplement to this chapter summarizes in detail women's representation in occupations more narrowly defined. Although women are found in all occupations, the extent of occupational segregation by sex is large. In broad outline, this situation does not appear to have undergone any dramatic change between 1950 and 1970, although there are several examples of large increases in the proportion of women in less typically "female" occupations (for example, busdrivers, bartenders, and compositors and typesetters).

TABLE 10–7.—*Occupational distribution of employed persons by education and sex, 1970*

[Percent]

Occupational groups	High school				College graduates	
	1–3 years		4 years		Men	Women
	Men	Women	Men	Women		
Total employed	100.0	100.0	100.0	100.0	100.0	100.0
Professional, technical, and kindred workers	2.8	3.6	7.6	7.1	58.9	77.4
Managers and proprietors	6.9	2.9	11.4	3.8	20.1	4.8
Salesworkers	5.6	10.2	7.5	8.1	8.6	2.3
Clerical and kindred workers	6.8	25.3	10.0	50.4	4.9	12.1
Craftsmen	25.6	2.4	26.4	1.8	3.3	.4
Operatives	27.3	22.5	20.6	11.4	1.4	.6
Nonfarm laborers	9.9	1.6	5.3	.8	.5	.1
Farm laborers and foremen	1.9	.6	.9	.3	.2	.1
Farmers and farm managers	2.2	.2	2.9	.2	.8	.1
Service workers excluding private household	10.8	25.4	7.5	14.5	1.4	1.9
Private household service workers	.2	5.2	(1)	1.7	(1)	.3

1 Less than one tenth of 1 percent.

Note.—Detail may not add to totals because of rounding.

Source: Department of Commerce, Bureau of the Census.

Casual observation of individual occupations cannot, of course, provide a comprehensive indication of whether the occupational distributions of men and women, involving numerous occupations, have moved closer together or further apart. To help answer this question, an index was constructed and calculated for 1960 and 1970 which reflects the difference (for 197 occupations) between the occupational distributions of men and women. The index displays a small move toward occupational similarity between 1960 and 1970. (See the supplement to this chapter.)

Another question of interest is whether the changes in the occupational distributions of men and women were in the direction of higher economic status and, if so, how far they went. Some insight into this question is obtained by calculating an index which reflects what earnings would have been in 1950, 1960, and 1970, if earnings were the same in all 3 years and only the occupational distributions changed. Median earnings for year-round, full-time workers in each of 11 broad occupational categories were used as the constant weights to calculate such an index. The results indicated that the occupational distributions of both men and women shifted in the direction of higher-earnings occupations from 1950 to 1960 and from 1960 to 1970. However, in the earlier period men moved ahead in this respect faster than women while in the second period the changes were similar for both.

EARNINGS

In 1971 annual median earnings for women 14 years old and over were $2,986, or 40 percent of the median earnings of men. But women work fewer hours per week and fewer weeks per year. If the comparison is restricted to year-round, full-time workers, women's earnings are 60 percent of men's, that is, $5,593 compared to $9,399. An additional adjustment for differences in the average full-time workweek—full-time hours for men were about 10 percent higher than for women—brings the female-male ratio to 66 percent in 1971.

Differentials of this order of magnitude appear to have persisted since 1956 (Table 10–8). Indeed, a slight increase in the differential seems to have occurred from 1956 to 1969. Part of the source of the increasing differential was the relatively low rate of growth in the earnings of female clerical workers and female operatives, who in 1970 accounted for 32 percent and 14 percent, respectively, of all women workers. On the other hand, the rate of growth of earnings of women in the professions was high (a 5.1-percent annual compound rate between 1955 and 1968) relative to all workers; more recently it was even high relative to male professionals. [See Chapter 2 for more detailed discussion of the widening of the male-female earnings differential.]

A large differential is also evident when the comparison is restricted to men and women of the same age and education. As Chart 10–2 indicates, the incomes of women do not increase with age in anything like the same way men's do. Thus the differential widens with age through much of the working life.

One important factor influencing the differential is experience. The lack of continuity in women's attachment to the labor force means that they will not have accumulated as much experience as men at a given age. The relatively steeper rise of men's income with age has been attributed to their greater accumulation of experience, of "human capital" acquired on the job. Since very few women have participated in the labor force to the same degree as men, it is difficult to set up direct comparisons between the earnings of men and women with the same lifetime pattern of work. Using data from the Labor

TABLE 10–8.—*Ratio of total money earnings of civilian women workers to earnings of civilian men workers, selected years, 1956–71*

Occupational group	Actual ratios					Adjusted ratios [1]	
	1956	1960	1965	1969	1971	1969	1971
Total [2]	63.3	60.7	59.9	58.9	59.5	65.9	66.1
Professional and technical workers	62.4	61.3	65.2	62.2	66.4	67.9	72.4
Teachers, primary and secondary schools	(3)	75.6	79.9	72.4	82.0	(3)	(3)
Managers, officials, and proprietors	59.1	52.9	53.2	53.1	53.0	57.2	56.8
Clerical workers	71.7	67.6	67.2	65.0	62.4	70.0	66.9
Sales workers	41.8	40.9	40.5	40.2	42.1	45.7	47.4
Craftsmen and foreman	(4)	(4)	56.7	56.7	56.4	60.8	60.2
Operatives	62.1	59.4	56.6	58.7	60.5	65.4	66.6
Service workers excluding private household workers	55.4	57.2	55.4	57.4	58.5	62.5	63.2

[1] Adjusted for differences in average full-time hours worked since full-time hours for women are typically less than full-time hours for men.
[2] Total includes occupational groups not shown separately.
[3] Not available.
[4] Base too small to be statistically significant.

Note.—Data relate to civilian workers who are employed full-time, year-round. Data for 1956 include salaried workers only, while data for later years include both salaried and self-employed workers.

Sources: Department of Commerce, Bureau of the Census, Department of Labor, Bureau of Labor Statistics, and Council of Economic Advisers.

Department's longitudinal study of women, referred to above, one study was able to compare the earnings of women working different amounts of time throughout their lives with the earnings of men, most of whom are presumed to work continuously after leaving school. The figures for men were taken from census data. The women's lifetime work experience was measured as the percentage of years each had worked since leaving school. However, a work year was crudely defined as one in which the women had worked at least 6 months. Thus no adjustment could be made for whether the years worked had been truly full-time commitments with respect to both hours worked per week and weeks worked per year.

Among the women 30–44 years old in the survey, the gain from continuous work was apparently very large. If we look only at those women who had worked year-round, full-time in 1966, the median wage and salary income for the group who had worked each year since leaving school was $5,618; for those who had worked less than 50 percent of the years since leaving school (almost half the group) the median income was $3,655. The median wage and salary income of men in the same age group who had worked full-time, year-round in 1966 was $7,529. The men are presumed to have worked continuously since leaving school. Thus the women who had worked less than half of the years since leaving school earned only 49 percent as much as men, while the small group of women who had worked each year earned 75 per-

Chart 10–2

Annual Income by Age, for Male and Female High School and College Graduates

DOLLARS ¹/ (RATIO SCALE)

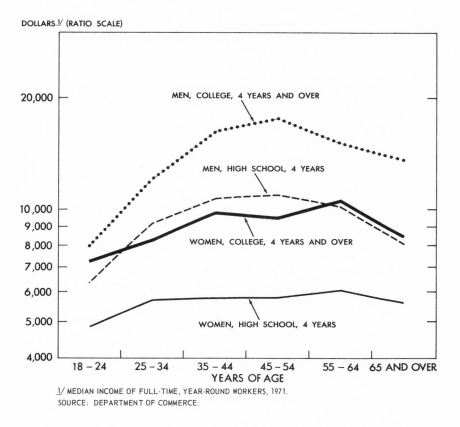

MEN, COLLEGE, 4 YEARS AND OVER

MEN, HIGH SCHOOL, 4 YEARS

WOMEN, COLLEGE, 4 YEARS AND OVER

WOMEN, HIGH SCHOOL, 4 YEARS

20,000

10,000
9,000
8,000
7,000
6,000
5,000
4,000

18 – 24   25 – 34   35 – 44   45 – 54   55 – 64 65 AND OVER
YEARS OF AGE

1/ MEDIAN INCOME OF FULL-TIME, YEAR-ROUND WORKERS, 1971.
SOURCE: DEPARTMENT OF COMMERCE.

cent as much as men. Interestingly, single women who had worked each year since leaving school earned slightly more than single men. More sophisticated comparisons, adjusting for additional differences in training, continuity at work, and education, can be made. One recent study found that the earnings differential was reduced to below 20 percent after taking account of such differences.

The importance of lifetime accumulated experience in influencing women's earnings suggests one possible explanation for the small decline in the ratio of women's to men's earnings between 1956 and 1969. Since the labor force participation of women has been rising rapidly, an increasing proportion of new entrants and of those with few accumulated years in the labor force could have resulted in a decline in the average experience level of all women. This drop would in turn temporarily push down the average level of earnings for all women. Unfortunately the data are not available to compare the ratio over a period of time between the earnings of women having a given number of years' experience and the earnings of men.

DIRECT DISCRIMINATION VERSUS ROLE DIFFERENTIATION

A differential, perhaps on the order of 20 percent, between the earnings of men and women remains after adjusting for factors such as education, work experience during the year, and even lifelong work experience. How much of this differential is due to differences in experience or in performance on the job which could not be measured adequately, and how much to discrimination? The question is difficult to answer, in part because there are differences of opinion about what should be classified as discrimination.

Some studies have succeeded in narrowing the male-female differential well below 20 percent. Indeed, Department of Labor surveys have found that the differential almost disappears when men's and women's earnings are compared within detailed job classifications and within the same establishment. In the very narrow sense of equal pay for the same job in the same plant there may be little difference between women and men. However, in this way the focus of the problem is shifted but not eliminated, for then we must explain why women have such a different job structure from men and why they are employed in different types of establishments.

There is clearly prejudice against women engaging in particular activities. Some patients reject women doctors, some clients reject women lawyers, some customers reject automobile saleswomen, and some workers reject women bosses. Employers also may have formulated discriminatory attitudes about women, exaggerating the risk of job instability or client acceptance and therefore excluding women from on-the-job training which would advance their careers.

In fact, even if employers do estimate correctly the average job turnover of women, women who are strongly committed to their jobs may suffer from "statistical discrimination" by being treated as though their own behavior resembled the average. The extent to which this type of discrimination occurs depends on how costly it is for employers to distinguish women who will have a strong job commitment from those who will not. Finally, because some occupations restrict the number of newcomers they take in and because women move in and out of the labor force more often, more women than men tend to fall into the newcomer category and to be thus excluded. For example, restrictive entry policies may have kept women out of the skilled crafts.

On the other hand, as discussed above, some component of the earnings differential and of the occupational differential stems from differences in role orientation which start with differences in education and continue through marriage, where women generally are expected to assume primary responsibility for the home and subordinate their own outside work to their household responsibilities.

It is not now possible to distinguish in a quantitative way between the discrimination which bars women from jobs solely because of their sex, and the role differentiation whereby women, either through choice or necessity, restrict their careers because of the demands of their homes. Some may label the latter as a pervasive societal discrimination which starts in the cradle; nonetheless, it is useful to draw the distinction.

One other missing link in our chain of understanding of these problems is the value of the work done at home by women. One study has found that women college graduates tend to reduce their outside work when their children are small more than less educated women, and that they also devote more time to the training of their children. Of course this pattern is undoubtedly facilitated by the higher income of their husbands. However, this pattern also results in a considerable sacrifice of earnings, and one may infer that these women have therefore placed a very high value on the personal attention they can give their children. Without more information, it is difficult to evaluate the full extent to which women's capabilities have actually been underutilized by society.

THE FEMALE-HEADED HOUSEHOLD

In 1975, some 7 million families, about 13 percent of all families, were headed by women. These women are widowed, divorced, separated, or single, and many have responsibilities for the support of children in fatherless families or of other relatives. About two-thirds of all female-headed families include children.

As a result of the division of labor within families, the average woman who has been married has not had the same labor market experience or vocationally oriented training as her husband. Unless she has a substantial alimony or pension, she is likely to face financial difficulties. The median income of female-headed families was $7,651 in 1975, slightly more than half the income of male-headed families ($15,094 in 1975). When women who head families were full-time, year-round workers, the family's median income was $10,684 in 1975; but only 31 percent of women heading families were full-time, year-round workers. Furthermore, the woman who heads a family and works has additional expenses of child care and other home care expenses.

The problems faced by the woman who heads a household are particularly acute if the woman is black, and 27 percent of women heading households are black. For this group, median family income was only $4,898 in 1975. Although at higher education levels, black women now earn amounts comparable to white women, those black women who head families are at a disadvantage compared to white women. The median personal income of white women heading households and working year-round, full-time was $7,967 in 1974, compared to $6,496 for black women in the same position.

As a result of the combination of a large number of dependents and the difficulty of maintaining the dual responsibility of monetary support and home care, many female-headed families fall below the low-income level. In 1975, 33 percent of female-headed families were below the low-income level, compared to 6 percent for male-headed families. Among black households with a female head, 50 percent were below the low-income level. A large proportion receive public assistance. In 1971, 30 percent of the women heading households received public assistance payments. [This proportion is undoubtedly a gross underestimate of the proportion receiving welfare. It is known from other sources, such as administrative records, that only about 60 percent of welfare payments are included in the family income reported to the Bureau of the Census. And, as indicated in Table 4–2, the number of AFDC families (excluding those in the unemployed fathers' program) has been close to 80 percent of the total number of female-headed families with children under the age of 18.]

It has been suggested, though not proved, that widespread availability of public assistance has encouraged husbands to desert their wives or wives to leave their husbands in families where the husband earns little more than the amount of welfare benefits his family would be entitled to in his absence. Remarriage may also be discouraged because the low-income mother would then lose her entire public stipend, including the child support portion, and without some outside child support a man might be reluctant to marry a woman with several children.[2]

Among the women who are now welfare recipients many are handicapped by lack of education and training and are not in a position to earn an income that would lift them and their families above poverty levels. A program established in 1967, the Work Incentive Program, now gives many mothers currently on welfare, training and placement assistance so that they can improve their ability to support themselves and their dependents.

2. For some recent evidence on this point see Chapter 4. [Editors]

THE INCOME TAX

Devising a tax system which is equitable and efficient has always posed formidable problems, and often the best solution is one involving compromise with one or more of the objectives. The tax treatment of working wives is one of the more difficult problems. The income tax law as such treats men and women equally and, indeed, its effects on single men and single women are the same. However, some of the features of the tax structure, which have been considered desirable for other purposes, have, as a by-product, unequal effects on the second earner of a married couple, who is usually the wife.

Only income arising from market transactions is taxed. Indeed, there is no practical way to assign a market value to the unpaid work performed at home and then subject it to the tax. As a result, the tax system imposes a general bias in the economy favoring unpaid work at home compared to paid work in the market. However, the bias and the resulting disincentive toward market work are particularly relevant for the married woman who traditionally has done more work at home.

An equity problem also arises from this situation. To use a hypothetical example, a husband and wife each earning $8,000 would pay the same income tax as a couple where the husband alone works and earns $16,000, although the couple with two earners will have the additional expenses of buying the services which would be produced at home and untaxed if the wife did not work.

There is the further problem that a married couple may pay more or less income tax than two single persons whose combined income equals the couple's, depending upon how the income is divided between the two individuals. This problem reflects a basic ambivalence about whether the appropriate unit of taxation is the individual or the family.

Remedies for the situation are not easy to find. One suggestion has been to allow working wives to deduct a given percentage of their earnings from their income for tax purposes. However, this would be unfair to single persons, who also incur expenses of going to work. A general earned income credit has also been suggested, but this creates a bias against investments in capital and in favor of wage income.

As discussed below, the Revenue Act of 1971 has given expanded tax relief to working wives with children by allowing more liberalized child care deductions to couples within a given income range. This provision, however, does not affect couples without children or couples with combined incomes outside the allowable income range.[3]

3. Starting in 1976, as a result of subsequent legislation, a tax *credit* of up to $400 per year ($800 for two or more) is substituted for the deduction. The credit is available to working parents and there is no income restriction. [Editors]

CHILD CARE

Provision for child care is a cost to working mothers and a major obstacle to the employment of many other mothers who would work outside the home if they could find satisfactory arrangements for taking care of their children. As more mothers have taken jobs outside the home, and more weigh the possibility of doing so, several major questions about child care have become intense national issues.

One question is whether the Government should pay for part or all of the cost of child care. This question is usually raised about the Federal Government, but it could be equally asked about State or local governments. According to one view of the matter parents have chosen to have children, which implies a certain allocation of their resources, therefore they have no reason to burden other taxpayers to look after the children. Another view of the matter is that Government subsidies can be justified and different groups have cited different reasons. The point has been made that the pressures of custom result in a bias against the wife going to work while the husband stays home with the children. A child-care subsidy for working mothers would help remove any harmful effects of this cultural bias. Another reason given is that there is a national interest in the proper care of children, who are, of course, the future nation, and that this case justifies Government subsidies. The analogy commonly given is to public education.

Government has given subsidies to families with children but there has been no consistent philosophy behind them. At the extreme, with respect to children in very poor families, we have long recognized the need for public assistance in the form of the program of Aid to Families with Dependent Children. This program is not specifically addressed to children with working mothers. In fact, until recently it was tilted *against* helping working mothers. The Federal Government also provides a form of assistance for child care through the income tax. With the Revenue Act of 1971, a much more liberal deduction than had ever been provided was instituted specifically for child-care expenses incurred by working wives. Below a combined husband-wife income of $18,000, a working wife can now deduct up to $400 a month for child care expenses. The deduction is scaled downwards to zero as combined income goes from $18,000 to $27,600. [These amounts were raised to $35,000 and $44,600, effective in 1976.] The two groups not covered are women whose family income is too low to benefit from a tax deduction and women at the other end of the income scale.

Public discussion of Government support for child care has not clearly distinguished among several possible objectives:

(a) To reward and assist the care of all small children;

(b) To assist the care of small children whose parents might not be otherwise able to care for them;

(c) To assist the care of the small children of working mothers;

(d) To assist in the care of small children in a particular way— through day-care institutions, or at home, etc.

Both the amount of Government support that is desirable, and the form it should take if it is to be provided, depend on the choice made among these objectives.

Recently, publicly supported institutional group care, or day care, has received considerable attention as one approach to helping the working mother. Some have also stressed day care as a developmental program. It may be noted that a very small proportion of working women have depended on group day care in an institutional center. A Government-sponsored survey of 1965 found that, among employed mothers of children under 6, only 6.4 percent depended on school or group care centers. About 47 percent of the women arranged to have their children cared for at home, often by a relative. The rest mainly arranged for care in someone else's home (31 percent) or looked after the child while working (15 percent).

Some have attributed the low use of day care to a failure of the market to provide a service that would be utilized if financing were available. Others have interpreted it as an indication that the true demand for institutional day care is low. Even among more affluent and knowledgeable working mothers who presumably could afford it, dependence on institutional group care is low. A survey of college graduates found that in 1964, among those who worked and who had children under 6 years, 9 percent used group care, which included nursery schools, kindergartens, and day-care centers. Most (73 percent) arranged for care in their own home.

Whether institutional day care provides the best use of dollars spent on child care has yet to be established. While this issue has not been resolved, it is clear that the problems of mothers who want and need to work require serious attention and continuing search for new solutions.

GOVERNMENT ACTION

Government has been profoundly concerned with promoting full equality of opportunity for women within both the public and the private sectors. Two approaches have been followed. The first involves the use of law and regulations where they are both applicable and compatible with other goals of a democratic society.

A number of laws have been passed and Executive Orders issued which deal with discrimination by employers. Included are the Equal

Pay Act of 1963, requiring employers to compensate men and women in the same establishment equally for work of equivalent skill and responsibility, and Title VII of the Civil Rights Act of 1964, which prohibits discrimination in hiring, discharging, compensation, and other aspects of employment. Title VII is administered by the Equal Employment Opportunity Commission (EEOC). The Equal Employment Opportunity Act, signed by the President in 1972, gave the EEOC enforcement power through the courts in sex-discrimination cases. In December 1971, Order No. 4, under Executive Order 11216, was extended to women. This Order requires Federal contractors employing more than 50 workers and holding contracts of $50,000 or more to formulate written affirmative action plans, with goals and timetables, to ensure equal opportunities. Title IX of the Education Amendments of 1972 prohibits discrimination in educational programs or activities on the basis of sex. [Further Government action has been taken since this section was written in January 1973.]

If ratified by the states, The Equal Rights Amendment to the Constitution, would provide that "equality of rights under the law shall not be denied or abridged by the United States or by any State on account of sex," and would authorize the Congress and the States to enforce the amendment by appropriate legislation.[4] The purpose of the proposed amendment would be to provide constitutional protection against laws and official practices that treat men and women differently.

The other approach of Government to providing equality to women has been through leadership. The Women's Bureau in the Department of Labor has for 50 years been concerned with the problems of women at work. Recently, several new groups, each concerned with different areas affecting women, have been formed. The formation of the Advisory Committee on the Economic Role of Women is one such effort.[5] The Citizen's Advisory Council on the Status of Women is another. The latter is a council of private citizens appointed by the President, which surveys the social and political issues of particular interest to women and makes recommendations for legislation or other suitable social action. In an effort to recruit women to top-level jobs in the Government, the President in 1971 appointed to the White House staff a special assistant for this purpose. As a result many women have been placed in key policy making positions, positions never before held by women.

4. As of 1975 it had been ratified in 35 States. For it to become an amendment to the Constitution, ratification by at least three-quarters of the States is required within seven years of the 1972 passage by the Senate. [Editors]

5. This Committee provided assistance to the Council of Economic Advisers during 1973 and 1974. Among other activities, the Committee sponsored a symposium on women in industry and issued a set of guidelines for employers to combat discrimination in the private sector. [Editors]

It is only in the past few years that the problems women face as a group have been given the widespread recognition they deserve. There is much to be learned before we can even ask all the appropriate questions. Many of the problems involve profound issues of family and social organization. By listening to diverse groups and to the discussion of the public it is hoped that Government will be able to find its appropriate role.

SUPPLEMENT TO CHAPTER 10

In order to answer the question whether the occupational distribution of women has moved closer to that of men's, an index of occupational dissimilarity was constructed for 1960 and 1970. The particular measure of dissimiliarity used here is calculated by taking the absolute difference (for each of 197 occupations) between the percentage of the female experienced civilian labor force in a given occupation and the percentage of the male experienced civilian labor force in the same occupation, summing these differences across the 197 occupations, and then dividing this sum by 2. Those persons in the experienced labor force who did not report their occupation were excluded from the denominator. If men and women were to have the identical occupational distributions then the value of the index would be 0. At the other extreme, if men and women were completely occupationally segregated, so that they were never in the same occupation, the index would have a value of 1.

The values of the occupational dissimilarity index, calculated as described, were as follows:

$$1960 \text{ — — — —} .629$$
$$1970 \text{ — — — —} .598$$

The index therefore indicates a very small change in the direction of increased occupational similarity between 1960 and 1970. The data for the calculations were taken from the decennial censuses of 1960 and 1970.

In Table 10–9, women's representation in a group of detailed occupations is given for 1950, 1960, and 1970.

TABLE 10–9.—*Women in experienced civilian labor force, 1950, 1960 and 1970*

(14 years of age and over)

Occupational group	Number of women (thousands)			Women as percent of all persons in occupation		
	1950	1960	1970	1950	1960	1970
TOTAL	16,481.9	22,303.7	30,601.0	28.1	32.8	38.0
Professional and technical workers	1,896.9	2,723.9	4,397.6	39.0	38.4	39.9
Accountants	57.0	81.9	187.0	14.9	16.5	26.2
Architects	.9	.8	2.0	3.8	2.1	3.6
Engineers	6.7	7.2	20.3	1.3	.8	1.6
Farm and home management advisers	5.0	6.4	6.5	46.1	47.2	49.7
Lawyers and Judges	7.0	7.5	13.4	4.1	3.5	4.9
Librarians	50.7	64.6	101.5	88.8	85.4	82.0
Life and physical scientists	12.6	15.2	29.2	11.0	9.2	13.7
Personnel and labor relations workers	15.0	34.2	91.7	28.3	33.1	30.9
Pharmacists	7.4	7.2	13.3	8.7	7.5	12.0
Physicians, medical and osteopathic	12.3	16.2	26.1	6.7	6.9	9.3
Dietitians	21.7	24.8	37.8	96.5	92.7	92.0
Registered nurses	399.2	613.7	819.3	97.6	97.5	97.3
Therapists	(¹)	16.4	48.5	(¹)	63.4	63.5
Health technicians	46.3	88.0	184.1	57.4	68.2	69.7
Clergymen	7.3	4.7	6.3	4.4	2.3	2.9
Other religious workers	28.7	38.6	20.1	69.9	63.3	55.7

TABLE 10–9.—*Women in experienced civilian labor force,*
1950, 1960, and 1970—Continued

(14 years of age and over)

Occupational group	Number of women (thousands)			Women as percent of all persons in occupation		
	1950	1960	1970	1950	1960	1970
Professional and technical workers—Cont'd.						
Social scientists	11.3	15.1	32.0	32.9	25.4	23.2
Social workers	54.0	59.4	138.9	69.3	62.8	62.8
Recreation workers	7.7	14.9	22.5	45.4	51.2	42.0
Teachers, elementary	(¹)	851.2	1,199.4	(¹)	85.8	83.7
Teachers, secondary	(¹)	280.5	498.7	(¹)	49.3	49.3
Teachers, college and university	27.8	46.5	140.4	22.4	23.9	28.6
Engineering and science technicians	(¹)	43.5	68.7	(¹)	11.1	12.9
Draftsmen	7.2	12.3	23.6	6.0	5.6	8.0
Radio operators	1.7	3.1	7.6	10.2	16.7	25.9
Authors	5.8	7.3	7.7	36.5	25.5	29.1
Dancers	(¹)	3.9	5.7	(¹)	86.0	81.3
Designers	10.7	13.4	27.2	26.7	19.3	24.2
Editors and reporters	29.4	39.0	61.5	32.1	36.6	40.6
Musicians and composers	(¹)	29.8	33.5	(¹)	38.6	34.8
Photographers	8.6	6.5	9.5	16.2	12.2	14.2
Other professional, technical, and kindred workers	(¹)	270.1	513.9	(¹)	33.9	32.9
Managers and administrators, except farm	680.8	844.5	1,034.3	13.7	14.8	16.6
Buyers, wholesale and retail trade	35.5	34.2	52.8	24.6	35.6	29.8
Credit men	6.6	12.0	17.0	19.2	25.1	28.3
Public administrators and postal inspectors	2.5	3.1	6.2	4.4	3.9	6.1
Managers and superintendents, building	22.9	20.0	34.0	34.2	43.6	40.2
Administrators, n.e.c., Federal	5.2	12.1	20.4	10.6	15.3	16.9
Administrators, n.e.c., State	2.1	4.8	6.5	9.5	12.8	13.4
Administrators, n.e.c., local	18.8	17.2	20.6	22.9	21.8	26.2
Officials of societies and unions	3.2	5.1	8.2	10.9	11.8	16.2
Postmasters and mail superintendents	17.3	15.0	11.3	44.9	39.3	31.8
Purchasing agents and buyers, n.e.c.	6.2	10.3	22.5	9.5	9.2	13.7
Restaurant, cafeteria and bar managers	93.9	95.5	112.6	26.9	32.5	34.2
Other specified managers and administrators, except farm	(¹)	72.4	223.4	(¹)	14.9	18.4
Managers and administrators, n.e.c., salaried:						
Construction	2.0	5.0	8.0	2.2	3.4	3.1
Manufacturing	27.8	45.0	43.0	6.8	7.1	6.3
Transportation	4.2	10.8	17.6	4.4	8.7	12.3
Communication and utilities	5.7	11.3	13.3	9.7	11.0	11.8
Wholesale trade	8.3	14.3	18.9	5.4	7.0	7.4
Retail, hardware, etc	1.4	2.3	2.7	3.3	4.3	5.1
Retail, general merchandise	13.6	23.6	25.4	23.2	26.2	24.6
Retail, foodstores	12.7	9.5	17.3	12.8	8.9	12.3
Retail, motor vehicles and accessories	2.4	3.9	5.7	4.3	4.4	5.4
Retail, apparel and accessories	14.1	17.0	19.9	33.5	33.5	34.2
Retail, furniture, etc.	3.1	3.4	5.3	11.2	10.7	12.1
Other retail trade	13.7	14.7	24.2	12.4	11.9	13.1
Finance, insurance and real estate	25.4	47.9	32.8	13.9	14.7	17.5
Business and repair services	6.1	16.1	19.8	10.8	16.8	14.0
Personal services	21.2	28.7	36.0	33.7	35.8	26.8
All other industries	39.6	64.5	64.0	25.3	27.8	26.8
Managers and administrators, n.e.c., self-employed:						
Construction	2.6	2.9	2.8	1.3	1.3	1.9
Manufacturing	15.2	11.8	6.0	6.5	6.9	9.1
Transportation	2.4	4.6	2.1	4.6	10.6	9.8
Wholesale trade	7.1	6.9	4.5	4.0	5.0	8.1
Retail, hardware, etc	3.8	3.4	2.4	4.7	5.1	8.4
Retail, general merchandise	15.1	10.8	8.0	23.6	23.3	32.4
Retail, food	70.6	42.7	30.1	18.4	19.4	26.1
Retail, gas service stations	5.2	4.1	3.5	3.6	2.7	3.4
Retail, apparel and accessories stores	24.4	19.2	10.0	29.5	33.7	41.9
Retail, furniture, etc	4.9	4.5	3.7	7.3	9.2	13.6
Other retail trade	38.8	32.8	27.4	14.3	15.9	25.1
Finance, insurance and real estate	7.2	8.3	3.0	10.9	11.5	12.6
Business and repair services	7.4	8.1	6.2	6.0	8.4	11.9
Personal services	39.5	43.6	27.8	28.0	33.1	31.3
All other industries	14.7	21.3	7.4	14.2	20.3	22.1

TABLE 10–9.—*Women in experienced civilian labor force,*
1950, 1960, and 1970—Continued

(14 years of age and over)

Occupational group	Number of women (thousands)			Women as percent of all persons in occupation		
	1950	1960	1970	1950	1960	1970
Sales workers	1,374.7	1,736.0	2,096.7	34.2	36.2	38.6
Advertising agents and salesmen	5.3	4.9	13.0	15.1	13.9	20.1
Demonstrators	11.0	26.7	36.7	77.5	93.2	91.1
Hucksters and peddlers	3.5	37.7	96.4	14.9	60.5	78.7
Insurance agents, brokers, and underwriters	27.3	36.1	57.6	8.9	9.7	12.5
Newsboys	4.1	8.6	13.9	3.8	4.3	7.4
Real estate agents and brokers	22.1	46.8	85.2	15.6	23.9	32.0
Sales representatives, manufacturing	23.0	50.8	36.8	7.2	10.7	8.8
Sales representatives, wholesale	15.3	21.3	42.8	3.8	4.2	6.6
Salesmen and clerks, retail	1,228.9	1,451.4	1,619.4	48.9	54.4	56.5
Other salesworkers	34.3	51.8	94.8	23.0	20.2	27.0
Clerical and kindred workers	4,343.4	6,407.0	9,910.0	61.9	67.9	73.6
Bank tellers	27.7	94.6	218.6	44.6	70.2	86.2
Bookkeepers	566.3	793.6	1,291.7	77.4	83.4	82.0
Cashiers	193.7	393.1	734.8	81.4	77.1	83.7
Collectors, bill and account	3.9	6.7	19.2	16.0	20.0	36.2
Dispatchers and starters, vehicle	4.1	5.2	10.5	12.7	10.8	17.1
Library attendants and assistants	9.1	28.1	101.2	76.7	75.7	78.6
Mail carriers, post office	3.4	4.4	20.5	2.0	2.2	8.0
Messengers and office boys	10.9	9.3	12.1	18.6	14.7	19.7
Office machine operators	119.5	239.1	423.1	81.6	74.4	74.0
Shipping and receiving clerks	20.3	26.4	62.9	6.8	8.1	14.7
Stenographers, typists, and secretaries	1,524.9	2,233.5	3,786.9	94.6	96.5	96.6
Telegraph operators	7.6	4.7	3.7	21.6	22.8	29.4
Telephone operators	349.2	356.2	398.3	95.8	95.8	94.5
Ticket, station, and express agents	7.9	16.2	36.7	12.7	21.8	36.7
Other clerical workers	1,494.9	2,196.0	2,789.8	47.2	54.6	58.9
Craftsmen	247.3	295.3	524.1	3.1	3.1	5.0
Bakers	13.9	21.4	33.9	11.6	18.2	30.0
Bookbinders	19.5	17.6	20.9	58.1	58.9	58.1
Compositors and typesetters	12.2	16.2	24.9	6.9	8.4	15.3
Decorators and window dressers	14.0	24.4	41.9	31.9	46.3	57.7
Electricians	2.1	2.8	9.3	.6	.8	1.9
Linemen and servicemen, telegraph, telephone, and power	5.1	5.6	10.7	2.4	2.1	2.7
Engravers, except photoengravers	1.4	2.1	2.5	14.5	17.9	27.5
Foremen, nonmanufacturing	18.2	22.8	51.1	5.3	4.4	7.5
Foremen, manufacturing	51.2	58.2	80.9	10.0	8.8	8.7
Inspectors	7.3	6.6	9.7	7.7	6.5	8.0
Machinists	7.6	7.4	12.8	1.5	1.4	3.3
Mechanics and repairmen, except air, auto	16.6	15.4	35.0	1.6	1.1	2.5
Aircraft mechanics	1.0	1.9	4.5	1.3	1.6	3.1
Auto mechanics	4.3	2.4	12.9	.6	.4	1.4
Opticians, lensgrinders and polishers	2.4	3.2	6.5	12.1	15.3	23.1
Painters, construction and maintenance	9.1	7.1	14.8	2.1	1.8	4.1
Pressmen and plate printers, printing	2.5	5.1	14.1	4.8	6.1	8.8
Stationary engineers	1.8	1.6	2.6	.8	.6	1.5
Tailors	16.3	23.1	22.5	19.3	26.5	31.7
Upholsterers	5.5	6.2	10.7	8.7	9.9	16.5
Other craftsmen	35.3	44.2	101.8	1.1	1.3	2.8
Operatives	3,190.8	3,521.2	4,222.6	27.4	28.7	31.5
Dressmakers and seamstresses, except factory	140.3	121.7	96.9	97.3	96.7	95.0
Filers, polishers, sanders and buffers	7.3	21.0	26.9	4.8	13.8	21.8
Laundry and drycleaning operatives	302.7	282.9	261.0	67.6	65.3	69.8
Meatcutters and butchers, except manufacturing	3.8	5.8	11.2	2.2	3.1	5.4
Milliners	12.5	3.9	2.1	89.4	90.7	89.4
Painters, manufactured articles	14.8	16.5	18.6	12.1	13.5	15.3
Photographic process workers	13.5	21.5	31.4	43.7	45.8	46.9
Sawyers	2.6	2.4	9.6	2.6	2.3	8.9
Textile operatives	(¹)	278.5	247.6	(¹)	53.2	54.8
Bus drivers	4.5	18.6	67.1	2.9	10.1	28.0
Deliverymen and routemen	4.3	15.0	21.3	1.7	3.3	3.3
Taxicab drivers and chauffeurs	3.4	4.6	9.0	1.6	2.7	5.7
Truckdrivers	8.6	8.3	21.6	.6	.5	1.5
Other specified operatives	(¹)	2,060.6	2,602.1	(¹)	36.7	39.1 ₁

TABLE 10–9.—*Women in experienced civilian labor force,*
1950, 1960, and 1970—Continued

(14 years of age and over)

Occupational group	Number of women (thousands)			Women as percent of all persons in occupation		
	1950	1960	1970	1950	1960	1970
Operatives—Cont'd.						
Miscelleneous and not specified operatives, n.e.c.	(1)	660.0	796.2	(1)	25.7	29.6
Lumber and wood products	(1)	10.6	11.7	(1)	11.4	15.1
Furniture and fixtures	(1)	8.3	14.9	(1)	15.6	28.1
Stone, clay, and glass products	(1)	16.5	19.7	(1)	15.1	18.7
Primary metal industries	(1)	6.9	12.7	(1)	3.8	7.1
Fabricated metal industries	(1)	27.9	33.1	(1)	19.7	22.9
Machinery, except electrical	(1)	16.3	25.7	(1)	11.8	16.0
Electrical machinery, equipment, and supplies	(1)	79.3	113.8	(1)	50.3	55.2
Transportation equipment	(1)	15.4	27.1	(1)	10.7	16.1
Professional and photographic equipment, and watches	(1)	15.8	19.5	(1)	42.6	48.8
Miscellaneous manufacturing industries	(1)	57.2	66.5	(1)	34.2	39.0
Food and kindred products	(1)	91.8	76.6	(1)	31.5	34.8
Tobacco manufactures	(1)	17.7	10.3	(1)	54.9	51.6
Apparel and other fabricated textile products	(1)	87.4	74.5	(1)	74.0	75.5
Paper and allied products	(1)	46.4	43.0	(1)	25.5	23.7
Printing, publishing, etc	(1)	32.4	36.7	(1)	42.4	45.5
Chemicals, etc	(1)	18.5	25.5	(1)	12.4	17.0
Rubber and miscellaneous plastic	(1)	31.9	60.7	(1)	26.4	35.1
Leather products	(1)	18.2	26.3	(1)	43.9	57.6
Wholesale and retail	(1)	35.5	47.1	(1)	31.4	30.6
Business and repair services	(1)	5.4	8.1	(1)	10.9	14.7
Public administration	(1)	2.3	3.7	(1)	13.3	16.2
Other nonmanufacturing	(1)	18.2	38.9	(1)	12.0	21.0
Laborers, except farm	134.1	193.1	294.6	3.6	5.1	8.4
Miscellaneous and not specified laborers	(1)	61.2	75.0	(1)	5.3	10.9
Lumber and wood products, except furniture	(1)	.6	1.8	(1)	1.3	7.0
Stone, clay, and glass products	(1)	2.5	1.6	(1)	4.7	6.6
Metal industries	(1)	4.5	6.3	(1)	2.1	6.1
Electrical machinery, equipment, and supplies	(1)	4.2	4.3	(1)	18.3	32.7
Food and kindred products	(1)	10.1	6.5	(1)	11.2	14.9
Textile mill products	(1)	1.9	2.6	(1)	13.9	22.1
Apparel and other fabricated textile products	(1)	1.7	1.8	(1)	43.0	49.3
Leather and leather products	(1)	1.6	1.4	(1)	19.2	34.8
Other manufacturing	(1)	16.0	17.1	(1)	7.6	14.4
Transportation, communication, and public utilities	(1)	2.9	3.2	(1)	1.5	3.0
Wholesale and retail trade	(1)	3.9	11.5	(1)	3.0	11.8
Public administration	(1)	.4	1.5	(1)	1.1	7.3
Other nonmanufacturing industries	(1)	11.0	15.4	(1)	7.7	13.1
Other nonfarm laborers	(1)	132.1	220.0	(1)	5.1	7.8
Farm workers	602.2	394.8	222.3	8.8	9.6	9.5
Farmers, owners, and tenants	118.3	119.0	59.9	2.8	4.8	4.6
Farm managers	2.4	.7	2.7	6.5	2.9	4.4
Farm laborers, wage workers	148.9	147.6	117.7	9.5	11.5	13.9
Farm laborers, unpaid family workers	330.7	126.8	39.3	35.1	44.4	36.2
Other farm laborers	2.0	.7	2.7	7.2	2.2	7.1

TABLE 10–9.—*Women in experienced civilian labor force,*
1950, 1960, and 1970—Continued

(14 years of age and over)

Occupational group	Number of women (thousands)			Women as percent of all persons in occupation		
	1950	1960	1970	1950	1960	1970
Service workers	3,564.1	4,890.3	5,751.9	58.1	61.9	60.0
Cleaners and charwomen	75.3	167.7	266.1	60.5	41.7	56.6
Janitors and sextons	56.5	91.3	165.2	12.0	11.6	12.7
Bartenders	13.1	20.5	41.9	6.4	11.1	21.1
Cooks, except private household	257.1	385.4	550.5	55.2	63.9	62.1
Counter and fountain workers	47.4	119.4	126.3	50.9	70.9	75.0
Waiters and waitresses	579.8	780.0	1,002.4	81.8	86.8	89.0
Practical nurses	138.4	166.5	233.2	96.4	95.4	96.4
Other health services	232.0	445.0	847.4	72.6	73.4	86.2
Attendants, recreation and amusement	5.2	13.0	19.7	7.9	17.6	23.8
Attendants, personal service, n.e.c.	33.5	46.8	40.9	67.2	55.6	62.6
Boarding and lodging housekeepers	23.6	26.4	5.4	75.6	88.5	71.9
Elevator operators	27.0	24.9	10.2	29.1	32.5	27.6
Barbers, hairdressers, and cosmetologists	193.2	278.0	442.4	49.2	56.9	68.0
Housekeepers, except private household	85.8	51.0	76.6	77.2	73.6	71.8
Guards and watchmen	5.3	5.2	17.0	2.1	2.0	5.2
Policemen and detectives	3.9	7.0	13.5	2.0	2.7	3.6
Other protective service workers	2.1	14.2	28.7	1.5	7.1	11.0
Other service workers, except private household	345.2	496.8	761.5	45.4	68.8	66.0
Housekeepers, private household	147.4	149.0	101.5	97.6	95.5	96.2
Laundresses, private household	73.3	40.7	11.9	97.0	98.2	94.8
Other private household workers	1,219.1	1,561.9	989.7	94.5	96.5	96.6
Occupation not reported	447.6	1,297.7	2,147.1	35.2	37.6	41.5

[1] Data are not available because of changes in classification.
n.e.c. = not elsewhere classified.

Note: Occupational classifications in this table are not exactly comparable with Census classifications because of re-grouping detailed occupations.
Detail for 1950 is not always strictly comparable with later years because of changes in classification.
The data are based on samples drawn from the decennial censuses. The sample sizes are: 1950, 3½ percent; 1960, 25 percent; 1970, 20 percent.
Detail may not add to totals because of rounding.

Sources: Department of Commerce, Bureau of the Census, and Council of Economic Advisers.

Part IV

Education and Health

[E DUCATION IS AN IMPORTANT FACTOR influencing income and unemployment. Although the financing of education
has been primarily a State and local government responsibility, the
Federal Government has maintained financial support particularly for
the academic education of the disadvantaged as well as for the vocational training. Chapter 11 contains a brief statement of the Federal
interest from the 1965 Economic Report with some comments on more
recent developments.

Chapter 12 offers a comprehensive examination of health and medical care. This includes discussions of the relation between medical
care, other factors, and health status and of the access to medical care
and medical expenditures of groups at different income levels. The
chapter examines the escalation in medical expenditures over the past
decade and suggests some reasons for that phenomenon. The pros and
cons of national health insurance have been widely discussed in recent years, and the editors have added a section on that subject.]

CHAPTER 11

Education

[The following section on Education is from the *1965 Economic Report*. None of the Economic Reports of the 1970s contain a section exclusively devoted to education finance or educational attainment, although education is routinely discussed as a variable related to income, unemployment and other aspects of economic performance. Because education is financed primarily by State and local governments, it is perhaps less consistently viewed as a Federal concern than other areas. The section from the 1965 Report came at a time when new education programs at the Federal level were being established. It was also a time when the baby-boom cohort of school children were creating financial pressures, a situation which has reversed as a result of declining birthrates.

The section from the 1965 Report expresses considerable optimism that additional Government spending on schooling and other training programs and new methods of teaching can raise the level of skill, particularly for the most disadvantaged. This optimism is less prevalent in the late 1970s. There is now greater awareness of the difficulties in narrowing skill differences. Factors outside the control of schools have been shown to have strong if not overwhelming effects on the outcome of public spending on education. The disadvantaged groups that Government programs aim particularly to help are just those groups for whom education is least likely to be effective because of the adverse effects of family background and other non-school factors.]

The education of our people is the most basic resource of our society. Education equips man to think rationally and creatively in his quest for knowledge, for beauty, and for the full life; it provides the basis for effective political democracy; and it is the most important force behind economic growth, by advancing technology and raising the productivity of workers.

This country has led the way in making education available to all. It has the highest level of educational attainment and allocates almost 6 percent of its gross national product to direct expenditures on education. By 1975 this proportion increased to almost 8 percent of GNP.

In the last seven years, since the launching of the first sputnik [1957], there has been a great concern about both the quantity and the quality of American education. Major efforts were made to strengthen education for science and technology, including the National Defense Education Act of 1958. In 1963 and 1964, major Federal programs were enacted to aid higher education through grants and loans, to improve and expand facilities for the sharply rising numbers of students about to reach college age, to support teacher training and language study, and to strengthen vocational education.

Most recently, the drive for improvement has focused on meeting the educational needs of disadvantaged groups, to equip them to escape from poverty and to become full participants in our productive effort and standard of living. The President has proposed a new program to help education this year aimed primarily—though not exclusively—at this effort.

RETURNS TO EDUCATION

The impact of education on economic productivity, though long recognized, has recently come to be more widely appreciated. Expenditures on education produce a wide and important array of direct and indirect economic benefits to individuals and to society.

Evidence on the effects of education on productivity is mounting. Increases in the conventional inputs of labor and capital explain only about half the growth of output in the economy over the past half-century. The rising level of education appears to account for between one-quarter and one-half of the otherwise unexplained growth of output. Despite the great expansion of the better-educated population, the pattern of income differentials associated with education has remained substantially unchanged over the past quarter-century. In 1963 the median income of male high school graduates 25 years of age and over was $6,000, compared with $5,153 for those with 1–3 years of high school and only $4,076 for elementary school graduates.

[By 1974 the median income of males 25 years of age and over was $16,162 for those with 5 or more years of college, $14,401 for college graduates (4 years), $11,290 for high school graduates, $9,017 for those with 1 to 3 years of high school and only $6,621 for elementary school graduates. (Some of the increase in income from 1963 to 1974 is due to inflation, since the Consumer Price Index increased by 61 percent.)] Moreover, the incidence of poverty is closely related to educational attainment—the chance that families headed by elementary school graduates will be poor is over twice as great as for families headed by high school graduates.

Other effects defy both easy cataloging and quantification. They include the impact of education on research and the development of new products and processes, and the economic efficiencies that result from general literacy and substantial educational attainment.

The direct and indirect benefits to society exceed those to individuals or specific communities. The operation of the market frequently makes it impossible for the individual to capture all of the gains produced by his work; the successful inventor, scientist, or artist creates benefits to society not measured by their financial reward. And communities which lose some of their better educated young people—as many rural communities are doing—are unable to reap the benefits of increased productivity which their investment in the education of those leaving makes possible. The presence of these public benefits warrants a social investment in education above and beyond what the single individual or his family or his area might be prepared to spend, and argues that the Federal Government should assist the efforts of States and localities.[1]

Even when viewed in the narrow perspective of economic benefit alone, expenditures on education yield high rates of return. The rate of return to society on its total expenditure for the public and private education of males is estimated at more than 10 percent at both the high school and college levels; this rate compares favorably with the return on other investment opportunities in the economy.

AVAILABILITY OF EDUCATION

The quality and availability of education vary greatly. For example, in 1961–62 current expenditures per child in average daily school attendance were $438 in the Great Lakes and Plains States, compared with $295 in the Southeast. Differences in teachers' salaries alone cannot account for such variations. Differences in fiscal resources are resulting in differences in quality of education. New York State historically has the highest expenditure per pupil in average daily attendance, and Mississippi the lowest. From 1964 to 1975 expenditures increased from $790 to $2,005 in New York and from $273 to $854 in Mississippi.

In 1964, about 40 percent of the total population over age 25 in the South had completed high school; in the Nation as a whole, almost half of the total population had a high school education. Nonwhite males over age 25 averaged 8.7 years of schooling, compared with 11.9 years for white males. Although these differences are narrowing among the young, they are still large. Even in the age group 25–29, only 6 percent of nonwhite males have completed 4 or more years of college; the

1. The magnitude of these external benefits has never been documented. However, there seems to be more skepticism today about their importance. [Editors]

equivalent figure for white males is 18 percent. Moreover, the education available to Negroes has been inferior in many cases.

[Since the early 1960's the educational level of the population has increased and geographic and racial differences in schooling have narrowed. By 1974, 61 percent of all persons 25 years old and over had completed at least high school; in the South, 55 percent had done so. (As noted above, these percentages were 50 percent and 40 percent respectively in 1964.) The data for 1974 on the median years of school completed for men age 25 and over, are 10.5 years for blacks and 12.4 years for whites. In 1960 the medians were 7.7 years and 10.7 years, respectively. The change is more striking for the young. Among persons 25 to 29 years of age, the median years of school completed were 12.4 for blacks and 12.8 for the total population, while in 1960 the medians were 9.9 and 12.3 years, respectively.]

Increasing the resources devoted to education will help to eliminate the disparities in the amount and quality of education offered in different sections of the Nation and to different segments of the population. In addition to making education available, it is necessary to insure that low family incomes do not bar individuals from taking full advantage of these expanded opportunities. Many individuals fail to develop their talents fully, often for economic reasons. In 1960, one-third of the top 25 percent of youths did not go on to college; 5 percent did not even finish high school. This is a serious waste of talent.

The quality of our education must be continuously improved. Many school systems are already adopting strengthened curricula, and demonstration and experimental programs are being evaluated. But increased support is needed for innovation, adaptation, and the speedy dissemination of new research.

THE PRESIDENT'S PROGRAM FOR EDUCATION

In his Education Message, the President [Lyndon Johnson] has recommended a program that will broaden the scope of the educational system, will make educational opportunities more equal, and will raise the quality of education at all levels.

The major proposal for equalizing and expanding educational opportunity is a $1 billion program to aid elementary and secondary schools to improve the education of the poor. This program will supplement by 50 percent the resources devoted to educating the children from families with incomes below $2,000. It will contribute greatly to the resources of poor school districts as much as 30 percent beyond present expenditures in the very poorest areas and 3 to 10 percent of total operating costs in the larger cities. A program of preschool training under the Community Action Program of the Office of Economic Opportunity will enable children from low-income families to take better advantage of elementary and secondary education.

To increase the quality of education, the President has recommended the establishment of a new program of grants for supplementary educational centers to be set up by a consortium of schools and other agencies in a community. They will provide special services—advanced science courses and laboratories, remedial reading, television instruction, summer courses, after school help, music and language training, and other types of aid—for all of the participating schools, public and private. In addition, proposals, have been made for strengthening educational research and innovation, library resources, and State departments of education.

A new program will seek to identify, early in their high school career, students of the greatest promise and the greatest need. It will provide scholarships to encourage them to decide in favor of higher education in order to develop their talents. Low-interest loans and an expanded Work Study Program will help college students continue their studies.

The President has proposed a program for strengthening smaller and less developed colleges through exchange arrangements with large universities. College libraries will be enriched by a grant program for the purchase of books, and universities through their extension services will be encouraged to tackle problems of the city.

[In the last decade the Government has been an important source of funds for manpower training and development. Prior to the Comprehensive Employment and Training Act of 1973 (CETA) the Federal Government controlled the allocation of funds among the various manpower training programs. Under CETA, which is a form of manpower revenue sharing, the State and local government prime sponsors decide the allocation of funds among programs.[2] In fiscal year 1975, the first full year of the CETA program, over 1 million persons received training under Title I at a cost of $1.6 billion. There are, however, other Federal training programs. The military, directly and through the voucher approach in the GI Bill, provides vocational (technical) and college training, primarily for young men. The Basic Opportunity Grants program provides financial assistance to high school graduates from low-income families for vocational training and college schooling. The AFDC Work Incentive Program (WIN) provides training, job

2. Some manpower training programs are still under Federal control, for example, Job Corps (CETA Title IV) and the special programs for Indians, migrant and seasonal farm workers, and youths (CETA Title III). CETA Titles II and VI (enacted in December 1974) provide Federal funding of State and local government public service employment programs. For an evaluation of PSE programs see Chapter 8.

placement services and employment subsidies for mothers in the AFDC program.

Although numerous evaluations have been made of the different programs, they have generally not been sufficiently refined to produce useful results. Typically the evaluations have compared earnings "before" and "after" for program participants. Since programs often last six months or more, and since earnings typically rise with inflation and for the young with age, earnings "after" would tend to be above earnings "before" even if the program had no effect. In addition, there is a tendency for those who are unemployed or who otherwise have temporarily low earnings to join these training programs. Then their earnings would tend to be higher "after" than "before", if only because their before training earnings were temporarily low. When the groups receiving the training are compared with those with similar characteristics who did not receive training, the effects of the programs are ambiguous. Moreover, for the training to be a good investment, the earnings gain must not only exist but be sufficiently high to produce a return commensurate with the costs, which include the direct Government expenditure plus the earnings foregone while the individual was in training. It is unlikely that trainees would have remained unemployed for the entire duration of training.

Far more careful research is needed before we can identify the kinds of training programs and the types of candidates for whom these programs are most effective in increasing earnings and the stability of employment. In addition, at this time it is not known to what extent Federal manpower training programs simply provide Federal subsidies to persons for training that they would undertake in any case. For these reasons, we do not know whether the current Federal programs are the most effective use of the available funds.]

CHAPTER 12

Health and Medical Care

The provision of medical care services in the United States is largely private, but Government plays a major and increasing role in the financing of medical expenditures. Between fiscal 1950 and fiscal 1975 total health expenditures rose from 4.5 percent to 8.3 percent of GNP (Table 12–1). During the same period the Federal share of the total health bill rose from 12 percent to 29 percent, an expenditure in fiscal 1975 of $34 billion. Federal funding of the hospital component of health expenditures has increased even more dramatically, paying 39 percent of the Nation's hospital bill in fiscal 1975. As a result of the ex-

TABLE 12–1.—*Total health expenditures and personal health expenditures by source of funds, selected fiscal years, 1940–75*

[Fiscal years; percent, except as noted]

Type of expenditure and source of funds	1940	1950	1960	1965	1970	1975
Total health expenditures:						
Amount (billions of dollars)	3.9	12.0	25.9	38.9	69.2	118.5
Percent of GNP	4.1	4.5	5.2	5.9	7.2	8.3
Percent funded by public	20.2	25.5	24.7	24.5	36.5	42.2
Personal health expenditures:						
Amount (billions of dollars)	3.4	10.4	22.7	33.5	60.1	103.2
Percent distribution by source of funds:						
Total	100.0	100.0	100.0	100.0	100.0	100.0
Direct payments	82.0	68.3	55.3	52.5	40.4	32.6
Third party payments	18.0	31.7	44.6	47.5	59.7	67.4
Private insurance		8.5	20.7	24.7	24.0	26.5
Other private	2.7	3.0	2.3	2.0	1.5	1.2
Federal	3.9	9.4	9.2	8.5	22.3	27.7
State and local	11.4	10.8	12.4	12.3	11.9	12.0
Hospital expenditures:						
Amount (billions of dollars)		3.7	8.5	13.2	25.9	46.6
Percent distribution by source of funds:						
Total funds		100.0	100.0	100.0	100.0	100.0
Direct payments		34.2	18.6	18.5	12.3	8.0
Third party payments		65.8	81.4	81.5	87.7	92.0
Private		20.1	39.4	44.0	36.9	37.0
Public		45.7	42.0	37.5	50.8	55.0

Note.—Detail may not add to totals because of rounding.

Source: Department of Health, Education, and Welfare (Social Security Administration).

pansion of Federal and State funds and of private insurance, consumers directly paid only 8 percent of all hospital expenditures. Consumers paid nearly all of the remainder indirectly through taxes and insurance premiums.

The two major Federal programs are medicare and medicaid, which were enacted as part of the Social Security Amendments of 1965. Medicare is a Federal program with uniform benefits available to the aged, to certain disabled persons covered by social security, and to those with end-stage renal (kidney) disease. Medicare includes hospital insurance financed through social security taxes, with benefits subject to a $104 deductible as well as various copayments after the 60th day of hospitalization. A physician reimbursement program is included which requires a monthly premium of $6.70, with benefits subject to a $60 deductible and 20 percent coinsurance. Federal expenditures on medicare doubled from 1970 to 1975. In fiscal 1976 they are expected to reach $17.4 billion. Fiscal 1976 Federal expenditures per enrollee are estimated at $717, but expenditures per beneficiary receiving hospital insurance benefits are estimated at $2,082 and for those receiving supplementary medical insurance benefits, $355.

Medicaid is funded by the States with Federal contributions accounting for from 50 to 78 percent of costs. The law provides categorical coverage of participants in the AFDC program; in 1974, 90 percent of AFDC recipients obtained medicaid benefits. Also covered are most of the aged, blind, and disabled in the supplemental security income program. Many States have also extended coverage to the medically indigent. Medicaid benefits and the population covered vary considerably across the States. In 1974, two States, California and New York, received 30 percent of all medicaid benefits, although they had only about 17 percent of the poverty population. Federal expenditures on medicaid have also increased rapidly and are estimated to be $8.2 billion in fiscal 1976, averaging $606 per participant. In addition to medicare and medicaid the Federal Government provides health care for veterans and military personnel (costing $6.5 billion in fiscal 1976), as well as for Indians and other groups ($2 billion in fiscal 1976), and it subsidizes medical research and physician education ($3 billion in fiscal 1976).

The influence of Government on medical care extends beyond its spending programs, however. For example, by exempting from taxable income an employer's contributions for health insurance, the Government indirectly encourages the purchase of more insurance. Federal and State governments impose regulatory controls on hospitals, and States regulate the training and licensing of physicians and other health professionals. Thus Government has considerable direct and indirect influence on the quantity, quality, distribution, and price of medical care in the United States.

This review of medical care and the role of Federal programs centers on: (1) The relation between changes in health status and changes in medical expenditures; (2) the personal financial impact of medical expenses; and (3) the relation between health insurance and resource allocation.

HEALTH STATUS AND MEDICAL EXPENDITURES

The medical care system is clearly important in maintaining the Nation's health. But the relation between various measures of health status and expenditures on medical care suggests that medical care is only one of a large number of factors affecting health.

Dramatic declines in mortality occurred during the first 50 years of this century mainly because of improved sanitation, heating, and other amenities, along with significant breakthroughs in medical technology. The development of vaccines, penicillin, and other drugs led to the control of many infectious diseases. Despite a relatively low level of medical expenditures and little public financing, access to medical care was apparently sufficient to ensure a general dissemination of these medical gains.

Since 1960 there have been substantial increases in expenditures on medical care. Infant mortality rates have declined—from 24.7 deaths in the first year of life per 1,000 live births in 1965 to 16.5 in 1974—partly because of the decline in high-risk births (e.g., births that are a mother's fifth or more). However, life expectancy at age one has barely changed for males since 1960, though for females there has been some increase.

Studies of the relation between income and mortality among the States indicate that higher income actually tends to be positively associated with higher mortality, even though expenditures on medical care increase with income. Many of the factors increasing mortality, such as pollution and sedentary white-collar work, are also associated with high income. Research studies show that, after controlling for these factors as well as education and income, increases in health expenditures are associated with declines in morality, but the effect is very slight. Moreover, at the same level of income and health expenditure, increases in educational attainment are strongly associated with lower mortality.

Comparisons across developed countries also indicate that there is no simple relation between health and income or health expenditures. Among the OECD countries, life expectancy for males at age 10 tends to fall somewhat as income measured by gross domestic product (GDP) increases, even though health expenditures seem to be strongly related to GDP. A fairly strong negative relation is found, however, between infant mortality and income. These patterns are illustrated by the con-

trast between Greece and the United States. Although per capita GDP is
about 4 times higher in the United States and per capita health expenditures are 10 times as high, life expectancy at birth is 72 years
for Greek males and 67 years for American males. For females, the difference is smaller: 76 years for Greeks and 75 years for Americans. And
infant mortality rates are higher in Greece: 25.3 in 1973 compared to
17.6 in the United States.

There are wide differences among the developed countries with respect to public funding and provision of care, which some believe has
an important effect on health, particularly of the poor. The United
States tends to rely more on private insurance or personal expenditures than do most developed countries. But there is no indication that
access to physicians' and hospital services in the United States is actually more restricted than in countries with nationalized health insurance or health care. For example, one study of visits to physicans in
1964 compared the situation in the United States before medicare and
medicaid with that in Sweden, where a substantially greater proportion
of physicians' services are paid for by national health insurance. The
incidence of reported symptoms of sickness was higher in Sweden, but
the percentage who saw a doctor when they had a symptom was the
same in both countries (16 percent). The ratio of visits to the incidence of symptoms was, however, somewhat lower in the United
States for low-income persons (42 percent versus 46 percent for Sweden)
and higher for high-income persons in 1964 (51 percent versus 48 percent in Sweden). In 1971 a second survey showed an increase in the ratio
for all income levels in the United States (50 percent), with the lowest
income group close to the level of the highest income group (52 percent and 54 percent respectively). No data are available for Sweden in
1971. These general findings—that in the United States there are a
similar number of visits to physicians per reported symptom as in other
developed countries with greater subsidization of medical care—are confirmed by other studies comparing a broader range of countries, including those with nationalized health services.

The United States, however, has high mortality rates despite seem-
ingly low sickness rates and high utilization of medical resources. One
possible explanation is that the higher mortality in the United States is
not the result of chronic illness susceptible to medical treatment, but is
due to illness less readily affected by medical technology. The unusually
high rates of mortality in the United States from cardiovascular diseases give this hypothesis some support. These diseases, it should be
noted, are more likely to be influenced by life-style and environmental
factors.

When health and income are compared across families in the United
States, persons with low incomes are found to have poorer health, as

measured by such indexes as days spent in bed and infant mortality rates, than those with high income who live in the same area. In part, the relation occurs because sickness can cause low income. But as was the case with international and State comparisons, detailed studies cast doubt that income or access to medical resources plays a significant role in explaining these differences in health. In fact, in recent years the poor have spent more days in the hospital and visited doctors at least as often as those who were not poor. Moreover, as noted above, a similar incidence of visits to physicians per reported symptom was found for high- and for low-income levels in 1971. Even taking account of differences in sickness, overall access to treatment seems fairly equalized.

Education has been found to be strongly associated with health in the United States and seems to account for the positive relation between income and health among persons living in the same area. Even when health expenditures are held constant, the relation between education and health is important. Education could affect health because those with more education are more aware of the effects on health of smoking, diet, and exercise. Evidence suggests that people with more education are more skilled in using medical resources and are better able to detect warning signals of illness. Of course, to some extent the chain of causation may also run the other way: those with better health may also obtain more schooling.

These studies of the factors affecting health status suggest that large additional expenditures on medical care may be a very costly way of obtaining small improvements in measured health status for this country. Apart from medical care, there are other ways in which the Nation's health may be improved. New advances are likely to result from research on medical technology and drugs, as in the past. Rising levels of education should tend to improve the health of the population. More important may be further research on, and the spread of current knowledge about, the effect of life-style and environment on health status.

HEALTH INSURANCE, HEALTH EXPENDITURES, AND FAMILY INCOME

Given the current level of medical resources, it is important to distinguish between the effects on health of small changes in medical expenditures and the effects of the absence of any medical care at all. Because medical care is beneficial, and the incidence of serious illness is generally unpredictable, people prefer to have medical insurance so that large unpredictable expenditures can be more easily budgeted on a routine basis.

A large proportion of the U.S. population is covered by private health insurance. On the basis of a survey of households, it is estimated that about 78 percent of the population have private health insurance for hospital care and 76 percent have surgical benefits.

Virtually all persons 65 years old and over are covered by medicare. The percentage of this group with private insurance dropped from 54 percent in 1962 to 45 percent in 1967 after medicare was introduced. Since then, however, an increasing proportion have been purchasing private insurance which supplements medicare by paying for deductibles and coinsurance. The low-income elderly are eligible for medicaid, which supplemented medicare for close to one-fifth of the elderly in 1974.

According to household survey estimates, in 1974 about 38 million Americans under age 65 had no private insurance against hospital costs, and 41 million were without surgical insurance. An estimated 40 percent (15 million) of the uninsured under 65 years of age were from families with an annual income below $6,400.

However, an unknown proportion of the uninsured have other sources of coverage or access to free or low-cost care provided by public sources. No unduplicated count of those receiving benefits under all programs is available. In 1974, 23 million persons received medicaid benefits at some time during the year, of whom about 19 million were under age 65, including 14 million AFDC recipients. In fiscal 1975, Veteran's hospitals provided free hospitalization to 1.1 million persons and 14.8 million doctors' visits on an outpatient basis. The military provided care for the 2 million men and women in the Armed Forces; 7 million ex-military personnel and their dependents, and the dependents of current military personnel were eligible for care under the civilian health and medical care program for the uniformed services (CHAMPUS). Care was also provided to Indians and others through the Public Health Service. State and local government spending for health, excluding medicaid, exceeded $8.5 billion in 1975.

Another way to evaluate the extent of coverage for high-cost medical expenses among the poor is to examine the data on expenditures incurred and sources of payment. In 1970, persons in lower-income families (defined here as an annual income of $5,700 or less for a family of four) incurred expenditures of $229 per year on medical care, compared to expenditures of $254 by those who were not poor (Table 12–2). Sources of funding differed, however: medicare, medicaid, and other government programs paid for 46 percent of the expenditures of lower-income families, compared to 12 percent for other families, who, as expected, relied more on private health insurance. Out-of-pocket medical care payments averaged $77 for those with lower income and $127 for those with higher income.

Hospital expenditures are likely to be less discretionary than other

TABLE 12–2.—*Expenditures per person for different health services by family income status and source of payments, 1970*

Type of expenditure and family income status [1]	Health expenditures (dollars)		Payment as percent of total health expenditures					
	Total	Out of pocket	Total	Medicaid and other free care	Medicare	Voluntary insurance	Out of pocket	Other sources[2]
Total expenditures per person__	248	116	100	11	8	29	47	4
Below near poverty_____	229	77	100	28	18	16	34	5
Above near poverty_____	254	127	100	6	6	33	50	5
Inpatient hospital expenditures_____	104	16	100	17	15	46	15	6
Below near poverty_____	113	14	100	30	28	23	12	6
Above near poverty_____	101	16	100	13	11	53	16	7
Physician expenditures_____	65	33	100	8	6	31	51	5
Below near poverty_____	57	22	100	28	14	16	39	4
Above near poverty_____	67	36	100	1	4	34	54	6
Other health expenditures[3]__	79	67	100	6	1	6	85	1
Below near poverty_____	59	41	100	22	2	3	69	3
Above near poverty_____	86	75	100	2	1	8	87	1

[1] Near poverty is a measure above the poverty threshold used by the Bureau of the Census. It was $5,700 for a family of four in 1970.

[2] Includes free and non-free care provided by Veterans Administration hospitals, workers' compensation, and military and civilian health and medical care programs for the uniformed services and their families.

[3] Includes expenditures on prescription and nonprescription drugs, dental care, appliances such as eyeglasses, care by nonphysician medical practitioners (nurses, psychologists, Christian Science practitioners), ambulance service, other outpatient services, and supplies.

Note.—Detail may not add to totals because of rounding.

Source: Department of Health, Education, and Welfare (Bureau of Health Services Research and Evaluation).

medical expenses, and the poor incurred somewhat higher hospital expenditures than those with higher incomes. However, both groups were liable for only a small fraction of hospital bills. Mean out-of-pocket hospital expenses for those requiring a hospital stay were only $14 for the poor and $16 for others.

Although lower-income groups seemed to have obtained the same amount of health resources as others in 1970, mostly subsidized by public sources, outlays on health consumed a larger proportion of their income. Outlays including both out-of-pocket expenditures and payments for health insurance premiums were estimated to be 9 percent of income on average for lower-income families and 4 percent for higher-income families.

It appears that a small proportion of the population experiences catastrophic medical expenditures relative to their income in any year. In 1970, 1 percent of all families were estimated to incur medical and psychiatric expenditures of $5,000 or more. Eighty percent of the expenditures over $5,000 were paid for by private insurance, medicare, medicaid, and sources other than the family. About 8 percent of all families had outlays (out-of-pocket expenses plus insurance premiums) of $1,000 or more, of which 40 percent represented routine payments for insurance premiums. For lower-income families, 2 percent had outlays of $1,000 or more during the year; and at higher income levels, 10 percent had such outlays. These medical outlays which include out-of-pocket expenses and insurance premiums exceeded 15 percent of income for 10 percent of all families, and the proportion was 25 percent for lower-income families and 4.5 percent for higher-income families. These estimates overstate the relation between outlays and income, however, because lower-income families with large health outlays are more likely to have a current income that is temporarily depressed below the usual level because of the sickness of an earner.

The data reviewed on expenditures and outlays refer to 1970. Since then, medicaid has expanded: from serving 15.5 million persons, it served 23 million persons in 1974, and third-party payments (both public and private) have accounted for a larger share of all expenditures.

Most Americans do have some coverage for health expenditures through public or private insurance or publicly provided care. However, it is believed that a substantial proportion do not have coverage for very large medical expenses relative to their income and assets, although it is also believed that such coverage is spreading rapidly. The Administration has proposed providing catastrophic health insurance coverage for medicare participants. This proposal is discussed below.

RESOURCE ALLOCATION AND COSTS

One of the major concerns about medical care is the sharp rise in costs. Since 1950 the medical component of the CPI has increased much faster than the overall CPI (Table 12–3).

Prices of hospital services have increased at a much faster rate than physicians' fees or other medical services. In part this is the result of an increase in the quality of hospital services not fully reflected in the CPI. As indicated in Table 12–3, when total hospital expenditures per patient day are deflated by a crude price index for hospital inputs, it appears that increases in real resources explain a substantial amount of the rate of increase in expenditures per patient day. During the 5-year period since medicare and medicaid were introduced, 1965 to 1970, the rate of increase of real resources per patient day nearly doubled and accounted for about one-half of the nominal increase in hospital expenses per patient day.

Resistance by taxpayers to the increasing burden of medicare and medicaid, and pressures to restrain medical costs have led in the past to pressures for a more formal mechanism to control costs. During the period of the Economic Stabilization Program, starting in August 1971 and ending April 1974, the health industry was placed under more stringent price controls than most industries. In addition to price ceil-

TABLE 12–3.—*Changes in prices of various medical and hospital services and expenses, 1950–75*

[Percent change; annual rate]

Period	Consumer prices					Hospital expenses and services per patient day [1]		
	All items	All services less medical care services	Medical care services			Expenses [3]	Real expenses [4]	
			All [2]	Semiprivate room	Physicians' fees		Assumption A [5]	Assumption B [6]
Annual average:								
1950 to 1955	2.2	[7] 3.8	4.2	6.9	3.4	8.2	3.3	4.3
1955 to 1960	2.0	[7] 3.3	4.4	6.3	3.3	6.9	3.3	3.5
1960 to 1965	1.3	1.8	3.1	5.8	2.8	6.7	3.3	4.2
1965 to 1970	4.2	5.4	7.3	13.9	6.6	12.7	6.0	7.4
1970 to 1975	6.7	6.3	7.6	10.2	6.9	12.5	4.8	5.1
Change from preceding year:								
1971	4.3	5.3	7.3	12.2	6.9	13.2	4.5	6.6
1972	3.3	3.8	3.7	6.6	3.1	13.4	6.5	7.8
1973	6.2	4.3	4.4	4.7	3.3	7.6	2.8	1.6
1974	11.0	9.2	10.3	10.7	9.2	11.2	3.7	2.5
1975	9.1	9.1	12.6	17.2	12.3	17.6	6.5	7.3

[1] Beginning 1965, patient days have been adjusted for outpatient visits.
[2] Includes some medical care services not shown separately.
[3] Based on data reported by the American Hospital Association for community hospitals for year ending September 30.
[4] Labor and nonlabor inputs adjusted for price changes.
[5] Deflated by a weighted average of the consumer price index and an index of hospital wages.
[6] Deflated by a weighted average of the consumer price index and adjusted hourly earnings index in the private nonfarm economy.
[7] Change for all services.

Sources: Department of Labor (Bureau of Labor Statistics), American Hospital Association, and Council of Economic Advisers.

ings on individual services, controls were also placed on the increase in total annual hospital expenditures. These controls in effect curtailed the amount as well as the price of the service provided. From 1972 to 1973 increases in hospital resource use per patient day did slow. However, it is not clear whether the slower growth rate represented a gain in efficiency through a more careful use of resources, a curtailment of quality improvements that would have been desirable, or less efficiency through a greater rate of admission of less serious cases. Since the end of controls, real hospital resources have increased at a very rapid rate, partly to "catch up" and perhaps partly in anticipation of a permanent controls program. Hospital expenses per patient day increased at the very high rate of 18 percent from 1974 to 1975.

Some of this expansion in medical resources is probably a desired quality improvement. There is considerable evidence, however, that much is a consequence of the growth of private insurance and public funding, which has led to a system where "third parties" pay for an increasing share of medical services, particularly hospital services. The most common form of health insurance has low or no deductibles and low cost-sharing (coinsurance), especially for hospital care. This type of coverage has been shown to have a substantial effect on the price and quantity of services. For example, families with insurance have a greater number and longer length of stays in hospitals and more visits to physicians. The patients may themselves prefer this extra health care because the extra cost to them is small. In addition, hospitals and doctors, knowing that most of the costs will be paid by third parties who are not in a position to decide on what services should be provided, are also likely to expand the quality, quantity, and price of their services. As a result, patients receive services that they would not value enough to pay for if they were given additional income equal to the cost of the service. In this way too many resources, and probably not the optimal kind, are allocated to medical services. The system encourages the development and use of high-cost techniques and a reliance on institutional rather than home care.

Unlike most other forms of insurance, private health insurance is largely purchased through the employer in a group policy. This practice has been substantially encouraged by the income tax and payroll tax systems, which exempt from taxation the employer's contribution for this form of insurance even though it is really an addition to the worker's income. Up to a point, it is to the mutual benefit of employer and employee to favor wage increases in the form of untaxed fringe benefits rather than in cash. As workers have moved into increasingly higher marginal tax brackets, this incentive has increased. In 1953 employers paid all of the costs for health insurance premiums for 10 percent of employees and none of the costs for 41 percent. By 1970 employers paid all of the costs for 39 percent and none of the costs for only 8 percent. The Government further reduces the cost of insurance by allowing a deduction under the personal income tax of half the cost of premiums paid by the taxpayer up to $150. All medical expenditures, including the other half of the premium cost, that exceed 3 percent of income may also be deducted. Estimated tax losses in fiscal 1977 are $4.2 billion for exclusion of employers' contributions and $2.1 billion for itemized medical deductions, including insurance premiums.

As a result of these tax subsidies, the cost to the consumer of paying for medical care indirectly through insurance is sharply reduced. Indeed, it has been estimated that in 1975 the Federal Government paid 20 to 22 percent of the premium costs of insurance through forgone tax receipts. Even taking into account the insurance companies' administrative costs and the costs of induced additional medical care, a result of the tax subsidy is that families with group coverage, paid for at least in part by the employer, spend less on medical care by buying insurance than they would have done by paying directly. In an unsubsidized market, consumers would have the incentive to pay out of pocket for routine budgetable medical care and to confine their insurance to very large and unpredictable expenditures. Faced with insurance at a substantial discount, they are induced to buy more comprehensive insurance, covering expenditures from the first dollar.

The problems of insurance are exacerbated in the case of medicare and medicaid because the mechanism of higher premiums, which may provide weak incentives to economize in our subsidized private insurance market, hardly works at all in the public system. Although there are medicare deductibles, there is no copayment for the first 60 days of hospital care. Under medicaid there are generally no deductibles and no coinsurance for hospital and physicians' services.

Perhaps the main feature that fosters cost increases is the method by which medicare, medicaid, and most Blue Cross policies reimburse the hospitals. These insurers pay a share of the hospital's costs, based on the percentage of all costs accounted for by their respective beneficiaries. Because hospitals have the assurance that a large percentage of their revenues will be based on cost reimbursement, there is little direct restraint to keep costs down. The Federal Government is now experimenting with prospective reimbursement schemes, whereby hospitals are told in advance how much they will be reimbursed per unit of service provided (e.g., patient admissions, patient days).

NATIONAL HEALTH INSURANCE

[Unlike several other developed economies, the United States does not have a Government-operated national health insurance or national health service covering the entire population. As indicated above, medicare provides comprehensive health insurance for the aged and medicaid and other programs provide health services to the poor. The bulk of the population, however, depends largely on private hospital and/or surgical insurance to finance large medical expenditures.

In recent years different aspects of the provision of health care have been criticized. Some feel that they do not have sufficient protection against the sometimes devastating financial effects of the rare catastrophic illnesses. Others have expressed a preference for a single health financing system to serve all, rather than separate programs for the poor, the aged, and others, and would like a more uniform distribution of health services throughout the country and between income groups. At the same time the rapid rate of increase in the use and the price of health services, particularly of in-hospital care, has been a source of substantial concern. These issues have led to wide-ranging proposals for the reform of the nation's system of financing health services.

Over the past few years several variants of national health insurance plans have been proposed. The Kennedy-Griffiths Bill (H.R. 22/S. 3) introduced in Congress in 1973 is representative of one approach which would radically alter the nature of medical care in the United States. Benefits under this bill would cover almost all medical and dental procedures, including checkups. Only certain psychiatric and nursing services would be subject to limitations on use. There would be no deductibles, co-payments or any other charge to the patient, regardless of income. All Americans would eventually be eligible for benefits and the system, which would replace medicare and medicaid, would be funded by a mandatory payroll tax.

The question that immediately comes to mind, however, is how resources would be allocated in a system where medical services are "free." It is reasonable to assume that demand for medical services would increase and, as discussed above, a number of studies support this assumption. The excess demand could be alleviated only if some other non-price rationing mechanism were adopted or if the public were willing to pay the increased taxes needed to finance a large increase in the share of national resources devoted to the health sector.

The Kennedy-Griffiths Bill addresses the issue of costs by setting fee limits on medical providers and by establishing overall expenditure limits. Doctors and other medical providers would be obliged to accept the fees set by the Government as full reimbursement if they in any way participated in the program. Patients could not supplement the set fees as they now are permitted to do for physician services under medicare (but not under medicaid). Doctors who chose to charge fees above the ceiling could receive no reimbursement from the Government plan and patients who used those doctors would pay them directly (i.e., out-of-pocket) or through private health insurance. Although it would be optional to use the benefits, it would be mandatory to pay the required taxes.[1] Costs would further be controlled through a system whereby the Federally appointed board determined an allocation of the medical trust funds among the regions. These regional ceilings would presumably determine the ceilings for doctor and hospital charges.

None of these efforts at cost control would, however, have any effect on the problem of excess demand, since the financial incentives for medical use induced by the program would remain. If taxes were not raised to pay for an expanding supply of resources, "queuing" time for doctor and hospital services would rise. This could take the form of increases in waiting time in doctors' offices, as well as delays

1. The situation would therefore resemble that of the public schools where parents who may choose not to send their children do not receive any public credit towards a private alternative. In the case of public schools, the argument is made that it is desirable to encourage the mingling of students from different socio-economic backgrounds. Whatever its merits for schooling, an analogous argument would not appear to have relevance for health care.

in scheduling appointments for physician and hospital services.[2] Waiting time is not free. The real costs of delayed or denied medical care may involve lost work time (and earnings), lost leisure and greater physical and psychic distress. For some individuals, health may be worsened and the probability of death increased.

Time costs do not have the same value for all individuals. In particular, those with high earnings would generally have higher time costs than others, thus giving them an incentive to use private providers. This incentive could be even greater if the providers outside the system (who would not accept the fee ceilings) were of higher quality. Rationing by time costs is therefore likely to result in changes in the distribution of medical resources. Those individuals with low earnings and low income who do not at present have access to medicaid, veterans' health programs or other subsidized medical care would be likely to be better off under a Kennedy-Griffith type system. Individuals with high time costs would be worse off, either because they would be deterred from receiving care or because, in addition to their taxes to finance medical care, they would pay more either in time costs or in the expense of going outside the system.

Would the overall level of medical care be higher in this country under a Kennedy-Griffiths type system? Pressures to keep taxes down could result in lower expenditures and in the long run, lower quality medical care than we now have, even for the poor. In England, which has had a nationalized health system for many years, medical expenditures are severely restricted; even the proportion of national income spent on health is considerably lower than in the United States.[3] In addition, critics of a nationalized system point out that resources may be inefficiently allocated under a system with chronic excess demand and where the ability to wait (or to go outside the system) would determine the use of services.

Other types of health plans have been suggested. Some would retain the governmentally administered nature of Kennedy-Griffiths but would impose deductibles and would require cost sharing of payments by patients, usually up to some ceiling on out of pocket expenditures. Some would relate the deductible and cost sharing to family income.

2. A study of waiting time in the year before and the year after the introduction of a universal health insurance plan in Montreal showed an increase from 6 to 11 days on average to see a doctor and an increase from 36 to 40 minutes waiting time in the doctor's office.

3. It is very difficult to make international comparisons of the quality of medical care. The suggestion that medical expenditures per capita are lower in England is, however, compatible with other data comparing real medical resources. For example, in the 1970–71 period, the U.S. had 1.7 physicians per 1,000 persons compared to 1.3 in the United Kingdom; and there were 138 hospital beds per 1,000 in the U.S. and 110 per 1,000 in the United Kingdom.

Others, unlike Kennedy-Griffiths, would allow the patient to supplement the payment to the provider if the charge exceeds the reimbursed amount. Still another version of national health insurance does not use the Federal Government to provide insurance for wage earners (though non-wage earners would be in a Federal system) but makes it mandatory for employers to provide a health insurance policy for their employees. Since the minimum specifications of the policy (coverage, deductibles, co-payments) would be determined by the Government, the mandatory purchase requirement is, in effect, a payroll tax. However, private insurance companies would administer the employee benefits, although with little scope for variation in insurance provisions.

Those proposals which require deductibles and co-payments would not contain as strong an incentive for excessive utilization and medical cost increases as the Kennedy-Griffith Bill. However, most of these proposals (as well as Kennedy-Griffith) extended coverage to levels of health service expenditures that are predictable and easily budgeted by the average American. Moreover, once everyone is required to pay the tax or buy the plan there would undoubtedly be pressure to reduce the deductibles and cost sharing amounts. Most proposals therefore include provisions for a decision-making process to restrict the use of resources. Elective care, for example, would be rationed on a queuing basis or by boards determining which cases should have the highest priorities.

There is, therefore, a national health insurance dilemma. No mechanism appears to exist for efficiently allocating health resources at zero or very low cost for the entire population without having either an increasingly large share of the real GNP devoted to the tax financed health sector, or substantial direct governmental intervention and arbitrary limits on the use of health resources.

Because of the enormous problems raised by national health insurance many have questioned its rationale. Critics point out that the bulk of the population already purchases health insurance. For this majority with the ability to pay, it would seem desirable to permit a choice of the kind of medical payment system they want rather than to compel them to purchase a particular insurance package. Because the incidence is rare, the cost of catastrophic health insurance is relatively low compared to the incomes of most families, and this form of insurance is growing in importance. A mechanism to subsidize the health care of those poor who are now excluded from medicaid need not involve the entire population.

As noted above, there are problems with our present private insurance system. The private insurance for physician, surgical and hospital services that most of the population buys is largely purchased through employer formed groups. Under current Treasury Department regulations employer contributions to health insurance plans for their workers are exempt from payroll and income taxation.[4] This encourages the formation of health insurance groups at the place of employment. As a result, some workers lose insurance coverage or face a large increase in premiums when they become unemployed or otherwise leave a job. By lowering the price of insurance the tax exemption also encourages the purchase of more coverage. Workers choose insurance packages covering the routine expenses that most families would incur; such insurance has high premiums.

As tax rates have increased over time so has the value of the untaxed fringe benefit. This has encouraged the purchase of more and more comprehensive health insurance through the employer. Moreover, it is this growth of insurance coverage which lowers the private cost of medical services to the patient and is apparently responsible for much of the increased utilization of services and price inflation in this sector.

It has been suggested that these problems would be less severe if employer contributions for health insurance were taxed as earnings (as they are now taxed for other forms of insurance), presumably in exchange for lower tax rates on earnings. When confronted with the full cost of the health insurance premium, workers would be likely to purchase insurance with higher deductibles and higher co-payments. The premiums for such insurance would be less costly than premiums for the zero deductible, low co-payment insurance that the tax shelter induces them to buy at the discount price. In addition, groups might be encouraged to form on bases other than place of employment. Thus, the problem of loss of employment leading to lapsed insurance coverage would be reduced and the ability of non-working individuals to buy low cost group insurance would be improved.]

4. It has been estimated that for fiscal year 1977 the Federal revenue loss from not taxing employer contributions will be $4.2 billion. There will be, in addition, a revenue loss of $2.1 billion from the itemized medical deductions allowed under the Federal income tax.

Statistical Appendix

TABLE A-1.—*Noninstitutional population and the labor force, 1929–75*

[Monthly data seasonally adjusted, except as noted]

Year or month	Noninstitutional population[1]	Total labor force (including Armed Forces)	Armed Forces[1]	Civilian labor force					Unemployment rate (percent of civilian labor force)	Labor force participation rate (total labor force as percent of noninstitutional population)
				Total	Employment			Unemployment		
					Total	Agricultural	Nonagricultural			
	Thousands of persons 14 years of age and over								Percent	
1929		49,440	260	49,180	47,630	10,450	37,180	1,550	3.2	
1933		51,840	250	51,590	38,760	10,090	28,670	12,830	24.9	
1939		55,600	370	55,230	45,750	9,610	36,140	9,480	17.2	
1940	100,380	56,180	540	55,640	47,520	9,540	37,980	8,120	14.6	56.0
1941	101,520	57,530	1,620	55,910	50,350	9,100	41,250	5,560	9.9	56.7
1942	102,610	60,380	3,970	56,410	53,750	9,250	44,500	2,660	4.7	58.8
1943	103,660	64,560	9,020	55,540	54,470	9,080	45,390	1,070	1.9	62.3
1944	104,630	66,040	11,410	54,630	53,960	8,950	45,010	670	1.2	63.1
1945	105,530	65,300	11,440	53,860	52,820	8,580	44,240	1,040	1.9	61.9
1946	106,520	60,970	3,450	57,520	55,250	8,320	46,930	2,270	3.9	57.2
1947	107,608	61,758	1,590	60,168	57,812	8,256	49,557	2,356	3.9	57.4
	Thousands of persons 16 years of age and over									
1947	103,418	60,941	1,591	59,350	57,039	7,891	49,148	2,311	3.9	58.9
1948	104,527	62,080	1,459	60,621	58,344	7,629	50,713	2,276	3.8	59.4
1949	105,611	62,903	1,617	61,286	57,649	7,656	49,990	3,637	5.9	59.6
1950	106,645	63,858	1,650	62,208	58,920	7,160	51,760	3,288	5.3	59.9
1951	107,721	65,117	3,100	62,017	59,962	6,726	53,239	2,055	3.3	60.4
1952	108,823	65,730	3,592	62,138	60,254	6,501	53,753	1,883	3.0	60.4
1953[2]	110,601	66,560	3,545	63,015	61,181	6,261	54,922	1,834	2.9	60.2
1954	111,671	66,993	3,350	63,643	60,110	6,206	53,903	3,532	5.5	60.0
1955	112,732	68,072	3,049	65,023	62,171	6,449	55,724	2,852	4.4	60.4
1956	113,811	69,409	2,857	66,552	63,802	6,283	57,517	2,750	4.1	61.0
1957	115,065	69,729	2,800	66,929	64,071	5,947	58,123	2,859	4.3	60.6
1958	116,363	70,275	2,636	67,639	63,036	5,586	57,450	4,602	6.8	60.4
1959	117,881	70,921	2,552	68,369	64,630	5,565	59,065	3,740	5.5	60.2
1960[2]	119,759	72,142	2,514	69,628	65,778	5,458	60,318	3,852	5.5	60.2
1961	121,343	73,031	2,572	70,459	65,746	5,200	60,546	4,714	6.7	60.2
1962[2]	122,981	73,442	2,828	70,614	66,702	4,944	61,759	3,911	5.5	59.7
1963	125,154	74,571	2,738	71,833	67,762	4,687	63,076	4,070	5.7	59.6
1964	127,224	75,830	2,739	73,091	69,305	4,523	64,782	3,786	5.2	59.6
1965	129,236	77,178	2,723	74,455	71,088	4,361	66,726	3,366	4.5	59.7
1966	131,180	78,893	3,123	75,770	72,895	3,979	68,915	2,875	3.8	60.1
1967	133,319	80,793	3,446	77,347	74,372	3,844	70,527	2,975	3.8	60.6
1968	135,562	82,272	3,535	78,737	75,920	3,817	72,103	2,817	3.6	60.7
1969	137,841	84,240	3,506	80,734	77,902	3,606	74,296	2,832	3.5	61.1
1970	140,182	85,903	3,188	82,715	78,627	3,462	75,165	4,088	4.9	61.3
1971	142,596	86,929	2,817	84,113	79,120	3,387	75,732	4,993	5.9	61.0
1972[2]	145,775	88,991	2,449	86,542	81,702	3,472	78,230	4,840	5.6	61.0
1973[2]	148,263	91,040	2,326	88,714	84,409	3,452	80,957	4,304	4.9	61.4
1974	150,827	93,240	2,229	91,011	85,936	3,492	82,443	5,076	5.6	61.8
1975	153,449	94,793	2,180	92,613	84,783	3,380	81,403	7,830	8.5	61.8

See footnotes at end of table.

Statistical Appendix

TABLE A-1.—*Noninstitutional population and the labor force, 1929-75*—Continued

[Monthly data seasonally adjusted, except as noted]

Year or month	Noninstitutional population [1]	Total labor force (including Armed Forces)	Armed Forces [1]	Civilian labor force					Unemployment rate (percent of civilian labor force)	Labor force participation rate (total labor force as percent of noninstitutional population)
				Total	Employment			Unemployment		
					Total	Agricultural	Nonagricultural			
	Thousands of persons 16 years cf age and over									
1974: Jan	149,656	92,659	2,258	90,401	85,865	3,737	82,128	4,536	5.0	61.9
Feb	149,857	92,837	2,258	90,579	85,948	3,735	82,213	4,631	5.1	62.0
Mar	150,066	92,800	2,251	90,549	86,033	3,661	82,372	4,516	5.0	61.8
Apr	150,283	92,715	2,243	90,472	85,990	3,576	82,414	4,482	5.0	61.7
May	150,507	92,982	2,229	90,753	86,154	3,502	82,652	4,599	5.1	61.8
June	150,710	93,206	2,212	90,994	86,167	3,372	82,795	4,827	5.3	61.8
July	150,922	93,519	2,220	91,299	86,292	3,425	82,867	5,007	5.5	62.0
Aug	151,135	93,377	2,220	91,157	86,170	3,447	82,723	4,987	5.5	61.8
Sept	151,367	93,791	2,217	91,574	86,155	3,460	82,695	5,419	5.9	62.0
Oct	151,593	93,810	2,214	91,596	86,012	3,428	82,584	5,584	6.1	61.9
Nov	151,812	93,939	2,213	91,726	85,549	3,385	82,164	6,177	6.7	61.9
Dec	152,020	93,854	2,212	91,642	85,053	3,338	81,715	6,589	7.2	61.7
1975: Jan	152,230	94,156	2,193	91,963	84,666	3,370	81,296	7,297	7.9	61.9
Feb	152,445	93,721	2,198	91,523	84,163	3,252	80,911	7,360	8.0	61.5
Mar	152,646	94,078	2,198	91,880	84,110	3,268	80,842	7,770	8.5	61.6
Apr	152,840	94,449	2,195	92,254	84,313	3,301	81,012	7,941	8.6	61.8
May	153,051	94,950	2,181	92,769	84,519	3,528	80,991	8,250	8.9	62.0
June	153,278	94,747	2,178	92,569	84,498	3,350	81,148	8,071	8.7	61.8
July	153,585	95,250	2,187	93,063	84,967	3,439	81,528	8,096	8.7	62.0
Aug	153,824	95,397	2,185	93,212	85,288	3,464	81,824	7,924	8.5	62.0
Sept	154,052	95,298	2,170	93,128	85,158	3,512	81,646	7,970	8.6	61.9
Oct	154,256	95,377	2,164	93,213	85,151	3,408	81,743	8,062	8.6	61.8
Nov	154,476	95,273	2,156	93,117	85,178	3,301	81,877	7,939	8.5	61.7
Dec	154,700	95,286	2,157	93,129	85,394	3,236	82,158	7,735	8.3	61.6

[1] Not seasonally adjusted.

[2] Not strictly comparable with earlier data due to population adjustments as follows: Beginning 1953, introduction of 1950 Census data added about 600,000 to population and about 350,000 to labor force, total employment, and agricultural employment. Beginning 1960, inclusion of Alaska and Hawaii added about 500,000 to population, about 300,000 to labor force, and about 240,000 to nonagricultural employment. Beginning 1962, introduction of 1960 Census data reduced population by about 50,000 and labor force and employment by about 200,000. Beginning 1972, introduction of 1970 Census data added about 800,000 to civilian noninstitutional population and about 333,000 to labor force and employment. A subsequent adjustment based on 1970 Census in March 1973 added 60,000 to labor force and to employment. Overall categories of the labor force other than those noted were not appreciably affected.

Note.—Labor force data in Tables B-22 through B-25 are based on household interviews and relate to the calendar week including the 12th of the month. For definitions of terms, area samples used, historical comparability of the data, comparability with other series, etc., see "Employment and Earnings."

Source: Department of Labor, Bureau of Labor Statistics.

TABLE A-2.—*Civilian employment and unemployment by sex and age, 1947-75*

[Thousands of persons 16 years of age and over; monthly data seasonally adjusted]

Year or month	Total	Employment Males Total	Employment Males 16-19 years	Employment Males 20 years and over	Employment Females Total	Employment Females 16-19 years	Employment Females 20 years and over	Total	Unemployment Males Total	Unemployment Males 16-19 years	Unemployment Males 20 years and over	Unemployment Females Total	Unemployment Females 16-19 years	Unemployment Females 20 years and over
1947___	57,039	40,994	2,218	38,776	16,045	1,691	14,354	2,311	1,692	270	1,422	619	144	475
1948___	58,344	41,726	2,345	39,382	16,618	1,683	14,937	2,276	1,559	255	1,305	717	152	564
1949___	57,649	40,926	2,124	38,803	16,723	1,588	15,137	3,637	2,572	352	2,219	1,065	223	841
1950___	58,920	41,580	2,186	39,394	17,340	1,517	15,824	3,288	2,239	318	1,922	1,049	195	854
1951___	59,962	41,780	2,156	39,626	18,182	1,611	16,570	2,055	1,221	191	1,029	834	145	689
1952___	60,254	41,684	2,106	39,578	18,570	1,612	16,958	1,883	1,185	205	980	698	140	559
1953 ¹__	61,181	42,431	2,135	40,296	18,750	1,584	17,164	1,834	1,202	184	1,019	632	123	510
1954___	60,110	41,620	1,985	39,634	18,490	1,490	17,000	3,532	2,344	310	2,035	1,188	191	997
1955___	62,171	42,621	2,095	40,526	19,550	1,548	18,002	2,852	1,854	274	1,580	998	176	823
1956___	63,802	43,380	2,164	41,216	20,422	1,654	18,767	2,750	1,711	269	1,442	1,039	209	832
1957___	64,071	43,357	2,117	41,239	20,714	1,663	19,052	2,859	1,841	299	1,541	1,018	197	821
1958___	63,036	42,423	2,012	40,411	20,613	1,570	19,043	4,602	3,098	416	2,681	1,504	262	1,242
1959___	64,630	43,466	2,198	41,267	21,164	1,640	19,524	3,740	2,420	398	2,022	1,320	256	1,063
1960 ¹__	65,778	43,904	2,360	41,543	21,874	1,769	20,105	3,852	2,486	425	2,060	1,366	286	1,080
1961___	65,746	43,656	2,314	41,342	22,090	1,793	20,296	4,714	2,997	479	2,518	1,717	349	1,368
1962 ¹__	66,702	44,177	2,362	41,815	22,525	1,833	20,693	3,911	2,423	407	2,016	1,488	313	1,175
1963___	67,762	44,657	2,406	42,251	23,105	1,849	21,257	4,070	2,472	500	1,971	1,598	383	1,216
1964___	69,305	45,474	2,587	42,886	23,831	1,929	21,903	3,786	2,205	487	1,718	1,581	386	1,195
1965___	71,088	46,340	2,918	43,422	24,748	2,118	22,630	3,366	1,914	479	1,435	1,452	395	1,056
1966___	72,895	46,919	3,252	43,668	25,976	2,469	23,510	2,875	1,551	432	1,120	1,324	404	921
1967___	74,372	47,479	3,186	44,293	26,893	2,497	24,397	2,975	1,508	448	1,060	1,468	391	1,078
1968___	75,920	48,114	3,255	44,859	27,807	2,525	25,281	2,817	1,419	427	993	1,397	412	985
1969___	77,902	48,818	3,430	45,388	29,084	2,686	26,397	2,832	1,403	441	963	1,429	412	1,016
1970___	78,627	48,960	3,407	45,553	29,667	2,734	26,933	4,088	2,235	599	1,636	1,853	506	1,347
1971___	79,120	49,245	3,470	45,775	29,875	2,725	27,149	4,993	2,776	691	2,086	2,217	567	1,650
1972 ¹__	81,702	50,630	3,750	46,880	31,072	2,972	28,100	4,840	2,635	707	1,928	2,205	595	1,610
1973 ¹__	84,409	51,963	4,017	47,946	32,446	3,219	29,228	4,304	2,240	647	1,594	2,064	579	1,485
1974 __	85,936	52,519	4,074	48,445	33,417	3,329	30,088	5,076	2,668	749	1,918	2,408	660	1,748
1975___	84,783	51,230	3,803	47,427	33,553	3,243	30,310	7,830	4,385	957	3,428	3,445	795	2,649
1974:														
Jan___	85,865	52,881	4,207	48,674	32,984	3,357	29,627	4,536	2,340	677	1,663	2,196	631	1,565
Feb__	85,948	52,755	4,164	48,591	33,193	3,376	29,817	4,631	2,441	694	1,747	2,190	614	1,576
Mar__	86,033	52,671	4,154	48,517	33,362	3,373	29,989	4,516	2,344	694	1,650	2,172	617	1,555
Apr__	85,990	52,573	4,116	48,457	33,417	3,343	30,074	4,482	2,385	681	1,704	2,097	546	1,551
May__	86,154	52,760	4,135	48,625	33,394	3,290	30,104	4,599	2,391	710	1,681	2,208	632	1,576
June_	86,167	52,606	4,075	48,531	33,561	3,344	30,217	4,827	2,522	767	1,755	2,305	673	1,632
July__	86,292	52,464	4,032	48,432	33,828	3,247	30,581	5,007	2,570	746	1,824	2,437	732	1,705
Aug__	86,170	52,492	4,021	48,471	33,678	3,314	30,364	4,987	2,655	705	1,950	2,332	593	1,739
Sept__	86,155	52,542	4,065	48,477	33,613	3,408	30,205	5,419	2,833	824	2,009	2,586	693	1,893
Oct__	86,012	52,481	4,056	48,425	33,531	3,368	30,163	5,584	3,044	803	2,241	2,540	731	1,810
Nov__	85,549	52,237	3,995	48,242	33,312	3,319	29,993	6,177	3,283	844	2,439	2,894	731	2,163
Dec__	85,053	51,815	3,948	47,867	33,238	3,246	29,992	6,589	3,558	852	2,706	3,031	733	2,298
1975:														
Jan___	84,666	51,387	3,849	47,538	33,279	3,295	29,984	7,297	3,901	942	2,959	3,396	823	2,573
Feb__	84,163	51,151	3,812	47,339	33,012	3,220	29,792	7,360	4,048	944	3,104	3,312	753	2,559
Mar__	84,110	50,952	3,794	47,158	33,158	3,199	29,959	7,770	4,261	952	3,309	3,509	809	2,700
Apr__	84,313	51,046	3,775	47,271	33,267	3,224	30,043	7,941	4,412	982	3,430	3,529	737	2,792
May__	84,519	51,195	3,859	47,336	33,324	3,247	30,077	8,250	4,637	970	3,667	3,613	842	2,771
June__	84,498	50,978	3,728	47,250	33,520	3,254	30,266	8,071	4,608	1,057	3,551	3,463	765	2,698
July__	84,967	51,280	3,799	47,481	33,687	3,234	30,453	8,096	4,657	1,015	3,642	3,439	795	2,644
Aug__	85,288	51,446	3,791	47,655	33,842	3,235	30,607	7,924	4,472	997	3,475	3,452	832	2,620
Sept__	85,158	51,334	3,818	47,516	33,824	3,273	30,551	7,970	4,604	912	3,692	3,366	796	2,570
Oct___	85,151	51,300	3,787	47,513	33,851	3,230	30,621	8,062	4,645	933	3,712	3,417	802	2,615
Nov__	85,178	51,325	3,804	47,521	33,853	3,234	30,619	7,939	4,538	883	3,655	3,401	764	2,637
Dec__	85,394	51,390	3,804	47,586	34,004	3,249	30,755	7,735	4,246	895	3,351	3,489	829	2,660

¹ See footnote 2, Table B-22.

Note.—See Note, Table B-22.

Source: Department of Labor, Bureau of Labor Statistics.

TABLE A-3.—*Selected unemployment rates, 1948–75*

[Percent [1]; monthly data seasonally adjusted]

Year or month	All workers	By sex and age			By color		By selected groups					Labor force time lost [5]
		Both sexes 16–19 years	Men 20 years and over	Women 20 years and over	White	Negro and other races	Experienced wage and salary workers	Household heads	Married men [2]	Full-time workers [3]	Blue-collar workers [4]	
1948	3.8	9.2	3.2	3.6	3.5	5.9	4.3	-------	-------	-------	4.2	-------
1949	5.9	13.4	5.4	5.3	5.6	8.9	6.8	-------	3.5	5.4	8.0	-------
1950	5.3	12.2	4.7	5.1	4.9	9.0	6.0	-------	4.6	5.0	7.2	-------
1951	3.3	8.2	2.5	4.0	3.1	5.3	3.7	-------	1.5	2.6	3.9	-------
1952	3.0	8.5	2.4	3.2	2.8	5.4	3.3	-------	1.4	2.5	3.6	-------
1953	2.9	7.6	2.5	2.9	2.7	4.5	3.2	-------	1.7	-----	3.4	-------
1954	5.5	12.6	4.9	5.5	5.0	9.9	6.2	-------	4.0	5.2	7.2	-------
1955	4.4	11.0	3.8	4.4	3.9	8.7	4.8	-------	2.8	3.8	5.8	4.8
1956	4.1	11.1	3.4	4.2	3.6	8.3	4.4	-------	2.6	3.7	5.1	5.1
1957	4.3	11.6	3.6	4.1	3.8	7.9	4.6	-------	2.8	4.0	6.2	5.3
1958	6.8	15.9	6.2	6.1	6.1	12.6	7.2	-------	5.1	7.2	10.2	8.1
1959	5.5	14.6	4.7	5.2	4.8	10.7	5.7	-------	3.6	-----	7.6	6.6
1960	5.5	14.7	4.7	5.1	4.9	10.2	5.7	-------	3.7	-----	7.8	6.7
1961	6.7	16.8	5.7	6.3	6.0	12.4	6.8	-------	4.6	6.7	9.2	8.0
1962	5.5	14.7	4.6	5.4	4.9	10.9	5.6	-------	3.6	-----	7.4	6.7
1963	5.7	17.2	4.5	5.4	5.0	10.8	5.5	3.7	3.4	5.5	7.3	6.4
1964	5.2	16.2	3.9	5.2	4.6	9.6	5.0	3.2	2.8	4.9	6.3	5.8
1965	4.5	14.8	3.2	4.5	4.1	8.1	4.3	2.7	2.4	4.2	5.3	5.0
1966	3.8	12.8	2.5	3.8	3.4	7.3	3.5	2.2	1.9	3.5	4.2	4.2
1967	3.8	12.8	2.3	4.2	3.4	7.4	3.6	2.1	1.8	3.4	4.4	4.2
1968	3.6	12.7	2.2	3.8	3.2	6.7	3.4	1.9	1.6	3.1	4.1	4.0
1969	3.5	12.2	2.1	3.7	3.1	6.4	3.3	1.8	1.5	3.1	3.9	3.9
1970	4.9	15.2	3.5	4.8	4.5	8.2	4.8	2.9	2.6	4.5	6.2	5.3
1971	5.9	16.9	4.4	5.7	5.4	9.9	5.7	3.6	3.2	5.5	7.4	6.4
1972	5.6	16.2	4.0	5.4	5.0	10.0	5.3	3.3	2.8	5.1	6.5	6.0
1973	4.9	14.5	3.2	4.8	4.3	8.9	4.5	2.9	2.3	4.3	5.3	5.2
1974	5.6	16.0	3.8	5.5	5.0	9.9	5.3	3.3	2.7	5.1	6.7	6.1
1975	8.5	19.9	6.7	8.0	7.8	13.9	8.2	5.8	5.1	8.1	11.7	9.1
1974: Jan	5.0	14.7	3.3	5.0	4.5	9.0	4.7	2.9	2.3	4.5	5.8	5.6
Feb	5.1	14.8	3.5	5.0	4.5	9.2	4.9	2.9	2.4	4.5	5.9	5.5
Mar	5.0	14.8	3.3	4.9	4.5	9.1	4.7	2.9	2.3	4.5	5.8	5.4
Apr	5.0	14.1	3.4	4.9	4.4	8.7	4.8	3.0	2.3	4.5	6.1	5.5
May	5.1	15.3	3.3	5.0	4.6	9.1	4.9	2.9	2.2	4.5	5.7	5.6
June	5.3	16.3	3.5	5.1	4.8	9.2	5.1	3.0	2.5	4.7	6.1	5.6
July	5.5	16.9	3.6	5.3	4.9	9.9	5.2	3.1	2.7	5.0	6.3	5.8
Aug	5.5	15.0	3.9	5.4	5.0	9.5	5.3	3.3	2.8	5.0	6.8	6.0
Sept	5.9	16.9	4.0	5.9	5.4	9.8	5.7	3.6	2.9	5.4	7.2	6.5
Oct	6.1	17.1	4.4	5.7	5.5	11.0	5.8	3.7	3.1	5.7	7.6	6.7
Nov	6.7	17.7	4.8	6.7	6.1	11.7	6.5	4.1	3.5	6.3	8.5	7.3
Dec	7.2	18.1	5.4	7.1	6.5	12.5	7.1	4.6	3.9	6.7	9.7	7.9
1975: Jan	7.9	19.8	5.9	7.9	7.3	13.0	7.7	5.2	4.4	7.5	10.6	8.7
Feb	8.0	19.4	6.2	7.9	7.3	13.3	7.8	5.3	4.7	7.6	10.6	8.7
Mar	8.5	20.1	6.6	8.3	7.8	13.8	8.3	5.7	5.0	8.0	12.0	9.3
Apr	8.6	19.7	6.8	8.5	7.9	14.1	8.7	5.8	5.3	8.3	12.6	9.4
May	8.9	20.3	7.2	8.4	8.3	14.2	9.0	6.1	5.7	8.5	12.8	9.7
June	8.7	20.7	7.0	8.2	8.0	14.0	8.7	6.1	5.5	8.4	12.4	8.9
July	8.7	20.5	7.1	8.0	8.1	13.4	8.6	6.1	5.5	8.5	12.3	8.9
Aug	8.5	20.7	6.8	7.9	7.8	14.3	8.5	5.7	5.2	8.1	11.9	8.9
Sept	8.6	19.4	7.2	7.8	7.8	14.4	8.5	6.0	5.5	8.4	11.9	9.1
Oct	8.6	19.8	7.2	7.9	8.0	14.3	8.5	6.0	5.3	8.5	11.6	9.4
Nov	8.5	19.0	7.1	7.9	7.8	13.9	8.4	5.8	5.1	8.3	11.3	9.3
Dec	8.3	19.6	6.6	8.0	7.6	13.8	8.2	5.7	4.8	7.9	10.7	8.9

[1] Unemployment as percent of civilian labor force in group specified, except as noted.
[2] Married men living with their wives. Data for 1949 and 1951–54 are for April; 1950, for March.
[3] Data for 1949–61 are for May.
[4] Includes craft and kindred workers, operatives, and nonfarm laborers. Data for 1948–57 are based on data for January, April, July, and October.
[5] Aggregate hours lost by the unemployed and persons on part-time for economic reasons as a percent of potentially available labor force hours.

Note.—See footnote 2 and Note, Table B–22.

Source: Department of Labor, Bureau of Labor Statistics.

TABLE A–4.—*Unemployment by duration, 1947–75*

[Monthly data seasonally adjusted [1]]

Year or month	Total un-employ-ment	Duration of unemployment				Average (mean) duration in weeks
		Less than 5 weeks	5–14 weeks	15–26 weeks	27 weeks and over	
	Thousands of persons 16 years of age and over					
1947	2,311	1,210	704	234	164	
1948	2,276	1,300	669	193	116	8.6
1949	3,637	1,756	1,194	428	256	10.0
1950	3,288	1,450	1,055	425	357	12.1
1951	2,055	1,177	574	166	137	9.7
1952	1,883	1,135	516	148	84	8.4
1953	1,834	1,142	482	132	78	8.0
1954	3,532	1,605	1,116	495	317	11.8
1955	2,852	1,335	815	366	336	13.0
1956	2,750	1,412	805	301	232	11.3
1957	2,859	1,408	891	321	239	10.5
1958	4,602	1,753	1,396	785	667	13.9
1959	3,740	1,585	1,114	469	571	14.4
1960	3,852	1,719	1,176	503	454	12.8
1961	4,714	1,806	1,376	728	804	15.6
1962	3,911	1,663	1,134	534	585	14.7
1963	4,070	1,751	1,231	535	553	14.0
1964	3,786	1,697	1,117	491	482	13.3
1965	3,366	1,628	983	404	351	11.8
1966	2,875	1,573	779	287	239	10.4
1967	2,975	1,634	893	271	177	8.8
1968	2,817	1,594	810	256	156	8.4
1969	2,832	1,629	827	242	133	7.9
1970	4,088	2,137	1,289	427	235	8.7
1971	4,993	2,234	1,578	665	517	11.3
1972	4,840	2,223	1,459	597	562	12.0
1973	4,304	2,196	1,296	475	337	10.0
1974	5,076	2,567	1,572	563	373	9.7
1975	7,830	2,894	2,452	1,290	1,193	14.1
1974: Jan	4,536	2,377	1,378	464	330	9.6
Feb	4,631	2,381	1,362	486	331	9.6
Mar	4,516	2,378	1,360	497	318	9.5
Apr	4,482	2,335	1,396	491	342	9.8
May	4,599	2,448	1,361	500	343	9.5
June	4,827	2,411	1,491	540	355	9.7
July	5,007	2,507	1,534	542	370	9.9
Aug	4,987	2,571	1,493	572	378	9.8
Sept	5,419	2,676	1,712	636	378	9.6
Oct	5,584	2,758	1,792	668	397	9.9
Nov	6,177	2,983	1,989	742	439	9.8
Dec	6,589	3,035	2,197	832	550	10.3
1975: Jan	7,297	3,267	2,599	940	632	10.8
Feb	7,360	2,866	2,484	1,107	721	11.7
Mar	7,770	3,165	2,540	1,240	738	11.4
Apr	7,941	2,935	2,590	1,341	937	12.8
May	8,250	3,081	2,589	1,479	1,050	13.3
June	8,071	2,733	2,511	1,480	1,271	15.3
July	8,096	2,868	2,141	1,600	1,354	15.1
Aug	7,924	2,758	2,449	1,431	1,447	15.5
Sept	7,970	2,820	2,444	1,352	1,582	16.2
Oct	8,062	3,015	2,446	1,238	1,481	15.6
Nov	7,939	2,641	2,469	1,286	1,718	16.9
Dec	7,735	2,648	2,244	1,413	1,667	17.0

[1] Because of independent seasonal adjustment of the various series, detail will not add to totals.

Note.—See footnote 2 and Note, Table B–22.

Source: Department of Labor, Bureau of Labor Statistics.

TABLE A-5.—*Unemployment insurance programs, selected data, 1946–75*

Year or month	All programs			State programs									
	Covered employment[1]	Insured unemployment (weekly average)[2][3]	Total benefits paid (millions of dollars)[2][4]	Insured unemployment		Initial claims		Exhaustions[5]	Insured unemployment as percent of covered employment		Benefits paid	
				Unadjusted	Seasonally adjusted	Unadjusted	Seasonally adjusted		Unadjusted	Seasonally adjusted	Total (millions of dollars)[4]	Average weekly check (dollars)[6]
	Thousands			Weekly average thousands					Percent			
1946	31,856	2,804	2,878.5	1,295	--------	189	--------	38	4.3	--------	1,094.9	18.50
1947	33,876	1,793	1,785.5	997	--------	187	--------	24	3.1	--------	775.1	17.83
1948	34,646	1,446	1,328.7	980	--------	200	--------	20	3.0	--------	789.9	19.03
1949	33,098	2,474	2,269.8	1,973	--------	340	--------	37	6.2	--------	1,736.0	20.48
1950	34,308	1,605	1,467.6	1,513	--------	236	--------	36	4.6	--------	1,373.1	20.76
1951	36,334	1,000	862.9	969	--------	208	--------	16	2.8	--------	840.4	21.09
1952	37,006	1,069	1,043.5	1,044	--------	215	--------	18	2.9	--------	998.2	22.79
1953	38,072	1,067	1,050.6	990	--------	218	--------	15	2.8	--------	962.2	23.58
1954	36,622	2,051	2,291.8	1,870	--------	304	--------	34	5.2	--------	2,026.9	24.93
1955	40,018	1,399	1,560.2	1,265	--------	226	--------	25	3.5	--------	1,350.3	25.04
1956	42,751	1,323	1,540.6	1,215	--------	227	--------	20	3.2	--------	1,380.7	27.02
1957	43,436	1,571	1,913.0	1,446	--------	270	--------	23	3.6	--------	1,733.9	28.17
1958	44,411	3,269	4,290.6	2,526	--------	369	--------	50	6.4	--------	3,512.7	30.58
1959	45,728	2,099	2,854.3	1,684	--------	277	--------	33	4.4	--------	2,279.0	30.41
1960	46,334	2,071	3,022.8	1,908	--------	331	--------	31	4.8	--------	2,726.7	32.87
1961	46,266	2,994	4,358.1	2,290	--------	350	--------	46	5.6	--------	3,422.7	33.80
1962	47,776	1,946	3,145.1	1,783	--------	302	--------	32	4.4	--------	2,675.4	34.56
1963	48,434	[7] 1,973	3,025.9	[7] 1,806	--------	[7] 298	--------	30	4.3	--------	2,774.7	35.27
1964	49,637	1,753	2,749.2	1,605	--------	268	--------	26	3.8	--------	2,522.1	35.92
1965	51,580	1,450	2,360.4	1,328	--------	232	--------	21	3.0	--------	2,166.0	37.19
1966	54,739	1,129	1,890.9	1,061	--------	203	--------	15	2.3	--------	1,771.3	39.75
1967	56,342	1,270	2,221.5	1,205	--------	226	--------	17	2.5	--------	2,092.3	41.25
1968	57,977	1,187	2,191.0	1,111	--------	201	--------	16	2.2	--------	2,031.6	43.43
1969	59,999	1,177	2,298.6	1,101	--------	200	--------	16	2.1	--------	2,127.9	46.17
1970	59,526	2,070	4,209.3	1,805	--------	296	--------	25	3.4	--------	3,848.5	50.34
1971	59,375	2,608	6,214.9	2,150	--------	295	--------	39	4.1	--------	4,957.0	53.23
1972	66,458	2,192	5,491.1	1,848	--------	261	--------	35	3.5	--------	4,471.0	56.76
1973	69,897	1,793	4,517.3	1,632	--------	246	--------	29	2.7	--------	4,007.6	59.00
1974 p	[8] 71,905	2,558	6,933.9	2,262	--------	363	--------	37	3.5	--------	5,974.9	64.25
1975 p		4,920	--------	3,973	--------	472	--------		6.0	--------		
1974: Jan	--------	2,739	622.7	2,561	1,965	446	426	32	4.1	3.1	570.8	62.28
Feb	--------	2,824	599.3	2,630	2,045	359	382	32	4.2	3.2	553.3	63.35
Mar	--------	2,751	652.4	2,502	2,099	293	366	35	4.0	3.3	593.9	63.85
Apr	--------	2,564	639.3	2,217	2,099	263	294	38	3.5	3.3	552.7	63.62
May	--------	2,278	584.5	1,934	2,093	237	251	39	3.0	3.3	486.4	62.69
June	--------	2,161	472.4	1,834	2,103	269	272	40	2.9	3.3	383.4	62.50
July	--------	2,290	541.6	1,989	2,113	340	315	41	3.1	3.3	459.1	62.93
Aug	--------	2,153	530.3	1,874	2,132	283	272	40	2.9	3.3	444.9	64.14
Sept	--------	2,081	463.6	1,783	2,251	274	308	35	2.7	3.5	381.0	64.23
Oct	--------	2,246	530.3	1,947	2,478	348	338	34	3.0	3.8	442.0	65.20
Nov	--------	2,825	571.0	2,499	2,808	480	447	36	3.8	4.3	485.0	65.49
Dec	--------	3,910	848.3	3,550	3,291	703	552	42	5.4	5.0	745.9	67.22
1975: Jan	--------	5,213	1,256.6	4,752	3,652	795	565	50	7.2	5.5	1,128.2	67.83
Feb	--------	5,751	1,312.3	5,108	3,955	609	546	58	7.8	6.0	1,164.2	68.73
Mar	--------	5,886	1,490.4	5,091	4,216	510	545	66	7.7	6.4	1,290.6	69.07
Apr	--------	5,647	1,539.7	4,775	4,522	463	525	84	7.2	6.8	1,301.2	69.08
May	--------	5,202	1,395.2	4,281	4,628	401	494	92	6.4	7.0	1,145.1	69.33
June	--------	4,892	1,256.7	3,878	4,427	427	487	104	5.8	6.7	984.0	69.58
July	--------	4,990	1,406.6	3,871	4,128	480	421	105	5.8	6.2	1,086.9	71.58
Aug	--------	4,590	1,199.0	3,436	3,898	375	443	97	5.1	5.8	881.3	70.98
Sept p	--------	4,254	1,095.2	3,077	3,885	340	449	84	4.6	5.8	763.8	71.22
Oct p	--------	4,044	1,046.3	2,924	3,718	367	439	73	4.4	5.6	734.2	72.18
Nov p	--------	4,120	--------	3,045	3,429	402	386	73	4.6	5.2	--------	--------
Dec p	--------	4,460	--------	3,409	3,193	501	375	--------	5.1	4.8	--------	--------

[1] Includes persons under the State, UCFE (Federal employee, effective January 1955), and RRB (Railroad Retirement Board) programs. Beginning October 1958, also includes the UCX program (unemployment compensation for ex-servicemen).

[2] Includes State, UCFE, RR, UCX, UCV (unemployment compensation for veterans, October 1952–January 1960), and SRA (Servicemen's Readjustment Act, September 1944–September 1951) programs. Also includes Federal and State extended benefit programs. Does not include FSB (Federal Supplemental Benefits) and SUA (Special Unemployment Assistance) programs.

[3] Covered workers who have completed at least 1 week of unemployment.

[4] Annual data are net amounts and monthly data are gross amounts.

[5] Individuals receiving final payments in benefit year.

[6] For total unemployment only.

[7] Programs include Puerto Rican sugarcane workers for initial claims and insured unemployment beginning July 1963.

[8] Latest data available for all programs combined. Workers covered by State programs account for about 92 percent of the total.

Source: Department of Labor, Employment and Training Administration.

TABLE A-6.—*Wage and salary workers in nonagricultural establishments, 1929-75*

[All employees; thousands of persons; monthly data seasonally adjusted]

| Year or month | Total wage and salary workers | Manufacturing | | | Mining | Contract construction | Transportation and public utilities | Wholesale and retail trade | Finance, insurance, and real estate | Services | Government | |
		Total	Durable goods	Nondurable goods							Federal	State and local
1929	31,339	10,702			1,087	1,497	3,916	6,123	1,509	3,440	533	2,532
1933	23,711	7,397			744	809	2,672	4,755	1,295	2,873	565	2,601
1939	30,618	10,278	4,715	5,564	854	1,150	2,936	6,426	1,462	3,517	905	3,090
1940	32,376	10,985	5,363	5,622	925	1,294	3,038	6,750	1,502	3,681	996	3,206
1941	36,554	13,192	6,968	6,225	957	1,790	3,274	7,210	1,549	3,921	1,340	3,320
1942	40,125	15,280	8,823	6,458	992	2,170	3,460	7,118	1,538	4,084	2,213	3,270
1943	42,452	17,602	11,084	6,518	925	1,567	3,647	6,982	1,502	4,148	2,905	3,174
1944	41,883	17,328	10,856	6,472	892	1,094	3,829	7,058	1,476	4,163	2,928	3,116
1945	40,394	15,524	9,074	6,450	836	1,132	3,906	7,314	1,497	4,241	2,808	3,137
1946	41,674	14,703	7,742	6,962	862	1,661	4,061	8,376	1,697	4,719	2,254	3,341
1947	43,881	15,545	8,385	7,159	955	1,982	4,166	8,955	1,754	5,050	1,892	3,582
1948	44,891	15,582	8,326	7,256	994	2,169	4,189	9,272	1,829	5,206	1,863	3,787
1949	43,778	14,441	7,489	6,953	930	2,165	4,001	9,264	1,857	5,264	1,908	3,948
1950	45,222	15,241	8,094	7,147	901	2,333	4,034	9,386	1,919	5,382	1,928	4,098
1951	47,849	16,393	9,089	7,304	929	2,603	4,226	9,742	1,991	5,576	2,302	4,087
1952	48,825	16,632	9,349	7,284	898	2,634	4,248	10,004	2,069	5,730	2,420	4,188
1953	50,232	17,549	10,110	7,438	866	2,623	4,290	10,247	2,146	5,867	2,305	4,340
1954	49,022	16,314	9,129	7,185	791	2,612	4,084	10,235	2,234	6,002	2,188	4,563
1955	50,675	16,882	9,541	7,340	792	2,802	4,141	10,535	2,335	6,274	2,187	4,727
1956	52,408	17,243	9,834	7,409	822	2,999	4,244	10,858	2,429	6,536	2,209	5,069
1957	52,894	17,174	9,856	7,319	828	2,923	4,241	10,886	2,477	6,749	2,217	5,399
1958	51,363	15,945	8,830	7,116	751	2,778	3,976	10,750	2,519	6,806	2,191	5,648
1959	53,313	16,675	9,373	7,303	732	2,960	4,011	11,127	2,594	7,130	2,233	5,850
1960	54,234	16,796	9,459	7,336	712	2,885	4,004	11,391	2,669	7,423	2,270	6,083
1961	54,042	16,326	9,070	7,256	672	2,816	3,903	11,337	2,731	7,664	2,279	6,315
1962	55,596	16,853	9,480	7,373	650	2,902	3,906	11,566	2,800	8,028	2,340	6,550
1963	56,702	16,995	9,616	7,380	635	2,963	3,903	11,778	2,877	8,325	2,358	6,868
1964	58,331	17,274	9,816	7,458	634	3,050	3,951	12,160	2,957	8,709	2,348	7,248
1965	60,815	18,062	10,406	7,656	632	3,186	4,036	12,716	3,023	9,087	2,378	7,696
1966	63,955	19,214	11,284	7,930	627	3,275	4,151	13,245	3,100	9,551	2,564	8,227
1967	65,857	19,447	11,439	8,008	613	3,208	4,261	13,606	3,225	10,099	2,719	8,679
1968	67,951	19,781	11,626	8,155	606	3,306	4,311	14,099	3,381	10,622	2,737	9,109
1969	70,442	20,167	11,895	8,272	619	3,525	4,435	14,704	3,562	11,228	2,758	9,444
1970	70,920	19,349	11,195	8,154	623	3,536	4,504	15,040	3,687	11,621	2,731	9,830
1971	71,222	18,572	10,597	7,975	609	3,639	4,457	15,352	3,802	11,903	2,696	10,192
1972	73,714	19,090	11,006	8,084	625	3,831	4,517	15,975	3,943	12,392	2,684	10,656
1973	76,896	20,068	11,839	8,229	644	4,015	4,644	16,674	4,091	13,021	2,663	11,075
1974	78,413	20,046	11,895	8,151	694	3,957	4,696	17,017	4,208	13,617	2,724	11,453
1975 p	76,983	18,344	10,676	7,668	745	3,455	4,499	16,950	4,222	13,997	2,748	12,023

See footnotes at end of table.

TABLE A–6.—*Wage and salary workers in nonagricultural establishments,*
1929–75—Continued

[All employees; thousands of persons; monthly data seasonally adjusted]

| Year or month | Total wage and salary workers | Manufacturing | | | Min-ing | Con-tract con-struc-tion | Trans-porta-tion and pub-lic utili-ties | Whole-sale and retail trade | Fi-nance, insur-ance, and real estate | Serv-ices | Government | |
		Total	Dura-ble goods	Non-dura-ble goods							Fed-eral	State and local
1973: Jan___	75, 516	19, 717	11, 522	8, 195	628	3, 899	4, 596	16, 382	4, 018	12, 724	2, 671	10, 881
Feb___	75, 915	19, 851	11, 633	8, 218	629	3, 940	4, 604	16, 486	4, 034	12, 788	2, 661	10, 922
Mar___	76, 159	19, 920	11, 686	8, 234	629	3, 962	4, 614	16, 541	4, 049	12, 829	2, 662	10, 953
Apr__	76, 367	19, 975	11, 735	8, 240	630	3, 955	4, 627	16, 573	4, 061	12, 887	2, 660	10, 999
May___	76, 569	20, 010	11, 788	8, 222	632	3, 987	4, 630	16, 626	4, 072	12, 919	2, 664	11, 029
June__	76, 878	20, 085	11, 844	8, 241	637	4, 028	4, 635	16, 673	4, 081	12, 985	2, 655	11, 099
July___	76, 940	20, 068	11, 862	8, 206	644	4, 059	4, 639	16, 689	4, 095	13, 022	2, 626	11, 098
Aug___	77, 207	20, 116	11, 907	8, 209	649	4, 047	4, 658	16, 739	4, 114	13, 100	2, 651	11, 133
Sept__	77, 366	20, 131	11, 925	8, 206	651	4, 070	4, 670	16, 776	4, 127	13, 169	2, 659	11, 113
Oct___	77, 673	20, 245	12, 001	8, 244	666	4, 049	4, 690	16, 836	4, 136	13, 208	2, 662	11, 181
Nov___	77, 973	20, 324	12, 058	8, 266	665	4, 064	4, 686	16, 894	4, 145	13, 288	2, 671	11, 236
Dec___	78, 058	20, 367	12, 097	8, 270	668	4, 080	4, 682	16, 854	4, 157	13, 310	2, 682	11, 258
1974: Jan___	78, 068	20, 324	12, 047	8, 277	672	4, 064	4, 710	16, 864	4, 172	13, 313	2, 681	11, 268
Feb___	78, 196	20, 222	11, 966	8, 256	674	4, 116	4, 721	16, 875	4, 186	13, 400	2, 696	11, 306
Mar___	78, 236	20, 185	11, 947	8, 238	677	4, 089	4, 711	16, 898	4, 196	13, 453	2, 699	11, 328
Apr___	78, 351	20, 209	11, 996	8, 213	685	4, 049	4, 707	16, 933	4, 202	13, 488	2, 705	11, 373
May___	78, 486	20, 189	11, 975	8, 214	689	4, 029	4, 704	17, 009	4, 209	13, 559	2, 713	11, 385
June__	78, 530	20, 201	12, 004	8, 197	692	3, 969	4, 700	17, 038	4, 206	13, 608	2, 721	11, 395
July ___	78, 648	20, 202	12, 024	8, 178	698	3, 913	4, 695	17, 123	4, 206	13, 656	2, 730	11, 425
Aug___	78, 733	20, 134	11, 962	8, 172	701	3, 938	4, 703	17, 135	4, 217	13, 696	2, 740	11, 469
Sept __	78, 830	20, 104	11, 943	8, 161	708	3, 902	4, 683	17, 143	4, 224	13, 767	2, 746	11, 553
Oct___	78, 790	19, 972	11, 870	8, 102	728	3, 872	4, 686	17, 154	4, 228	13, 797	2, 745	11, 608
Nov___	78, 374	19, 638	11, 656	7, 982	722	3, 826	4, 683	17, 058	4, 226	13, 822	2, 742	11, 657
Dec___	77, 723	19, 190	11, 357	7, 833	686	3; 770	4, 659	16, 935	4, 229	13, 833	2, 738	11, 683
1975: Jan___	77, 319	18, 798	11, 099	7, 699	723	3, 749	4, 603	16, 903	4, 219	13, 857	2, 734	11, 733
Feb___	76, 804	18, 375	10, 813	7, 562	724	3, 592	4, 565	16, 879	4, 210	13, 865	2, 733	11, 861
Mar___	76, 468	18, 226	10, 728	7, 498	729	3, 467	4, 506	16, 851	4, 207	13, 864	2, 733	11, 885
Apr___	76, 462	18, 155	10, 637	7, 518	732	3, 441	4, 508	16, 847	4, 209	13, 878	2, 731	11, 961
May__	76, 510	18, 162	10, 595	7, 567	738	3, 439	4, 491	16, 857	4, 208	13, 889	2, 732	11, 994
June__	76, 343	18, 100	10, 527	7, 573	741	3, 392	4, 469	16, 877	4, 202	13, 871	2, 738	11, 953
July__	76, 679	18, 084	10, 465	7, 619	743	3, 395	4, 464	16, 984	4, 203	13, 990	2, 745	12, 071
Aug___	77, 023	18, 254	10, 563	7, 691	749	3, 415	4, 466	17, 016	4, 218	14, 050	2, 756	12, 099
Sept__	77, 310	18, 417	10, 650	7, 767	752	3, 432	4, 467	17, 045	4, 239	14, 113	2, 765	12, 080
Oct___	77, 555	18, 493	10, 661	7, 832	774	3, 402	4, 476	17, 043	4, 246	14, 157	2, 767	12, 197
Nov ᴾ_	77, 558	18, 471	10, 643	7, 828	767	3, 403	4, 501	17, 020	4, 248	14, 189	2, 761	12, 198
Dec ᴾ_	77, 798	18, 551	10, 697	7, 854	772	3, 389	4, 481	17, 096	4, 259	14, 251	2, 758	12, 241

Note.—Data in Tables B–27 through B–29 are based on reports from employing establishments and relate to full- and part-time wage and salary workers in nonagricultural establishments who worked during, or received pay for, any part of the pay period which includes the 12th of the month.

Not comparable with labor force data (Tables B–22 through B–25), which include proprietors, self-employed persons, domestic servants, and unpaid family workers; which count persons as employed when they are not at work because of industrial disputes, bad weather, etc.; and which are based on a sample of the working-age population, whereas the estimates in this table are based on reports from employing establishments.

For description and details of the various establishment data, see "Employment and Earnings."

Source: Department of Labor, Bureau of Labor Statistics.

TABLE A–7.—*Average weekly hours and hourly earnings in selected private nonagricultural industries, 1947–75*

[For production or nonsupervisory workers; monthly data seasonally adjusted]

Year or month	Average weekly hours				Average gross hourly earnings, current dollars				Adjusted hourly earnings, total private nonagricultural [3]			
									Index, 1967=100		Percent change from preceding period [5]	
	Total private nonagricultural [1]	Manufacturing	Contract construction	Retail trade [2]	Total private nonagricultural [1]	Manufacturing	Contract construction	Retail trade [2]	Current dollars	1967 dollars [4]	Current dollars	1967 dollars
1947	40.3	40.4	38.2	40.3	$1.131	$1.217	$1.541	$0.838	42.6	63.7		
1948	40.0	40.0	38.1	40.2	1.225	1.328	1.713	.901	46.0	63.8	8.0	0.2
1949	39.4	39.1	37.7	40.4	1.275	1.378	1.792	.951	48.2	67.5	4.8	5.8
1950	39.8	40.5	37.4	40.4	1.335	1.440	1.863	.983	50.0	69.3	3.7	2.7
1951	39.9	40.6	38.1	40.4	1.45	1.56	2.02	1.06	53.7	69.0	7.4	−.4
1952	39.9	40.7	38.9	39.8	1.52	1.65	2.13	1.09	56.4	70.9	5.0	2.8
1953	39.6	40.5	37.9	39.1	1.61	1.74	2.28	1.16	59.6	74.4	5.7	4.9
1954	39.1	39.6	37.2	39.2	1.65	1.78	2.39	1.20	61.7	76.6	3.5	3.0
1955	39.6	40.7	37.1	39.0	1.71	1.86	2.45	1.25	63.7	79.4	3.2	3.7
1956	39.3	40.4	37.5	38.6	1.80	1.95	2.57	1.30	67.0	82.3	5.2	3.7
1957	38.8	39.8	37.0	38.1	1.89	2.05	2.71	1.37	70.3	83.4	4.9	1.3
1958	38.5	39.2	36.8	38.1	1.95	2.11	2.82	1.42	73.2	84.5	4.1	1.3
1959	39.0	40.3	37.0	38.2	2.02	2.19	2.93	1.47	75.8	86.8	3.6	2.7
1960	38.6	39.7	36.7	38.0	2.09	2.26	3.08	1.52	78.4	88.4	3.4	1.8
1961	38.6	39.8	36.9	37.6	2.14	2.32	3.20	1.56	80.8	90.2	3.1	2.0
1962	38.7	40.4	37.0	37.4	2.22	2.39	3.31	1.63	83.5	92.2	3.3	2.2
1963	38.8	40.5	37.3	37.3	2.28	2.46	3.41	1.68	85.9	93.7	2.9	1.6
1964	38.7	40.7	37.2	37.0	2.36	2.53	3.55	1.75	88.3	95.1	2.8	1.5
1965	38.8	41.2	37.4	36.6	2.45	2.61	3.70	1.82	91.6	97.0	3.7	2.0
1966	38.6	41.3	37.6	35.9	2.56	2.72	3.89	1.91	95.4	98.1	4.1	1.1
1967	38.0	40.6	37.7	35.3	2.68	2.83	4.11	2.01	100.0	100.0	4.8	1.9
1968	37.8	40.7	37.3	34.7	2.85	3.01	4.41	2.16	106.3	102.0	6.3	2.0
1969	37.7	40.6	37.9	34.2	3.04	3.19	4.79	2.30	113.3	103.2	6.6	1.2
1970	37.1	39.8	37.3	33.8	3.22	3.36	5.24	2.44	120.8	103.9	6.6	.7
1971	37.0	39.9	37.2	33.7	3.44	3.57	5.69	2.57	129.4	106.7	7.1	2.7
1972	37.1	40.6	36.9	33.7	3.67	3.81	6.03	2.70	137.8	110.0	6.5	3.1
1973	37.1	40.7	37.0	33.3	3.92	4.08	6.37	2.87	146.6	110.1	6.4	.1
1974	36.6	40.0	36.9	32.7	4.22	4.41	6.75	3.09	158.6	107.4	8.2	−2.5
1975 ᵖ	36.1	39.4	36.6	32.4	4.54	4.81	7.24	3.33	172.6	107.1	8.8	−.3
1974: Jan	36.7	40.5	36.4	32.9	4.06	4.21	6.48	2.98	151.8	108.4	4.7	−8.0
Feb	36.9	40.4	37.6	33.0	4.08	4.23	6.51	2.98	152.8	107.9	8.2	−5.5
Mar	36.8	40.4	36.8	32.9	4.10	4.25	6.57	3.01	153.9	107.5	8.6	−3.8
Apr	36.4	39.3	36.4	33.1	4.12	4.26	6.60	3.00	154.7	107.4	6.4	−1.6
May	36.7	40.3	36.8	32.9	4.17	4.34	6.63	3.08	156.5	107.6	15.4	2.3
June	36.6	40.2	36.9	32.7	4.21	4.40	6.72	3.09	158.5	107.9	15.9	3.9
July	36.7	40.2	36.9	32.6	4.24	4.44	6.76	3.12	159.2	107.5	5.4	−4.8
Aug	36.6	40.1	36.6	32.6	4.27	4.49	6.89	3.14	160.6	107.2	11.2	−3.0
Sept	36.5	39.9	36.7	32.5	4.31	4.53	6.92	3.15	162.0	107.0	11.6	−3.0
Oct	36.5	40.0	37.1	32.4	4.34	4.57	6.90	3.18	163.3	106.8	9.8	−1.3
Nov	36.2	39.5	37.0	32.5	4.35	4.59	6.96	3.18	164.2	106.4	6.4	−4.8
Dec	36.3	39.4	37.4	32.5	4.38	4.62	7.00	3.20	165.4	106.4	9.7	−.1
1975: Jan	36.2	39.2	37.2	32.4	4.41	4.65	7.03	3.23	166.3	106.3	6.3	−1.5
Feb	36.1	38.8	36.8	32.3	4.43	4.68	6.98	3.26	167.8	106.6	11.4	4.3
Mar	35.9	38.9	34.9	32.5	4.46	4.72	7.18	3.27	169.1	107.2	9.7	6.1
Apr	35.9	39.1	36.8	32.3	4.47	4.73	7.18	3.29	169.4	106.8	2.6	−4.5
May	35.9	39.0	36.9	32.5	4.49	4.75	7.16	3.31	170.6	107.1	8.5	4.0
June	36.0	39.3	35.7	32.4	4.51	4.78	7.27	3.32	172.2	107.3	12.2	2.4
July	36.0	39.4	36.2	32.2	4.54	4.82	7.33	3.34	173.1	106.6	6.3	−7.3
Aug	36.2	39.7	36.7	32.3	4.57	4.86	7.30	3.37	174.6	107.4	11.1	8.9
Sept	36.1	39.8	36.7	32.2	4.60	4.88	7.32	3.38	175.2	107.3	4.1	−1.6
Oct	36.2	39.8	36.6	32.3	4.63	4.90	7.32	3.41	176.7	107.5	10.8	2.5
Nov ᵖ	36.3	39.9	36.8	32.5	4.67	4.93	7.38	3.42	178.0	107.5	8.9	.3
Dec ᵖ	36.5	40.3	37.5	32.4	4.67	4.95	7.38	3.41	178.0	107.0	.3	−5.4

[1] Also includes other private industry groups shown in Table B–27.
[2] Includes eating and drinking places.
[3] Adjusted for overtime (in manufacturing only) and for interindustry employment shifts.
[4] Current dollar earnings index divided by the consumer price index.
[5] Monthly data are annual rates, computed from indexes to two decimal places.

Note.—See Note, Table B–27.

Source: Department of Labor, Bureau of Labor Statistics.

Statistical Appendix

NATIONAL INCOME OR EXPENDITURE

TABLE B-1.—*Gross national product, 1929-76*

[Billions of dollars, except as noted; quarterly data at seasonally adjusted annual rates]

Year or quarter	Gross national product	Personal consumption expenditures	Gross private domestic investment	Net exports of goods and services			Government purchases of goods and services					Percent change from preceding period, gross national product [2]
				Net exports	Exports	Imports	Total	Federal			State and local	
								Total	National defense [1]	Non-defense		
1929	103.4	77.3	16.2	1.1	7.0	5.9	8.8	1.4			7.4	
1933	55.8	45.8	1.4	.4	2.4	2.0	8.2	2.1			6.1	-4.2
1939	90.8	67.0	9.3	1.1	4.4	3.4	13.5	5.2	1.2	3.9	8.3	6.9
1940	100.0	71.0	13.1	1.7	5.4	3.6	14.2	6.1	2.2	3.9	8.1	10.1
1941	124.9	80.8	17.9	1.3	5.9	4.6	24.9	16.9	13.7	3.2	8.0	24.9
1942	158.3	88.6	9.9	.0	4.8	4.8	59.8	52.0	49.4	2.6	7.8	26.8
1943	192.0	99.4	5.8	-2.0	4.4	6.5	88.9	81.3	79.7	1.6	7.5	21.3
1944	210.5	108.2	7.2	-1.8	5.3	7.1	97.0	89.4	87.4	2.0	7.6	9.6
1945	212.3	119.5	10.6	-.6	7.2	7.8	82.8	74.6	73.5	1.1	8.2	.9
1946	209.6	143.8	30.7	7.6	14.8	7.2	27.5	17.6	14.8	2.8	9.9	-1.3
1947	232.8	161.7	34.0	11.6	19.8	8.2	25.5	12.7	9.0	3.7	12.8	11.1
1948	259.1	174.7	45.9	6.5	16.9	10.4	32.0	16.7	10.7	6.0	15.3	11.3
1949	258.0	178.1	35.3	6.2	15.9	9.6	38.4	20.4	13.2	7.2	18.0	-.4
1950	286.2	192.0	53.8	1.9	13.9	12.0	38.5	18.7	14.0	4.7	19.8	10.9
1951	330.2	207.1	59.2	3.8	18.9	15.1	60.1	38.3	33.5	4.8	21.8	15.4
1952	347.2	217.1	52.1	2.4	18.2	15.8	75.6	52.4	45.8	6.5	23.2	5.1
1953	366.1	229.7	53.3	.6	17.1	16.6	82.5	57.5	48.6	8.9	25.0	5.5
1954	366.3	235.8	52.7	2.0	18.0	16.0	75.8	47.9	41.1	6.8	27.8	.0
1955	399.3	253.7	68.4	2.2	20.0	17.8	75.0	44.5	38.4	6.0	30.6	9.0
1956	420.7	266.0	71.0	4.3	23.9	19.6	79.4	45.9	40.2	5.7	33.5	5.4
1957	442.8	280.4	69.2	6.1	26.7	20.7	87.1	50.0	44.0	5.9	37.1	5.2
1958	448.9	289.5	61.9	2.5	23.3	20.8	95.0	53.9	45.6	8.3	41.1	1.4
1959	486.5	310.8	77.6	.6	23.7	23.2	97.6	53.9	45.6	8.3	43.7	8.4
1960	506.0	324.9	76.4	4.4	27.6	23.2	100.3	53.7	44.5	9.3	46.5	4.0
1961	523.3	335.0	74.3	5.8	28.9	23.1	108.2	57.4	47.0	10.4	50.8	3.4
1962	563.8	355.2	85.2	5.4	30.6	25.2	118.0	63.7	51.1	12.7	54.3	7.7
1963	594.7	374.6	90.2	6.3	32.7	26.4	123.7	64.6	50.3	14.3	59.0	5.5
1964	635.7	400.4	96.6	8.9	37.4	28.4	129.8	65.2	49.0	16.2	64.6	6.9
1965	688.1	430.2	112.0	7.6	39.5	32.0	138.4	67.3	49.4	17.8	71.1	8.2
1966	753.0	464.8	124.5	5.1	42.8	37.7	158.7	78.8	60.3	18.5	79.8	9.4
1967	796.3	490.4	120.8	4.9	45.6	40.6	180.2	90.9	71.5	19.5	89.3	5.8
1968	868.5	535.9	131.5	2.3	49.9	47.7	198.7	98.0	76.9	21.2	100.7	9.1
1969	935.5	579.7	146.2	1.8	54.7	52.9	207.9	97.5	76.3	21.2	110.4	7.7
1970	982.4	618.8	140.8	3.9	62.5	58.5	218.9	95.6	73.5	22.1	123.2	5.0
1971	1,063.4	668.2	160.0	1.6	65.6	64.0	233.7	96.2	70.2	26.0	137.5	8.2
1972	1,171.1	733.0	188.3	-3.3	72.7	75.9	253.1	102.1	73.5	28.6	151.0	10.1
1973	1,306.6	809.9	220.0	7.1	101.6	94.4	269.5	102.2	73.5	28.7	167.3	11.6
1974	1,413.2	887.5	215.0	7.5	144.4	136.9	303.3	111.6	77.3	34.3	191.6	8.2
1975	1,516.3	973.2	183.7	20.5	148.1	127.6	339.0	124.4	84.3	40.1	214.5	7.3
1976 P	1,692.4	1,078.6	241.2	6.9	161.9	155.1	365.8	133.4	88.2	45.2	232.3	11.6
1974: I	1,372.7	853.3	216.4	15.0	133.2	118.2	288.0	106.1	74.9	31.2	181.9	5.3
II	1,399.4	878.7	218.8	3.9	142.2	138.3	298.0	108.9	75.9	33.0	189.1	8.0
III	1,431.6	906.8	213.3	2.9	148.4	145.5	308.6	113.5	78.2	35.3	195.1	9.5
IV	1,449.2	911.1	211.5	8.1	153.8	145.7	318.5	118.1	80.2	37.9	200.4	5.0
1975: I	1,446.2	933.2	172.4	15.0	147.5	132.5	325.6	120.3	82.0	38.3	205.3	-.8
II	1,482.3	960.3	164.4	24.4	142.9	118.5	333.2	122.4	83.4	39.0	210.9	10.4
III	1,548.7	987.3	196.7	21.4	148.2	126.8	343.2	124.6	84.6	40.0	218.6	19.1
IV	1,588.2	1,012.0	201.4	21.0	153.7	132.7	353.8	130.4	87.1	43.2	223.4	10.6
1976: I	1,636.2	1,043.6	229.6	8.4	154.1	145.7	354.7	129.2	86.2	42.9	225.5	12.6
II	1,675.2	1,064.7	239.2	9.3	160.3	151.0	362.0	131.2	86.9	44.2	230.9	9.9
III	1,709.8	1,088.5	247.0	4.7	167.7	163.0	369.6	134.5	88.5	46.0	235.0	8.5
IV P	1,748.5	1,117.5	249.0	5.2	165.6	160.4	376.8	138.9	91.3	47.6	238.0	9.4

[1] This category corresponds closely to the national defense classification in "The Budget of the United States Government, Fiscal Year 1978."

[2] Changes are based on unrounded data and therefore may differ slightly from those obtained from data shown here.

Source: Department of Commerce, Bureau of Economic Analysis.

TABLE B–27.—*Noninstitutional population and the labor force, 1929–76*

[Monthly data seasonally adjusted, except as noted]

Year or month	Nonin-stitu-tional popu-lation[1]	Total labor force (includ-ing Armed Forces)	Armed Forces[1]	Civilian labor force					Unem-ploy-ment rate (percent of civilian labor force)	Labor force partici-pation rate (total labor force as percent of non-institu-tional popu-lation)
				Total	Employment			Unem-ploy-ment		
					Total	Agri-cul-tural	Non-agri-cul-tural			
	Thousands of persons 14 years of age and over								Percent	
1929		49,440	260	49,180	47,630	10,450	37,180	1,550	3.2	
1933		51,840	250	51,590	38,760	10,090	28,670	12,830	24.9	
1939		55,600	370	55,230	45,750	9,610	36,140	9,480	17.2	
1940	100,380	56,180	540	55,640	47,520	9,540	37,980	8,120	14.6	56.0
1941	101,520	57,530	1,620	55,910	50,350	9,100	41,250	5,560	9.9	56.7
1942	102,610	60,380	3,970	56,410	53,750	9,250	44,500	2,660	4.7	58.8
1943	103,660	64,560	9,020	55,540	54,470	9,080	45,390	1,070	1.9	62.3
1944	104,630	66,040	11,410	54,630	53,960	8,950	45,010	670	1.2	63.1
1945	105,530	65,300	11,440	53,860	52,820	8,580	44,240	1,040	1.9	61.9
1946	106,520	60,970	3,450	57,520	55,250	8,320	46,930	2,270	3.9	57.2
1947	107,608	61,758	1,590	60,168	57,812	8,256	49,557	2,356	3.9	57.4
	Thousands of persons 16 years of age and over									
1947	103,418	60,941	1,591	59,350	57,038	7,890	49,148	2,311	3.9	58.9
1948	104,527	62,080	1,459	60,621	58,343	7,629	50,714	2,276	3.8	59.4
1949	105,611	62,903	1,617	61,286	57,651	7,658	49,993	3,637	5.9	59.6
1950	106,645	63,858	1,650	62,208	58,918	7,160	51,758	3,288	5.3	59.9
1951	107,721	65,117	3,100	62,017	59,961	6,726	53,235	2,055	3.3	60.4
1952	108,823	65,730	3,592	62,138	60,250	6,500	53,749	1,883	3.0	60.4
1953[2]	110,601	66,560	3,545	63,015	61,179	6,260	54,919	1,834	2.9	60.2
1954	111,671	66,993	3,350	63,643	60,109	6,205	53,904	3,532	5.5	60.0
1955	112,732	68,072	3,049	65,023	62,170	6,450	55,722	2,852	4.4	60.4
1956	113,811	69,409	2,857	66,552	63,799	6,283	57,514	2,750	4.1	61.0
1957	115,065	69,729	2,800	66,929	64,071	5,947	58,123	2,859	4.3	60.6
1958	116,363	70,275	2,636	67,639	63,036	5,586	57,450	4,602	6.8	60.4
1959	117,881	70,921	2,552	68,369	64,630	5,565	59,065	3,740	5.5	60.2
1960[2]	119,759	72,142	2,514	69,628	65,778	5,458	60,318	3,852	5.5	60.2
1961	121,343	73,031	2,572	70,459	65,746	5,200	60,546	4,714	6.7	60.2
1962[2]	122,981	73,442	2,828	70,614	66,702	4,944	61,759	3,911	5.5	59.7
1963	125,154	74,571	2,738	71,833	67,762	4,687	63,076	4,070	5.7	59.6
1964	127,224	75,830	2,739	73,091	69,305	4,523	64,782	3,786	5.2	59.6
1965	129,236	77,178	2,723	74,455	71,088	4,361	66,726	3,366	4.5	59.7
1966	131,180	78,893	3,123	75,770	72,895	3,979	68,915	2,875	3.8	60.1
1967	133,319	80,793	3,446	77,347	74,372	3,844	70,527	2,975	3.8	60.6
1968	135,562	82,272	3,535	78,737	75,920	3,817	72,103	2,817	3.6	60.7
1969	137,841	84,240	3,506	80,734	77,902	3,606	74,296	2,832	3.5	61.1
1970	140,182	85,903	3,188	82,715	78,627	3,462	75,165	4,088	4.9	61.3
1971	142,596	86,929	2,817	84,113	79,120	3,387	75,732	4,993	5.9	61.0
1972[2]	145,775	88,991	2,449	86,542	81,702	3,472	78,230	4,840	5.6	61.0
1973[2]	148,263	91,040	2,326	88,714	84,409	3,452	80,957	4,304	4.9	61.4
1974	150,827	93,240	2,229	91,011	85,935	3,492	82,443	5,076	5.6	61.8
1975	153,449	94,793	2,180	92,613	84,783	3,380	81,403	7,830	8.5	61.8
1976	156,048	96,917	2,144	94,773	87,485	3,297	84,188	7,288	7.7	62.1

See footnotes at end of table.

TABLE B–27.—*Noninstitutional population and the labor force, 1929–76*—Continued

[Monthly data seasonally adjusted, except as noted]

Year or month	Nonin-stitu-tional popu-lation[1]	Total labor force (includ-ing Armed Forces)	Armed Forces[1]	Civilian labor force					Unem-ploy-ment rate (percent of civilian labor force)	Labor force partici-pation rate (total labor force as percent of non-institu-tional popu-lation)
				Total	Employment			Unem-ploy-ment		
					Total	Agri-cul-tural	Non-agri-cul-tural			
	Thousands of persons 16 years of age and over								Percent	
1975: Jan	152,230	94,146	2,193	91,953	84,673	3,337	81,336	7,280	7.9	61.8
Feb	152,445	93,819	2,198	91,621	84,259	3,286	80,973	7,362	8.0	61.5
Mar	152,646	94,218	2,198	92,020	84,243	3,301	80,942	7,777	8.5	61.7
Apr	152,840	94,405	2,195	92,210	84,246	3,283	80,963	7,964	8.6	61.8
May	153,051	94,970	2,181	92,789	84,475	3,535	80,940	8,314	9.0	62.1
June	153,278	94,773	2,178	92,595	84,496	3,361	81,135	8,099	8.7	61.8
July	153,585	95,103	2,186	92,917	84,856	3,435	81,421	8,061	8.7	61.9
Aug	153,824	95,220	2,185	93,035	85,114	3,417	81,697	7,921	8.5	61.9
Sept	154,052	95,296	2,170	93,126	85,115	3,506	81,609	8,011	8.6	61.9
Oct	154,256	95,299	2,164	93,135	85,087	3,389	81,698	8,048	8.6	61.8
Nov	154,476	95,180	2,155	93,025	85,212	3,315	81,897	7,813	8.4	61.6
Dec	154,700	95,305	2,157	93,148	85,443	3,255	82,188	7,705	8.3	61.6
1976: Jan	154,915	95,613	2,140	93,473	86,226	3,305	82,921	7,247	7.8	61.7
Feb	155,106	95,743	2,146	93,597	86,471	3,198	83,273	7,126	7.6	61.7
Mar	155,325	96,009	2,148	93,862	86,845	3,215	83,630	7,017	7.5	61.8
Apr	155,516	96,520	2,144	94,376	87,329	3,398	83,931	7,047	7.5	62.1
May	155,711	96,693	2,142	94,551	87,640	3,332	84,308	6,911	7.3	62.1
June	155,925	96,841	2,137	94,704	87,533	3,313	84,220	7,171	7.6	62.1
July	156,142	97,329	2,140	95,189	87,783	3,333	84,450	7,406	7.8	62.3
Aug	156,367	97,498	2,147	95,351	87,834	3,372	84,462	7,517	7.9	62.4
Sept	156,595	97,387	2,145	95,242	87,794	3,278	84,516	7,448	7.8	62.2
Oct	156,788	97,449	2,147	95,302	87,738	3,310	84,428	7,564	7.9	62.2
Nov	157,006	98,020	2,149	95,871	88,220	3,248	84,972	7,651	8.0	62.4
Dec	157,176	98,106	2,146	95,960	88,441	3,257	85,184	7,519	7.8	62.4

[1] Not seasonally adjusted.
[2] Not strictly comparable with earlier data due to population adjustments as follows: Beginning 1953, introduction of 1950 Census data added about 600,000 to population and about 350,000 to labor force, total employment, and agricultural employment. Beginning 1960, inclusion of Alaska and Hawaii added about 500,000 to population, about 300,000 to labor force, and about 240,000 to nonagricultural employment. Beginning 1962, introduction of 1960 Census data reduced population by about 50,000 and labor force and employment by about 200,000. Beginning 1972, introduction of 1970 Census data added about 800,000 to civilian noninstitutional population and about 333,000 to labor force and employment. A subsequent adjustment based on 1970 Census in March 1973 added 60,000 to labor force and to employment. Overall categories of the labor force other than those noted were not appreciably affected.

Note.—Labor force data in Tables B–27 through B–30 are based on household interviews and relate to the calendar week including the 12th of the month. For definitions of terms, area samples used, historical comparability of the data, comparability with other series, etc., see "Employment and Earnings."

Source: Department of Labor, Bureau of Labor Statistics.

TABLE B-28.—*Civilian employment and unemployment by sex and age 1947-76*

[Thousands of persons 16 years of age and over; monthly data seasonally adjusted]

Year or month	Employment Total	Males Total	Males 16-19 years	Males 20 years and over	Females Total	Females 16-19 years	Females 20 years and over	Unemployment Total	Males Total	Males 16-19 years	Males 20 years and over	Females Total	Females 16-19 years	Females 20 years and over
1947___	57,038	40,994	2,218	38,776	16,045	1,691	14,354	2,311	1,692	270	1,422	619	144	475
1948___	58,343	41,726	2,345	39,382	16,618	1,683	14,937	2,276	1,559	255	1,305	717	152	564
1949___	57,651	40,926	2,124	38,803	16,723	1,588	15,137	3,637	2,572	352	2,219	1,065	223	841
1950___	58,918	41,580	2,186	39,394	17,340	1,517	15,824	3,288	2,239	318	1,922	1,049	195	854
1951___	59,961	41,780	2,156	39,626	18,182	1,611	16,570	2,055	1,221	191	1,029	834	145	689
1952___	60,250	41,684	2,106	39,578	18,570	1,612	16,958	1,883	1,185	205	980	698	140	559
1953 [1]__	61,179	42,431	2,135	40,296	18,750	1,584	17,164	1,834	1,202	184	1,019	632	123	510
1954___	60,109	41,620	1,985	39,634	18,490	1,490	17,000	3,532	2,344	310	2,035	1,188	191	997
1955___	62,170	42,621	2,095	40,526	19,550	1,548	18,002	2,852	1,854	274	1,580	998	176	823
1956___	63,799	43,380	2,164	41,216	20,422	1,654	18,767	2,750	1,711	269	1,442	1,039	209	832
1957___	64,071	43,357	2,117	41,239	20,714	1,663	19,052	2,859	1,841	299	1,541	1,018	197	821
1958___	63,036	42,423	2,012	40,411	20,613	1,570	19,043	4,602	3,098	416	2,681	1,504	262	1,242
1959___	64,630	43,466	2,198	41,267	21,164	1,640	19,524	3,740	2,420	398	2,022	1,320	256	1,063
1960 [1]__	65,778	43,904	2,360	41,543	21,874	1,769	20,105	3,852	2,486	425	2,060	1,366	286	1,080
1961___	65,746	43,656	2,314	41,342	22,090	1,793	20,296	4,714	2,997	479	2,518	1,717	349	1,368
1962 [1]__	66,702	44,177	2,362	41,815	22,525	1,833	20,693	3,911	2,423	407	2,016	1,488	313	1,175
1963___	67,762	44,657	2,406	42,251	23,105	1,849	21,257	4,070	2,472	500	1,971	1,598	383	1,216
1964___	69,305	45,474	2,587	42,886	23,831	1,929	21,903	3,786	2,205	487	1,718	1,581	386	1,195
1965___	71,088	46,340	2,918	43,422	24,748	2,118	22,630	3,366	1,914	479	1,435	1,452	395	1,056
1966___	72,895	46,919	3,252	43,668	25,976	2,469	23,510	2,875	1,551	432	1,120	1,324	404	921
1967___	74,372	47,479	3,186	44,293	26,893	2,497	24,397	2,975	1,508	448	1,060	1,468	391	1,078
1968___	75,920	48,114	3,255	44,859	27,807	2,525	25,281	2,817	1,419	427	993	1,397	412	985
1969___	77,902	48,818	3,430	45,388	29,084	2,686	26,397	2,832	1,403*	441	963	1,429	412	1,016
1970___	78,627	48,960	3,407	45,553	29,667	2,734	26,933	4,088	2,235	599	1,636	1,853	506	1,347
1971___	79,120	49,245	3,470	45,775	29,875	2,725	27,149	4,993	2,776	691	2,086	2,217	567	1,650
1972 [1]__	81,702	50,630	3,750	46,880	31,072	2,972	28,100	4,840	2,635	707	1,928	2,205	595	1,610
1973 [1]__	84,409	51,963	4,017	47,946	32,446	3,219	29,228	4,304	2,240	647	1,594	2,064	579	1,485
1974___	85,936	52,519	4,074	48,445	33,417	3,329	30,088	5,076	2,668	749	1,918	2,408	660	1,748
1975___	84,783	51,230	3,803	47,427	33,553	3,243	30,310	7,830	4,385	957	3,428	3,445	795	2,649
1976___	87,485	52,391	3,904	48,486	35,095	3,365	31,730	7,288	3,968	928	3,041	3,320	773	2,546
1975:														
Jan__	84,673	51,399	3,850	47,549	33,274	3,298	29,976	7,280	3,919	924	2,995	3,361	802	2,559
Feb__	84,259	51,192	3,806	47,386	33,067	3,232	29,835	7,362	4,070	943	3,127	3,292	755	2,537
Mar__	84,243	51,067	3,805	47,262	33,176	3,201	29,975	7,777	4,289	951	3,338	3,488	805	2,683
Apr__	84,246	50,960	3,753	47,207	33,286	3,223	30,063	7,964	4,445	972	3,473	3,519	751	2,768
May__	84,475	51,138	3,851	47,287	33,337	3,244	30,093	8,314	4,665	955	3,710	3,649	855	2,794
June__	84,496	51,024	3,758	47,266	33,472	3,245	30,227	8,099	4,602	1,066	3,536	3,497	769	2,728
July__	84,856	51,267	3,799	47,468	33,589	3,209	30,380	8,061	4,613	1,009	3,604	3,448	800	2,648
Aug__	85,114	51,365	3,775	47,590	33,749	3,245	30,504	7,921	4,458	988	3,470	3,463	825	2,638
Sept__	85,115	51,296	3,820	47,476	33,819	3,272	30,547	8,011	4,615	932	3,683	3,396	799	2,597
Oct__	85,087	51,244	3,785	47,459	33,843	3,221	30,622	8,048	4,598	935	3,663	3,450	802	2,648
Nov__	85,212	51,324	3,812	47,512	33,888	3,228	30,660	7,813	4,430	892	3,538	3,383	765	2,618
Dec__	85,443	51,401	3,794	47,607	34,042	3,275	30,767	7,705	4,256	922	3,334	3,449	821	2,628
1976:														
Jan__	86,226	51,789	3,848	47,941	34,437	3,296	31,141	7,247	3,949	946	3,003	3,298	779	2,519
Feb__	86,471	51,942	3,863	48,079	34,529	3,301	31,228	7,126	3,858	920	2,938	3,268	775	2,493
Mar__	86,845	52,078	3,877	48,201	34,767	3,353	31,414	7,017	3,798	924	2,874	3,219	775	2,444
Apr__	87,329	52,397	3,942	48,455	34,932	3,386	31,546	7,047	3,812	990	2,822	3,235	768	2,467
May__	87,640	52,490	3,948	48,542	35,150	3,479	31,671	6,911	3,830	937	2,893	3,081	753	2,328
June__	87,533	52,332	3,889	48,443	35,201	3,400	31,801	7,171	3,931	882	3,049	3,240	763	2,477
July__	87,783	52,507	3,963	48,544	35,276	3,423	31,853	7,406	4,020	889	3,131	3,386	752	2,634
Aug__	87,834	52,596	3,958	48,638	35,238	3,355	31,883	7,517	3,968	908	3,060	3,549	870	2,679
Sept__	87,794	52,546	3,845	48,701	35,248	3,342	31,906	7,448	4,060	910	3,150	3,388	754	2,634
Oct__	87,738	52,576	3,892	48,684	35,162	3,351	31,811	7,564	4,178	950	3,228	3,386	753	2,633
Nov__	88,220	52,643	3,870	48,773	35,577	3,369	32,208	7,651	4,244	951	3,293	3,407	767	2,640
Dec__	88,441	52,799	3,940	48,859	35,642	3,302	32,340	7,519	4,152	933	3,219	3,367	769	2,598

[1] See footnote 2, Table B-27.

Note.—See Note, Table B-27.

Source: Department of Labor, Bureau of Labor Statistics.

TABLE B-29.—*Selected unemployment rates, 1948-76*

[Percent [1]; monthly data seasonally adjusted]

Year or month	All workers	By sex and age			By color		By selected groups					Labor force time lost[5]
		Both sexes 16-19 years	Males 20 years and over	Females 20 years and over	White	Black and other	Experienced wage and salary workers	Household heads	Married men[2]	Full-time workers[3]	Blue-collar workers[4]	
1948	3.8	9.2	3.2	3.6	3.5	5.9	4.3	------	------	------	4.2	------
1949	5.9	13.4	5.4	5.3	5.6	8.9	6.8	------	3.5	5.4	8.0	------
1950	5.3	12.2	4.7	5.1	4.9	9.0	6.0	------	4.6	5.0	7.2	------
1951	3.3	8.2	2.5	4.0	3.1	5.3	3.7	------	1.5	2.6	3.9	------
1952	3.0	8.5	2.4	3.2	2.8	5.4	3.3	------	1.4	2.5	3.6	------
1953	2.9	7.6	2.5	2.9	2.7	4.5	3.2	------	1.7	------	3.4	------
1954	5.5	12.6	4.9	5.5	5.0	9.9	6.2	------	4.0	5.2	7.2	------
1955	4.4	11.0	3.8	4.4	3.9	8.7	4.8	------	2.8	3.8	5.8	4.8
1956	4.1	11.1	3.4	4.2	3.6	8.3	4.4	------	2.6	3.7	5.1	5.1
1957	4.3	11.6	3.6	4.1	3.8	7.9	4.6	------	2.8	4.0	6.2	5.3
1958	6.8	15.9	6.2	6.1	6.1	12.6	7.2	------	5.1	7.2	10.2	8.1
1959	5.5	14.6	4.7	5.2	4.8	10.7	5.7	------	3.6	------	7.6	6.6
1960	5.5	14.7	4.7	5.1	4.9	10.2	5.7	------	3.7	------	7.8	6.7
1961	6.7	16.8	5.7	6.3	6.0	12.4	6.8	------	4.6	6.7	9.2	8.0
1962	5.5	14.7	4.6	5.4	4.9	10.9	5.6	------	3.6	------	7.4	6.7
1963	5.7	17.2	4.5	5.4	5.0	10.8	5.5	3.7	3.4	5.5	7.3	6.4
1964	5.2	16.2	3.9	5.2	4.6	9.6	5.0	3.2	2.8	4.9	6.3	5.8
1965	4.5	14.8	3.2	4.5	4.1	8.1	4.3	2.7	2.4	4.2	5.3	5.0
1966	3.8	12.8	2.5	3.8	3.4	7.3	3.5	2.2	1.9	3.5	4.2	4.2
1967	3.8	12.8	2.3	4.2	3.4	7.4	3.6	2.1	1.8	3.4	4.4	4.2
1968	3.6	12.7	2.2	3.8	3.2	6.7	3.4	1.9	1.6	3.1	4.1	4.0
1969	3.5	12.2	2.1	3.7	3.1	6.4	3.3	1.8	1.5	3.1	3.9	3.9
1970	4.9	15.2	3.5	4.8	4.5	8.2	4.8	2.9	2.6	4.5	6.2	5.3
1971	5.9	16.9	4.4	5.7	5.4	9.9	5.7	3.6	3.2	5.5	7.4	6.4
1972	5.6	16.2	4.0	5.4	5.0	10.0	5.3	3.3	2.8	5.1	6.5	6.0
1973	4.9	14.5	3.2	4.8	4.3	8.9	4.5	2.9	2.3	4.3	5.3	5.2
1974	5.6	16.0	3.8	5.5	5.0	9.9	5.3	3.3	2.7	5.1	6.7	6.1
1975	8.5	19.9	6.7	8.0	7.8	13.9	8.2	5.8	5.1	8.1	11.7	9.1
1976	7.7	19.0	5.9	7.4	7.0	13.1	7.3	5.1	4.2	7.3	9.4	8.3
1975: Jan	7.9	19.5	5.9	7.9	7.3	13.0	7.7	5.2	4.4	7.5	10.6	8.7
Feb	8.0	19.4	6.2	7.8	7.3	13.3	7.7	5.3	4.7	7.7	10.7	8.7
Mar	8.5	20.0	6.6	8.2	7.8	13.9	8.2	5.7	5.0	8.1	12.0	9.2
Apr	8.6	19.8	6.9	8.4	7.9	14.2	8.5	5.9	5.4	8.4	12.4	9.3
May	9.0	20.3	7.3	8.5	8.3	14.3	8.9	6.2	5.7	8.7	12.8	9.7
June	8.7	20.8	7.0	8.3	8.1	14.1	8.6	6.1	5.5	8.4	12.5	9.1
July	8.7	20.5	7.1	8.0	8.0	13.5	8.4	6.0	5.4	8.4	12.4	9.1
Aug	8.5	20.5	6.8	8.0	7.8	14.3	8.3	5.8	5.3	8.2	12.0	9.0
Sept	8.6	19.6	7.2	7.8	7.8	14.5	8.4	6.0	5.4	8.4	12.0	9.2
Oct	8.6	19.9	7.2	8.0	7.9	14.2	8.4	6.0	5.3	8.4	11.7	9.2
Nov	8.4	19.1	6.9	7.9	7.7	13.8	8.2	5.7	5.0	8.2	11.2	9.1
Dec	8.3	19.8	6.5	7.9	7.6	13.6	8.0	5.6	4.8	7.9	10.6	8.8
1976: Jan	7.8	19.4	5.9	7.5	7.1	13.2	7.5	5.2	4.1	7.3	9.4	8.4
Feb	7.6	19.1	5.8	7.4	6.8	13.6	7.3	5.0	4.2	7.1	9.3	8.1
Mar	7.5	19.0	5.6	7.2	6.8	12.6	7.1	5.0	4.1	7.0	9.1	8.1
Apr	7.5	19.3	5.5	7.3	6.8	13.0	7.1	4.8	4.0	7.0	8.9	8.1
May	7.3	18.5	5.6	6.8	6.7	12.3	7.1	4.9	4.1	6.9	9.0	8.1
June	7.6	18.4	5.9	7.2	6.8	13.4	7.2	5.1	4.3	7.2	9.3	7.9
July	7.8	18.2	6.1	7.6	7.1	12.9	7.4	5.3	4.4	7.3	9.7	8.1
Aug	7.9	19.6	5.9	7.8	7.1	13.6	7.5	5.2	4.3	7.5	9.8	8.4
Sept	7.8	18.8	6.1	7.6	7.2	12.8	7.4	5.5	4.5	7.5	9.8	8.4
Oct	7.9	19.0	6.2	7.6	7.2	13.4	7.5	5.4	4.4	7.6	9.8	8.6
Nov	8.0	19.2	6.3	7.6	7.3	13.5	7.6	5.3	4.5	7.6	9.7	8.6
Dec	7.8	19.0	6.2	7.4	7.1	13.4	7.4	5.1	4.3	7.5	9.6	8.4

[1] Unemployment as percent of civilian labor force in group specified, except as noted.
[2] Married men living with their wives. Data for 1949 and 1951-54 are for April; 1950, for March.
[3] Data for 1949-61 are for May.
[4] Includes craft and kindred workers, operatives, and nonfarm laborers. Data for 1948-57 are based on data for January, April, July, and October.
[5] Aggregate hours lost by the unemployed and persons on part-time for economic reasons as a percent of potentially available labor force hours.

Note.—See footnote 2 and Note, Table B-27.

Source: Department of Labor, Bureau of Labor Statistics.

TABLE B–30.—*Unemployment by duration, 1947–76*

[Monthly data seasonally adjusted [1]]

Year or month	Total unemployment	Duration of unemployment				Average (mean) duration in weeks
		Less than 5 weeks	5–14 weeks	15–26 weeks	27 weeks and over	
	Thousands of persons 16 years of age and over					
1947	2,311	1,210	704	234	164	-------
1948	2,276	1,300	669	193	116	8.6
1949	3,637	1,756	1,194	428	256	10.0
1950	3,288	1,450	1,055	425	357	12.1
1951	2,055	1,177	574	166	137	9.7
1952	1,883	1,135	516	148	84	8.4
1953	1,834	1,142	482	132	78	8.0
1954	3,532	1,605	1,116	495	317	11.8
1955	2,852	1,335	815	366	336	13.0
1956	2,750	1,412	805	301	232	11.3
1957	2,859	1,408	891	321	239	10.5
1958	4,602	1,753	1,396	785	667	13.9
1959	3,740	1,585	1,114	469	571	14.4
1960	3,852	1,719	1,176	503	454	12.8
1961	4,714	1,806	1,376	728	804	15.6
1962	3,911	1,663	1,134	534	585	14.7
1963	4,070	1,751	1,231	535	553	14.0
1964	3,786	1,697	1,117	491	482	13.3
1965	3,366	1,628	983	404	351	11.8
1966	2,875	1,573	779	287	239	10.4
1967	2,975	1,634	893	271	177	8.8
1968	2,817	1,594	810	256	156	8.4
1969	2,832	1,629	827	242	133	7.9
1970	4,088	2,137	1,289	427	235	8.7
1971	4,993	2,234	1,578	665	517	11.3
1972	4,840	2,223	1,459	597	562	12.0
1973	4,304	2,196	1,296	475	337	10.0
1974	5,076	2,567	1,572	563	373	9.7
1975	7,830	2,894	2,452	1,290	1,193	14.1
1976	7,288	2,790	2,159	1,003	1,336	15.8
1975: Jan	7,280	3,196	2,578	939	627	10.8
Feb	7,362	2,818	2,536	1,122	721	11.7
Mar	7,777	3,198	2,558	1,234	767	11.5
Apr	7,964	2,936	2,621	1,404	952	12.9
May	8,314	3,038	2,621	1,515	1,071	13.5
June	8,099	2,829	2,465	1,467	1,251	15.3
July	8,061	2,850	2,200	1,535	1,344	14.9
Aug	7,921	2,783	2,445	1,405	1,418	15.4
Sept	8,011	2,839	2,419	1,341	1,581	16.1
Oct	8,048	2,960	2,448	1,261	1,473	15.5
Nov	7,813	2,662	2,373	1,253	1,696	16.8
Dec	7,705	2,651	2,200	1,349	1,632	16.9
1976: Jan	7,247	2,635	2,065	1,165	1,616	16.9
Feb	7,126	2,637	1,890	968	1,563	16.3
Mar	7,017	2,630	1,915	870	1,455	16.0
Apr	7,047	2,988	1,902	715	1,388	15.8
May	6,911	2,795	1,978	850	1,192	15.1
June	7,171	2,730	2,215	902	1,271	16.9
July	7,406	2,931	2,093	1,058	1,189	15.6
Aug	7,517	2,867	2,433	1,127	1,214	15.4
Sept	7,448	2,852	2,426	1,118	1,193	15.4
Oct	7,564	2,952	2,367	1,094	1,266	15.3
Nov	7,651	2,759	2,494	1,188	1,329	15.5
Dec	7,519	2,765	2,319	1,130	1,384	15.6

[1] Because of independent seasonal adjustment of the various series, detail will not add to totals.

Note.—See footnote 2 and Note, Table B–27.

Source: Department of Labor, Bureau of Labor Statistics.

TABLE B-31—*Unemployment insurance programs, selected data, 1946-76*

Year or month	All programs			State programs					
	Covered employment [1]	Insured unemployment (weekly average) [2][3]	Total benefits paid (millions of dollars) [2][4]	Insured unemployment	Initial claims	Exhaustions [5]	Insured unemployment as percent of covered employment	Benefits paid	
								Total (millions of dollars) [4]	Average weekly check (dollars) [6]
	Thousands			Weekly average; thousands					
1946	31,856	2,804	2,878.5	1,295	189	38	4.3	1,094.9	18.50
1947	33,876	1,793	1,785.5	997	187	24	3.1	775.1	17.88
1948	34,646	1,446	1,328.7	980	200	20	3.0	789.9	19.03
1949	33,098	2,474	2,269.8	1,973	340	37	6.2	1,736.0	20.43
1950	34,308	1,605	1,467.6	1,513	236	36	4.6	1,373.1	20.76
1951	36,334	1,000	862.9	969	208	16	2.8	840.4	21.09
1952	37,006	1,069	1,043.5	1,044	215	18	2.9	998.2	22.79
1953	38,072	1,067	1,050.6	990	218	15	2.8	962.2	23.58
1954	36,622	2,051	2,291.8	1,870	304	34	5.2	2,026.9	24.93
1955	40,018	1,399	1,560.2	1,265	226	25	3.5	1,350.3	25.04
1956	42,751	1,323	1,540.6	1,215	227	20	3.2	1,380.7	27.02
1957	43,436	1,571	1,913.0	1,446	270	23	3.6	1,733.9	28.17
1958	44,411	2,269	4,290.6	2,526	369	50	6.4	3,512.7	30.58
1959	45,728	2,099	2,854.3	1,684	277	33	4.4	2,279.0	30.41
1960	46,334	2,071	3,022.8	1,908	331	31	4.8	2,726.7	32.87
1961	46,266	2,994	4,358.1	2,290	350	46	5.6	3,422.7	33.80
1962	47,776	1,946	3,145.1	1,783	302	32	4.4	2,675.4	34.56
1963	48,434	[7] 1,973	3,025.9	[7] 1,806	[7] 298	30	4.3	2,774.7	35.27
1964	49,637	1,753	2,749.2	1,605	268	26	3.8	2,522.1	35.92
1965	51,580	1,450	2,360.4	1,328	232	21	3.0	2,166.0	37.19
1966	54,739	1,129	1,890.9	1,061	203	15	2.3	1,771.3	39.75
1967	56,342	1,270	2,221.5	1,205	226	17	2.5	2,092.3	41.25
1968	57,977	1,187	2,191.0	1,111	201	16	2.2	2,031.6	43.43
1969	59,999	1,177	2,298.6	1,101	200	16	2.1	2,127.9	46.17
1970	59,526	2,070	4,209.3	1,805	296	25	3.4	3,848.5	50.34
1971	59,375	2,608	6,214.9	2,150	295	39	4.1	4,957.0	53.23
1972	66,458	2,192	5,491.1	1,848	261	35	3.5	4,471.0	56.76
1973	69,897	1,793	4,517.3	1,632	246	29	2.7	4,007.6	59.00
1974	72,451	2,558	6,933.9	2,262	363	37	3.5	5,974.9	64.25
1975ᵖ	[8] 71,037	4,943	16,802.4	3,992	478	81	6.0	11,754.7	70.23
1976ᵖ		3,822		2,968	382		4.5		
				*	*		*		
1975: Jan		5,213	1,256.6	3,603	543	50	5.5	1,128.2	67.83
Feb		5,751	1,312.3	3,832	530	58	5.8	1,164.2	68.73
Mar		5,886	1,490.4	4,125	534	66	6.3	1,290.6	69.07
Apr		5,647	1,539.7	4,271	508	84	6.4	1,301.2	69.08
May		5,202	1,395.2	4,480	504	92	6.7	1,145.1	69.33
June		4,892	1,256.7	4,331	494	104	6.5	984.0	69.58
July		4,979	1,365.5	4,210	456	106	6.3	1,037.1	71.56
Aug		4,576	1,218.4	4,130	473	98	6.2	891.4	71.06
Sept		4,238	1,126.5	4,070	463	84	6.1	779.4	71.32
Oct		4,037	1,115.8	3,940	445	76	5.9	759.5	72.37
Nov		4,120	972.5	3,576	392	73	5.4	677.8	73.11
Dec		4,461	1,231.9	3,242	362	73	4.9	893.2	73.64
1976: Jan		4,962	1,344.9	2,961	371	76	4.5	1,018.6	74.71
Feb		4,721	1,231.9	2,859	343	74	4.3	945.1	75.66
Mar		4,366	1,334.4	2,759	350	71	4.2	1,018.2	75.69
Apr		3,917	1,150.7	2,717	361	69	4.1	869.6	75.61
May		3,564	945.7	2,862	398	66	4.4	698.7	74.79
June		3,457	981.7	2,947	397	64	4.5	719.3	74.16
July		3,642	960.5	3,086	403	61	4.7	711.5	73.66
Aug		3,446	951.5	3,203	417	59	4.9	698.7	73.83
Septᵖ		3,236	892.8	3,261	427	56	5.0	640.8	74.19
Octᵖ		3,227	821.6	3,328	437	53	5.1	610.5	75.50
Novᵖ		3,453		3,165	385		4.8		
Decᵖ				2,933	356		4.5		

* Monthly data are seasonally adjusted.
[1] Includes persons under the State, UCFE (Federal employee, effective January 1955), and RRB (Railroad Retirement Board) programs. Beginning October 1958, also includes the UCX program (unemployment compensation for ex-servicemen).
[2] Includes State, UCFE, RR, UCX, UCV (unemployment compensation for veterans, October 1952–January 1960), and SRA (Servicemen's Readjustment Act, September 1944–September 1951) programs. Also includes Federal and State extended benefit programs. Does not include FSB (Federal supplemental benefits) and SUA (special unemployment assistance) programs.
[3] Covered workers who have completed at least 1 week of unemployment.
[4] Annual data are net amounts and monthly data are gross amounts.
[5] Individuals receiving final payments in benefit year.
[6] For total unemployment only.
[7] Programs include Puerto Rican sugarcane workers for initial claims and insured unemployment beginning July 1963.
[8] Latest data available for all programs combined. Workers covered by State programs account for about 92 percent of the total.

Source: Department of Labor, Employment and Training Administration.

TABLE B–32.—*Wage and salary workers in nonagricultural establishments, 1929–76*

[Thousands of persons; monthly data seasonally adjusted]

| Year or month | Total wage and salary workers | Manufacturing | | | Mining | Contract construction | Transportation and public utilities | Wholesale and retail trade | Finance, insurance, and real estate | Services | Government | |
		Total	Durable goods	Nondurable goods							Federal	State and local
1929	31,339	10,702	--------	-------	1,087	1,497	3,916	6,123	1,509	3,440	533	2,532
1933	23,711	7,397	--------	-------	744	809	2,672	4,755	1,295	2,873	565	2,601
1939	30,618	10,278	4,715	5,564	854	1,150	2,936	6,426	1,462	3,517	905	3,090
1940	32,376	10,985	5,363	5,622	925	1,294	3,038	6,750	1,502	3,681	996	3,206
1941	36,554	13,192	6,968	6,225	957	1,790	3,274	7,210	1,549	3,921	1,340	3,320
1942	40,125	15,280	8,823	6,458	992	2,170	3,460	7,118	1,538	4,084	2,213	3,270
1943	42,452	17,602	11,084	6,518	925	1,567	3,647	6,982	1,502	4,148	2,905	3,174
1944	41,883	17,328	10,856	6,472	892	1,094	3,829	7,058	1,476	4,163	2,928	3,116
1945	40,394	15,524	9,074	6,450	836	1,132	3,906	7,314	1,497	4,241	2,808	3,137
1946	41,674	14,703	7,742	6,962	862	1,661	4,061	8,376	1,697	4,719	2,254	3,341
1947	43,881	15,545	8,385	7,159	955	1,982	4,166	8,955	1,754	5,050	1,892	3,582
1948	44,891	15,582	8,326	7,256	994	2,169	4,189	9,272	1,829	5,206	1,863	3,787
1949	43,778	14,441	7,489	6,953	930	2,165	4,001	9,264	1,857	5,264	1,908	3,948
1950	45,222	15,241	8,094	7,147	901	2,333	4,034	9,386	1,919	5,382	1,928	4,098
1951	47,849	16,393	9,089	7,304	929	2,603	4,226	9,742	1,991	5,576	2,302	4,087
1952	48,825	16,632	9,349	7,284	898	2,634	4,248	10,004	2,069	5,730	2,420	4,188
1953	50,232	17,549	10,110	7,438	866	2,623	4,290	10,247	2,146	5,867	2,305	4,340
1954	49,022	16,314	9,129	7,185	791	2,612	4,084	10,235	2,234	6,002	2,188	4,563
1955	50,675	16,882	9,541	7,340	792	2,802	4,141	10,535	2,335	6,274	2,187	4,727
1956	52,408	17,243	9,834	7,409	822	2,999	4,244	10,858	2,429	6,536	2,209	5,069
1957	52,894	17,174	9,856	7,319	828	2,923	4,241	10,886	2,477	6,749	2,217	5,399
1958	51,363	15,945	8,830	7,116	751	2,778	3,976	10,750	2,519	6,806	2,191	5,648
1959	53,313	16,675	9,373	7,303	732	2,960	4,011	11,127	2,594	7,130	2,233	5,850
1960	54,234	16,796	9,459	7,336	712	2,885	4,004	11,391	2,669	7,423	2,270	6,083
1961	54,042	16,326	9,070	7,256	672	2,816	3,903	11,337	2,731	7,664	2,279	6,315
1962	55,596	16,853	9,480	7,373	650	2,902	3,906	11,566	2,800	8,028	2,340	6,550
1963	56,702	16,995	9,616	7,380	635	2,963	3,903	11,778	2,877	8,325	2,358	6,868
1964	58,331	17,274	9,816	7,458	634	3,050	3,951	12,160	2,957	8,709	2,348	7,248
1965	60,815	18,062	10,406	7,656	632	3,186	4,036	12,716	3,023	9,087	2,378	7,696
1966	63,955	19,214	11,284	7,930	627	3,275	4,151	13,245	3,100	9,551	2,564	8,227
1967	65,857	19,447	11,439	8,008	613	3,208	4,261	13,606	3,225	10,099	2,719	8,679
1968	67,951	19,781	11,626	8,155	606	3,306	4,311	14,099	3,381	10,622	2,737	9,109
1969	70,442	20,167	11,895	8,272	619	3,525	4,435	14,704	3,562	11,228	2,758	9,444
1970	70,920	19,349	11,195	8,154	623	3,536	4,504	15,040	3,687	11,621	2,731	9,830
1971	71,222	18,572	10,597	7,975	609	3,639	4,457	15,352	3,802	11,903	2,696	10,192
1972	73,714	19,090	11,006	8,084	625	3,831	4,517	15,975	3,943	12,392	2,684	10,656
1973	76,896	20,068	11,839	8,229	644	4,015	4,644	16,674	4,091	13,021	2,663	11,075
1974	78,413	20,046	11,895	8,151	694	3,957	4,696	17,017	4,208	13,617	2,724	11,453
1975	76,985	18,347	10,679	7,668	745	3,457	4,498	16,947	4,223	13,995	2,748	12,025
1976ᵖ	79,115	18,954	11,028	7,926	783	3,370	4,507	17,490	4,316	14,607	2,736	12,352

See footnotes at end of table.

TABLE B–32.—*Wage and salary workers in nonagricultural establishments,*
1929–76—Continued

[All employees; thousands of persons; monthly data seasonally adjusted]

| Year or month | Total wage and salary workers | Manufacturing | | | Mining | Contract construction | Transportation and public utilities | Wholesale and retail trade | Finance, insurance, and real estate | Services | Government | |
		Total	Durable goods	Nondurable goods							Federal	State and local
1974: Jan___	78,033	20,305	12,037	8,268	673	4,050	4,705	16,864	4,172	13,313	2,683	11,268
Feb___	78,205	20,220	11,967	8,253	679	4,121	4,716	16,878	4,186	13,400	2,699	11,306
Mar___	78,275	20,196	11,957	8,239	680	4,098	4,711	16,911	4,196	13,453	2,702	11,328
Apr___	78,423	20,235	12,009	8,226	688	4,062	4,707	16,968	4,202	13,488	2,711	11,362
May___	78,559	20,220	11,989	8,231	692	4,037	4,708	17,029	4,209	13,573	2,717	11,374
Jun___	78,628	20,234	12,020	8,214	694	3,985	4,704	17,051	4,210	13,621	2,723	11,406
July___	78,660	20,209	12,026	8,183	700	3,921	4,699	17,111	4,210	13,656	2,729	11,425
Aug___	78,709	20,128	11,954	8,174	703	3,934	4,703	17,125	4,217	13,696	2,734	11,469
Sep___	78,774	20,074	11,927	8,147	707	3,891	4,683	17,139	4,220	13,753	2,742	11,565
Oct___	78,718	19,938	11,856	8,082	714	3,869	4,686	17,142	4,224	13,797	2,740	11,608
Nov___	78,339	19,635	11,658	7,977	718	3,818	4,674	17,049	4,226	13,822	2,740	11,657
Dec___	77,703	19,183	11,353	7,830	684	3,759	4,659	16,939	4,225	13,833	2,738	11,683
1975: Jan___	77,300	18,784	11,092	7,692	725	3,732	4,599	16,903	4,219	13,857	2,736	11,745
Feb___	76,804	18,375	10,816	7,559	728	3,596	4,556	16,878	4,210	13,865	2,735	11,861
Mar___	76,518	18,237	10,737	7,500	732	3,483	4,511	16,864	4,207	13,864	2,735	11,885
Apr___	76,491	18,183	10,650	7,533	734	3,455	4,508	16,856	4,205	13,878	2,735	11,937
May___	76,577	18,192	10,607	7,585	741	3,446	4,496	16,873	4,208	13,903	2,736	11,982
Jun___	76,444	18,131	10,539	7,592	743	3,405	4,474	16,882	4,206	13,885	2,741	11,977
July__	76,706	18,115	10,488	7,627	745	3,404	4,473	16,949	4,211	13,990	2,748	12,071
Aug___	76,988	18,272	10,578	7,694	750	3,412	4,466	16,968	4,218	14,050	2,753	12,099
Sep___	77,239	18,395	10,645	7,750	753	3,420	4,472	17,016	4,235	14,099	2,757	12,092
Oct___	77,470	18,452	10,644	7,808	759	3,399	4,472	17,043	4,242	14,157	2,761	12,185
Nov___	77,542	18,472	10,652	7,820	761	3,406	4,482	17,027	4,248	14,188	2,756	12,202
Dec___	77,764	18,555	10,709	7,846	766	3,392	4,477	17,084	4,260	14,229	2,753	12,248
1976: Jan___	78,142	18,704	10,810	7,894	767	3,409	4,489	17,207	4,266	14,307	2,749	12,244
Feb___	78,358	18,774	10,857	7,917	767	3,379	4,504	17,308	4,266	14,360	2,742	12,258
Mar___	78,692	18,897	10,956	7,941	773	3,380	4,507	14,399	4,276	14,422	2,735	12,303
Apr___	79,011	19,008	11,016	7,992	775	3,413	4,510	17,465	4,289	14,498	2,733	12,320
May___	79,006	19,000	11,062	7,938	776	3,393	4,503	17,461	4,282	14,529	2,730	12,332
Jun___	79,043	18,984	11,059	7,925	781	3,375	4,482	17,460	4,301	14,571	2,728	12,361
July___	79,183	18,945	11,034	7,911	791	3,382	4,508	17,531	4,312	14,623	2,723	12,368
Aug___	79,278	18,979	11,083	7,896	752	3,349	4,501	17,554	4,312	14,709	2,732	12,390
Sep___	79,572	19,100	11,146	7,954	798	3,330	4,528	17,625	4,338	14,758	2,728	12,367
Oct___	79,467	18,941	11,018	7,923	800	3,340	4,506	17,610	4,359	14,781	2,730	12,400
Nov ᴾ_	79,700	19,057	11,134	7,923	808	3,353	4,510	17,585	4,381	14,844	2,734	12,428
Dec ᴾ_	79,957	19,093	11,181	7,912	806	3,349	4,537	17,685	4,403	14,897	2,736	12,451

Note.—Data in Tables B–32 through B–34 are based on reports from employing establishments and relate to full- and part-time wage and salary workers in nonagricultural establishments who worked during, or received pay for, any part of the pay period which includes the 12th of the month.

Not comparable with labor force data (Tables B–27 through B–30), which include proprietors, self-employed persons, domestic servants, and unpaid family workers; which count persons as employed when they are not at work because of industrial disputes, bad weather, etc.; and which are based on a sample of the working-age population, whereas the estimates in this table are based on reports from employing establishments.

For description and details of the various establishment data, see "Employment and Earnings."

Source: Department of Labor, Bureau of Labor Statistics.

TABLE B–33.—*Average weekly hours and hourly earnings in selected private nonagricultural industries, 1947–76*

[For production or nonsupervisory workers; monthly data seasonally adjusted]

Year or month	Average weekly hours				Average gross hourly earnings, current dollars				Adjusted hourly earnings, total private nonagricultural [3]			
									Index, 1967=100		Percent change from a year earlier [5]	
	Total private nonagricultural [1]	Manufacturing	Contract construction	Retail trade [2]	Total private nonagricultural [1]	Manufacturing	Contract construction	Retail trade [2]	Current dollars	1967 dollars [4]	Current dollars	1967 dollars
1947	40.3	40.4	38.2	40.3	$1.131	$1.217	$1.541	$0.838	42.6	63.7		
1948	40.0	40.0	38.1	40.2	1.225	1.328	1.713	.901	46.0	63.8	8.0	0.2
1949	39.4	39.1	37.7	40.4	1.275	1.378	1.792	.951	48.2	67.5	4.8	5.8
1950	39.8	40.5	37.4	40.4	1.335	1.440	1.863	.983	50.0	69.3	3.7	2.7
1951	39.9	40.6	38.1	40.4	1.45	1.56	2.02	1.06	53.7	69.0	7.4	−.4
1952	39.9	40.7	38.9	39.8	1.52	1.65	2.13	1.09	56.4	70.9	5.0	2.8
1953	39.6	40.5	37.9	39.1	1.61	1.74	2.28	1.16	59.6	74.4	5.7	4.9
1954	39.1	39.6	37.2	39.2	1.65	1.78	2.39	1.20	61.7	76.6	3.5	3.0
1955	39.6	40.7	37.1	39.0	1.71	1.86	2.45	1.25	63.7	79.4	3.2	3.7
1956	39.3	40.4	37.5	38.6	1.80	1.95	2.57	1.30	67.0	82.3	5.2	3.7
1957	38.8	39.8	37.0	38.1	1.89	2.05	2.71	1.37	70.3	83.4	4.9	1.3
1958	38.5	39.2	36.8	38.1	1.95	2.11	2.82	1.42	73.2	84.5	4.1	1.3
1959	39.0	40.3	37.0	38.2	2.02	2.19	2.93	1.47	75.8	86.8	3.6	2.7
1960	38.6	39.7	36.7	38.0	2.09	2.26	3.08	1.52	78.4	88.4	3.4	1.8
1961	38.6	39.8	36.9	37.6	2.14	2.32	3.20	1.56	80.8	90.2	3.1	2.0
1962	38.7	40.4	37.0	37.4	2.22	2.39	3.31	1.63	83.5	92.2	3.3	2.2
1963	38.8	40.5	37.3	37.3	2.28	2.46	3.41	1.68	85.9	93.7	2.9	1.6
1964	38.7	40.7	37.2	37.0	2.36	2.53	3.55	1.75	88.3	95.1	2.8	1.5
1965	38.8	41.2	37.4	36.6	2.45	2.61	3.70	1.82	91.6	97.0	3.7	2.0
1966	38.6	41.3	37.6	35.9	2.56	2.72	3.89	1.91	95.4	98.1	4.1	1.1
1967	38.0	40.6	37.7	35.3	2.68	2.83	4.11	2.01	100.0	100.0	4.8	1.9
1968	37.8	40.7	37.3	34.7	2.85	3.01	4.41	2.16	106.3	102.0	6.3	2.0
1969	37.7	40.6	37.9	34.2	3.04	3.19	4.79	2.30	113.3	103.2	6.6	1.2
1970	37.1	39.8	37.3	33.8	3.22	3.36	5.24	2.44	120.8	103.9	6.6	.7
1971	37.0	39.9	37.2	33.7	3.44	3.57	5.69	2.57	129.4	106.7	7.1	2.7
1972	37.1	40.6	36.9	33.7	3.67	3.81	6.03	2.70	137.8	110.0	6.5	3.1
1973	37.1	40.7	37.0	33.3	3.92	4.08	6.37	2.87	146.6	110.1	6.4	.1
1974	36.6	40.0	36.9	32.7	4.22	4.41	6.75	3.09	158.6	107.4	8.2	−2.5
1975	36.1	39.4	36.6	32.4	4.54	4.81	7.25	3.34	172.7	107.1	8.9	−.3
1976 ᵖ	36.2	40.1	37.1	32.2	4.86	5.19	7.67	3.55	184.7		6.9	
1975: Jan	36.2	39.1	37.1	32.3	4.41	4.65	7.04	3.23	166.0	106.1	9.5	−1.9
Feb	36.0	38.9	36.6	32.3	4.43	4.68	6.98	3.26	167.4	106.4	9.8	−1.1
Mar	35.9	38.9	34.9	32.5	4.45	4.72	7.18	3.27	168.9	107.0	10.0	−.3
Apr	35.9	39.0	36.7	32.3	4.47	4.73	7.18	3.28	169.3	106.7	9.6	−.6
May	36.0	39.1	36.8	32.4	4.49	4.75	7.16	3.30	170.3	106.8	9.0	−.5
June	36.0	39.3	36.0	32.4	4.52	4.78	7.26	3.32	171.8	106.9	8.6	−.8
July	36.0	39.4	36.4	32.3	4.55	4.82	7.32	3.34	172.7	106.5	8.7	−.9
Aug	36.1	39.7	36.7	32.4	4.58	4.85	7.30	3.37	174.2	107.0	8.8	.1
Sept	36.1	39.8	36.7	32.3	4.60	4.88	7.32	3.38	174.8	106.9	8.1	.1
Oct	36.2	39.8	36.7	32.4	4.63	4.90	7.34	3.40	176.2	107.1	8.2	.5
Nov	36.3	39.9	36.9	32.4	4.67	4.93	7.40	3.42	177.6	107.3	8.4	1.0
Dec	36.4	40.3	37.2	32.4	4.68	4.96	7.45	3.43	178.0	107.0	7.9	.8
1976: Jan	36.4	40.4	37.6	32.5	4.72	5.00	7.48	3.46	179.4	107.3	8.0	1.2
Feb	36.4	40.3	37.7	32.3	4.74	5.04	7.47	3.47	180.3	107.8	7.7	1.3
Mar	36.2	40.3	37.0	32.2	4.77	5.08	7.57	3.48	181.1	108.0	7.2	1.0
Apr	36.1	39.4	37.4	32.5	4.79	5.08	7.57	3.49	182.1	108.2	7.6	1.4
May	36.3	40.3	37.1	32.2	4.83	5.13	7.66	3.51	183.3	108.3	7.7	1.4
June	36.2	40.2	37.3	32.0	4.85	5.16	7.68	3.52	184.0	108.1	7.1	1.1
July	36.2	40.1	36.9	32.1	4.88	5.21	7.77	3.55	185.2	108.4	7.3	1.8
Aug	36.1	40.0	36.8	32.0	4.90	5.25	7.74	3.57	186.4	108.5	7.0	1.4
Sept	36.0	39.7	35.9	32.1	4.92	5.29	7.71	3.60	187.2	108.5	7.1	1.5
Oct	36.1	39.9	37.3	32.0	4.95	5.29	7.76	3.63	188.2	108.7	6.8	1.5
Nov ᵖ	36.2	40.1	37.4	32.0	4.99	5.34	7.81	3.66	189.2	109.0	6.5	1.6
Dec ᵖ	36.3	40.1	37.3	32.2	5.01	5.37	7.85	3.67	190.0		6.7	

[1] Also includes other private industry groups shown in Table B–32.
[2] Includes eating and drinking places.
[3] Adjusted for overtime (in manufacturing only) and for interindustry employment shifts.
[4] Current dollar earnings index divided by the consumer price index.
[5] Monthly data are computed from indexes to two decimal places.

Note.—See Note, Table B–32.

Source: Department of Labor, Bureau of Labor Statistics.

Table B-34.—*Average weekly earnings in selected private nonagricultural industries, 1947-76*

[For production or nonsupervisory workers; monthly data seasonally adjusted]

Year or month	Average gross weekly earnings					Percent change from a year earlier, total private nonagricultural [4]	
	Total private nonagricultural [1]		Manu- facturing	Contract construc- tion	Retail trade [3]	Current dollars	1967 dollars
	Current dollars	1967 dollars [2]	Current dollars				
1947	$45.58	$68.13	$49.17	$58.87	$33.77		
1948	49.00	67.96	53.12	65.27	36.22	7.5	-0.2
1949	50.24	70.36	53.88	67.56	38.42	2.5	3.5
1950	53.13	73.69	58.32	69.68	39.71	5.8	4.7
1951	57.86	74.37	63.34	76.96	42.82	8.9	.9
1952	60.65	76.29	67.16	82.86	43.38	4.8	2.6
1953	63.76	79.60	70.47	86.41	45.36	5.1	4.3
1954	64.52	80.15	70.49	88.91	47.04	1.2	.7
1955	67.72	84.44	75.70	90.90	48.75	5.0	5.4
1956	70.74	86.90	78.78	96.38	50.18	4.5	2.9
1957	73.33	86.99	81.59	100.27	52.20	3.7	.1
1958	75.08	86.70	82.71	103.78	54.10	2.4	-.3
1959	78.78	90.24	88.26	108.41	56.15	4.9	4.1
1960	80.67	90.95	89.72	113.04	57.76	2.4	.8
1961	82.60	92.19	92.34	118.08	58.66	2.4	1.4
1962	85.91	94.82	96.56	122.47	60.96	4.0	2.9
1963	88.46	96.47	99.63	127.19	62.66	3.0	1.7
1964	91.33	98.31	102.97	132.06	64.75	3.2	1.9
1965	95.06	100.59	107.53	138.38	66.61	4.1	2.3
1966	98.82	101.67	112.34	146.26	68.57	4.0	1.1
1967	101.84	101.84	114.90	154.95	70.95	3.1	.2
1968	107.73	103.39	122.51	164.49	74.95	5.8	1.5
1969	114.61	104.38	129.51	181.54	78.66	6.4	1.0
1970	119.46	102.72	133.73	195.45	82.47	4.2	-1.6
1971	127.28	104.93	142.44	211.67	86.61	6.5	2.2
1972	136.16	108.67	154.69	222.51	90.99	7.0	3.6
1973	145.43	109.26	166.06	235.69	95.57	6.8	.5
1974	154.45	104.57	176.40	249.08	101.04	6.2	-4.3
1975 ᵖ	163.89	101.67	189.51	265.35	108.22	6.1	-2.8
1976 ᵖ	175.93		208.12	284.56	114.31	7.3	
1975: Jan	159.64	102.01	181.82	261.18	104.33	6.8	-4.4
Feb	159.48	101.39	182.05	255.47	105.30	6.2	-4.4
Mar	159.76	101.17	183.61	250.58	106.28	5.9	-4.0
Apr	160.47	101.12	184.47	263.51	105.94	7.0	-2.9
May	161.64	101.34	185.73	263.49	106.92	5.1	-4.0
June	162.72	101.32	187.85	261.36	107.57	5.4	-3.6
July	163.80	100.99	189.91	266.45	107.88	5.1	-4.2
Aug	165.34	101.56	192.55	267.91	109.19	5.9	-2.5
Sept	166.06	101.57	194.22	268.64	109.17	5.5	-2.2
Oct	167.61	101.89	195.02	269.38	110.16	5.8	-1.7
Nov	169.52	102.43	196.71	273.06	110.81	7.6	.3
Dec	170.35	102.37	199.89	277.14	111.13	7.1	.1
1976: Jan	171.81	102.82	202.00	281.25	112.45	8.2	1.3
Feb	172.54	103.13	203.11	281.62	112.08	8.1	1.7
Mar	172.67	103.03	204.72	272.52	112.06	7.9	1.6
Apr	172.92	102.74	200.15	283.12	113.43	7.5	1.4
May	175.33	103.56	206.74	284.19	113.02	8.5	2.1
June	175.57	103.22	207.43	286.46	112.54	7.6	1.6
July	176.66	103.37	208.92	286.71	113.96	7.9	2.3
Aug	176.89	102.96	210.00	284.83	114.24	7.0	1.3
Sept	177.12	102.68	210.01	276.79	115.55	6.6	1.0
Oct	178.70	103.24	211.07	289.45	116.16	6.9	1.5
Nov ᵖ	180.64	104.06	214.13	292.09	117.12	6.5	1.5
Dec ᵖ	181.86		215.34	292.81	118.17	6.8	

[1] Also includes other private industry groups shown in Table B-32.
[2] Earnings in current dollars divided by the consumer price index.
[3] Includes eating and drinking places.
[4] Based on unadjusted data.

Note.—See Note, Table B-32.

Source: Department of Labor, Bureau of Labor Statistics.

TABLE B-35.—*Productivity and related data, private business economy, 1947-76*

[1967 = 100; quarterly data seasonally adjusted]

Year or quarter	Output¹ Total private business	Output¹ Private nonfarm business	Hours of all persons² Total private business	Hours of all persons² Private nonfarm business	Output per hour of all persons Total private business	Output per hour of all persons Private nonfarm business	Compensation per hour³ Total private business	Compensation per hour³ Private nonfarm business	Unit labor costs Total private business	Unit labor costs Private nonfarm business	Implicit price deflator⁴ Total private business	Implicit price deflator⁴ Private nonfarm business
1947	48.6	47.5	92.9	80.9	52.3	58.7	35.1	37.5	67.1	63.9	65.1	62.3
1948	50.8	49.5	93.5	82.1	54.4	60.3	38.1	40.7	70.1	67.5	70.6	67.5
1949	49.9	48.7	90.3	78.9	55.3	61.7	38.8	42.0	70.2	68.1	69.8	68.0
1950	54.5	53.2	91.2	81.3	59.	65.5	41.6	44.5	69.6	67.9	70.8	69.1
1951	57.7	56.7	93.9	85.0	61.5	66.7	45.6	48.4	74.3	72.5	76.0	73.7
1952	59.1	58.4	93.9	85.8	63.0	68.1	48.6	51.0	77.1	75.0	77.4	75.2
1953	61.9	60.8	94.7	87.9	65.3	69.2	51.8	54.0	79.3	78.0	77.9	76.8
1954	60.8	59.6	91.5	84.7	66.5	70.3	53.5	55.8	80.5	79.3	78.6	77.8
1955	65.6	64.5	94.8	88.1	69.2	73.2	54.9	57.8	79.3	79.0	79.8	79.4
1956	67.5	66.5	96.2	90.3	70.2	73.6	58.6	61.4	83.5	83.3	82.2	81.9
1957	68.4	67.5	94.6	89.7	72.3	75.3	62.5	65.0	86.5	86.4	84.8	84.6
1958	66.9	65.8	90.2	85.8	74.2	76.8	65.5	67.7	88.2	88.1	86.4	85.9
1959	71.8	71.0	93.4	89.3	76.8	79.6	68.5	70.6	89.1	88.8	88.1	88.0
1960	73.1	72.2	93.6	89.9	78.1	80.3	71.4	73.7	91.4	91.7	89.3	89.2
1961	74.1	73.3	92.0	88.7	80.6	82.6	74.2	76.2	92.1	92.3	89.8	89.8
1962	78.8	78.1	93.4	90.5	84.4	86.2	77.7	79.4	92.1	92.0	90.6	90.5
1963	82.2	81.6	93.8	91.4	87.7	89.3	80.7	82.3	92.0	92.2	91.4	91.5
1964	86.8	86.4	95.1	93.3	91.3	92.6	85.1	86.2	93.2	93.1	92.7	92.9
1965	92.9	92.6	98.1	96.8	94.7	95.7	88.4	89.1	93.4	93.2	94.2	94.1
1966	98.0	98.1	100.3	100.0	97.8	98.1	94.7	94.5	96.8	96.4	97.2	96.8
1967	100.0	100.0	100.0	100.0	100.0	100.0	100.0	100.0	100.0	100.0	100.0	100.0
1968	105.1	105.4	101.7	102.1	103.3	103.2	107.6	107.3	104.1	103.9	103.9	104.0
1969	108.3	108.6	104.5	105.3	103.7	103.1	115.1	114.2	111.0	110.9	108.8	108.7
1970	107.4	107.4	102.8	104.0	104.5	103.2	123.3	121.9	118.1	118.1	113.9	114.0
1971	110.3	110.3	102.3	103.7	107.8	106.3	131.5	129.9	121.9	122.2	118.9	119.2
1972	117.6	117.9	106.0	107.6	110.9	109.5	138.9	137.4	125.2	125.5	123.2	122.9
1973	124.5	125.0	110.1	112.2	113.1	111.4	150.3	148.1	132.9	133.0	130.3	128.0
1974	120.8	121.1	110.6	112.7	109.2	107.5	164.3	162.0	150.4	150.8	143.8	142.0
1975	118.1	118.0	105.9	107.9	111.5	109.4	180.2	177.7	161.6	162.4	157.5	156.4
1974: I	123.0	123.7	111.3	113.2	110.5	109.3	157.1	155.3	142.1	142.1	137.4	134.7
II	121.8	122.1	111.3	113.5	109.4	107.6	161.8	159.6	147.9	148.3	141.5	140.1
III	120.6	121.0	110.9	113.3	108.7	106.7	166.7	164.0	153.3	153.6	146.0	144.6
IV	117.7	117.9	109.3	111.5	107.6	105.7	170.7	168.3	158.6	159.3	150.4	149.2
1975: I	114.2	114.4	105.7	107.9	108.1	106.0	176.0	173.1	162.9	163.3	154.5	154.0
II	116.7	116.6	104.8	106.7	111.4	109.2	179.0	176.4	160.7	161.6	155.9	155.0
III	120.1	119.9	105.7	107.4	113.6	111.6	181.3	179.3	159.5	160.6	158.4	157.0
IV	121.2	121.3	107.0	109.2	113.2	111.0	185.0	182.2	163.4	164.1	160.9	159.3
1976: I	124.2	124.3	107.7	110.4	115.3	112.6	189.8	186.4	164.7	165.7	161.7	161.0
II	125.8	126.0	108.2	110.4	116.3	114.1	193.3	190.4	166.1	166.9	163.8	162.5
III	126.9	127.1	108.2	110.6	117.2	114.9	196.7	193.6	167.8	168.5	165.4	164.8

¹ Output refers to gross domestic product originating in the sector in 1972 dollars.
² Hours of all persons in private industry engaged in production, including hours of proprietors and unpaid family workers. Estimates based primarily on establishment data.
³ Wages and salaries of employees plus employers' contributions for social insurance and private benefit plans. Also includes an estimate of wages, salaries, and supplemental payments for the self-employed.
⁴ Current dollar gross domestic product divided by constant dollar gross domestic product.

Source: Department of Labor, Bureau of Labor Statistics.

TABLE B-36.—*Changes in productivity and related data, private business economy, 1948-76*

[Percent change from preceding period; quarterly data at seasonally adjusted annual rates]

Year or quarter	Output [1]		Hours of all persons [2]		Output per hour of all persons		Compensation per hour [3]		Unit labor costs		Implicit price deflator [4]	
	Total private business	Private nonfarm business	Total private business	Private nonfarm business	Total private business	Private nonfarm business	Total private business	Private nonfarm business	Total private business	Private nonfarm business	Total private business	Private nonfarm business
1948	4.6	4.4	0.6	1.6	3.9	2.8	8.6	8.7	4.5	5.8	8.4	8.3
1949	-1.8	-1.7	-3.4	-4.0	1.7	2.3	1.8	3.2	.1	.8	-1.1	.7
1950	9.2	9.4	1.1	3.1	8.0	6.1	7.1	5.8	-.8	-.3	1.5	1.6
1951	5.9	6.5	2.9	4.6	2.9	1.8	9.8	8.7	6.7	6.7	7.3	6.5
1952	2.5	3.0	.0	1.0	2.5	2.0	6.4	5.6	3.8	3.5	1.9	2.1
1953	4.6	4.1	.9	2.4	3.7	1.6	6.6	5.7	2.9	4.0	.6	2.1
1954	-1.7	-1.9	-3.5	-3.6	1.8	1.7	3.4	3.3	1.5	1.6	.9	1.3
1955	8.0	8.2	3.7	4.0	4.1	4.1	2.6	3.7	-1.5	-.4	1.5	2.1
1956	2.8	3.1	1.4	2.4	1.4	.6	6.7	6.2	5.2	5.5	3.0	3.2
1957	1.3	1.5	-1.6	-.7	3.0	2.2	6.7	5.9	3.7	3.7	3.2	3.3
1958	-2.1	-2.4	-4.7	-4.3	2.7	2.0	4.7	4.0	1.9	2.0	1.9	1.5
1959	7.3	7.9	3.6	4.1	3.6	3.6	4.6	4.4	1.0	.7	2.0	2.4
1960	1.8	1.6	.2	.6	1.6	1.0	4.2	4.3	2.6	3.3	1.4	1.4
1961	1.5	1.5	-1.7	-1.3	3.3	2.8	4.0	3.5	.7	.6	.6	.6
1962	6.2	6.5	1.5	2.1	4.6	4.4	4.7	4.1	.1	-.3	.9	.8
1963	4.4	4.5	.4	1.0	4.0	3.5	3.9	3.7	-.1	.1	.9	1.0
1964	5.6	5.9	1.4	2.1	4.1	3.7	5.4	4.8	1.3	1.0	1.4	1.5
1965	7.0	7.1	3.1	3.7	3.7	3.3	3.9	3.4	.2	.1	1.6	1.3
1966	5.5	6.0	2.3	3.3	3.2	2.5	7.0	6.1	3.7	3.4	3.2	2.9
1967	2.0	1.9	-.3	-.0	2.3	1.9	5.6	5.8	3.3	3.8	2.9	3.3
1968	5.1	5.4	1.7	2.1	3.3	3.2	7.6	7.3	4.1	3.9	3.9	4.0
1969	3.0	3.0	2.7	3.2	.3	-.2	7.0	6.5	6.6	6.6	4.7	4.5
1970	-.9	-1.1	-1.6	-1.2	.7	.2	7.2	6.7	6.4	6.5	4.7	4.9
1971	2.8	2.7	-.4	-.3	3.2	2.9	6.6	6.6	3.2	3.5	4.4	4.5
1972	6.6	6.9	3.6	3.7	2.9	3.0	5.7	5.8	2.7	2.7	3.6	3.1
1973	5.9	6.0	3.9	4.3	1.9	1.7	8.2	7.8	6.2	6.0	5.8	4.1
1974	-3.0	-3.1	.4	.4	-3.4	-3.5	9.3	9.4	13.2	13.4	10.3	11.0
1975	-2.3	-2.6	-4.2	-4.3	2.1	1.8	9.7	9.7	7.5	7.7	9.5	10.1
1974: I	-6.4	-5.2	.3	-.9	-6.6	-4.3	8.0	9.3	15.6	14.3	9.1	9.4
II	-3.8	-4.8	-.0	1.2	-3.8	-5.9	12.7	11.5	17.1	18.5	12.5	17.0
III	-3.9	-3.8	-1.4	-.6	-2.6	-3.2	12.6	11.5	15.5	15.2	13.2	13.4
IV	-9.4	-9.9	-5.7	-6.2	-4.0	-3.9	9.9	10.9	14.5	15.5	12.9	13.5
1975: I	-11.2	-11.3	-12.7	-12.4	1.6	1.3	13.1	11.8	11.9	10.4	11.3	13.5
II	8.9	7.9	-3.3	-4.1	12.7	12.6	6.9	7.9	-5.1	-4.2	3.5	2.6
III	12.3	12.1	3.5	2.5	8.5	9.3	5.2	6.8	-3.0	-2.2	6.6	5.3
IV	3.6	4.5	5.2	6.9	-1.5	-2.2	8.3	6.6	10.0	9.0	6.6	6.2
1976: I	10.2	10.5	2.6	4.4	7.4	5.8	10.9	9.5	3.2	3.5	2.1	4.3
II	5.5	5.4	1.6	.1	3.8	5.4	7.5	8.9	3.6	3.3	5.2	3.6
III	3.4	3.4	.2	.5	3.1	2.9	7.3	6.9	4.1	3.9	3.9	5.8

[1] Output refers to gross domestic product originating in the sector in 1972 dollars.
[2] Hours of all persons in private industry engaged in production, including hours of proprietors and unpaid family workers. Estimates based primarily on establishment data.
[3] Wages and salaries of employees plus employers' contributions for social insurance and private benefit plans. Also includes an estimate of wages, salaries, and supplemental payments for the self-employed.
[4] Current dollar gross domestic product divided by constant dollar gross domestic product.

Note.—Percent changes are based on original data and therefore may differ slightly from percent changes based on indexes in Table B-35.

Source: Department of Labor, Bureau of Labor Statistics.

PRICES

Table B-47.—*Consumer price indexes by expenditure classes, 1929-76*

For urban wage earners and clerical workers

[1967 = 100]

Year or month	All items	Food	Housing		Apparel and upkeep	Trans- porta- tion	Medical care	Personal care	Reading and recrea- tion	Other goods and services
			Total	Rent						
1929	51.3	48.3	--------	76.0	48.5	--------	--------	--------	--------	--------
1933	38.8	30.6	--------	54.1	36.9	--------	--------	--------	--------	--------
1939	41.6	34.6	52.2	56.0	42.4	43.0	36.7	40.3	45.3	46.9
1940	42.0	35.2	52.4	56.2	42.8	42.7	36.8	40.2	46.1	48.3
1941	44.1	38.4	53.7	57.2	44.8	44.2	37.0	41.2	47 7	49.2
1942	48.8	45.1	56.2	58.5	52.3	48.1	38.0	45.2	50 0	50.7
1943	51.8	50.3	56.8	58.5	54.6	47.9	39.9	49.9	54.1	53.3
1944	52.7	49.6	58.1	58.6	58.5	47.9	41.1	53.4	60.0	54.7
1945	53.9	50.7	59.1	58.8	61.5	47.8	42.1	55.1	62.4	56.9
1946	58.5	58.1	60.6	59.2	67.5	50.3	44.4	59.0	64.5	58.8
1947	66.9	70.6	65.2	61.1	78.2	55.5	48.1	66.0	68.7	63.8
1948	72.1	76.6	69.8	65.1	83.3	61.8	51.1	68.5	72.2	66.8
1949	71.4	73.5	70.9	68.0	80.1	66.4	52.7	68.3	74.9	68.7
1950	72.1	74.5	72.8	70.4	79.0	68.2	53.7	68.3	74 4	69.9
1951	77.8	82.8	77.2	73.2	86.1	72.5	56.3	74.7	76.6	72.8
1952	79.5	84.3	78.7	76.2	85.3	77.3	59.3	75.6	76.9	76.6
1953	80.1	83.0	80.8	80.3	84.6	79.5	61.4	76.3	77.7	78.5
1954	80.5	82.8	81.7	83.2	84.5	78.3	63.4	76.6	76.9	79.8
1955	80.2	81.6	82.3	84.3	84.1	77.4	64.8	77.9	76.7	79.8
1956	81.4	82.2	83.6	85.9	85.8	78.8	67.2	81.1	77.8	81.0
1957	84.3	84.9	86.2	87.5	87.3	83.3	69.9	84.1	80.7	83.3
1958	86.6	88.5	87.7	89.1	87.5	86.0	73.2	86.9	83.9	84.4
1959	87.3	87.1	88.6	90.4	88.2	89.6	76.4	88.7	85.3	86.1
1960	88.7	88.0	90.2	91.7	89.6	89.6	79.1	90.1	87.3	87.8
1961	89.6	89.1	90.9	92.9	90.4	90.6	81.4	90.6	89.3	88.5
1962	90.6	89.9	91.7	94.0	90.9	92.5	83.5	92.2	91.3	89.1
1963	91.7	91.2	92.7	95.0	91.9	93.0	85.6	93.4	92.8	90.6
1964	92.9	92.4	93.8	95.9	92.7	94.3	87.3	94.5	95.0	92.0
1965	94.5	94.4	94.9	96.9	93.7	95.9	89.5	95.2	95.9	94.2
1966	97.2	99.1	97.2	98.2	96.1	97.2	93.4	97.1	97.5	97.2
1967	100.0	100.0	100.0	100 0	100.0	100.0	100.0	100.0	100.0	100.0
1968	104.2	103.6	104.2	102.4	105.4	103.2	106.1	104.2	104.7	104.6
1969	109.8	108.9	110.8	105.7	111.5	107.2	113.4	109.3	108.7	109.1
1970	116.3	114.9	118.9	110.1	116.1	112.7	120.6	113.2	113.4	116.0
1971	121.3	118.4	124.3	115.2	119.8	118.6	128.4	116.8	119.3	120.9
1972	125.3	123.5	129.2	119.2	122.3	119.9	132.5	119.8	122.8	125.5
1973	133.1	141.4	135.0	124.3	126.8	123.8	137.7	125.2	125.9	129.0
1974	147.7	161.7	150.6	130.6	136.2	137.7	150.5	137.3	133.8	137.2
1975	161.2	175.4	166.8	137.3	142.3	150.6	168.6	150.7	144.4	147.4
1975: Jan	156.1	170.9	161.3	134.5	139.4	143.2	161.0	146.5	141.0	144.8
Feb	157.2	171.6	162.8	135.1	140.2	143.5	163.0	147.8	141.8	145.9
Mar	157.8	171.3	163.6	135.5	140.9	144.8	164.6	148.9	142.0	146.5
Apr	158.6	171.2	164.7	135.9	141.3	146.2	165.8	149.5	143.5	146.8
May	159.3	171.8	165.3	136.4	141.8	147.4	166.8	149.9	143.8	147.1
June	160.6	174.4	166.4	136.9	141.4	149.8	168.1	150.3	144.1	147.3
July	162.3	178.6	167.1	137.3	141.1	152.6	169.8	151.2	144.4	147.6
Aug	162.8	178.1	167.7	138.0	142.3	153.6	170.9	151.4	144.7	148.1
Sept	163.6	177.8	168.9	138.4	143.5	155.4	172.2	152.1	146.0	148.0
Oct	164.6	179.0	169.8	139.3	144.6	156.1	173.5	152.9	146.6	148.5
Nov	165.6	179.8	171.3	139.9	145.5	157.4	173.3	153.6	147.0	148.9
Dec	166.3	180.7	172.2	140.6	145.2	157.6	174.7	154.6	147.5	149.8
1976: Jan	166.7	180.8	173.2	141.2	143.3	158.1	176.6	155.7	148.2	150.5
Feb	167.1	180.0	173.8	142.1	144.0	158.5	178.8	157.0	148.5	151.3
Mar	167.5	178.7	174.5	142.7	145.0	159.8	180.6	157.4	149.0	151.8
Apr	168.2	179.2	174.9	143.2	145.7	161.3	181.6	158.3	149.5	152.5
May	169.2	180.0	175.6	143.8	146.8	163.5	182.6	158.9	150.3	152.9
June	170.1	180.9	176.5	144.4	146.9	165.9	183.7	159.8	150.9	153.2
July	171.1	182.1	177.5	145.0	146.5	167.6	185.5	160.5	151.2	153.6
Aug	171.9	182.4	178.4	145.6	148.1	168.5	186.8	161.6	151.4	153.8
Sept	172.6	181.6	179.5	146.2	150.2	169.5	187.9	162.8	152.8	153.9
Oct	173.3	181.6	180.1	146.9	150.9	170.9	188.9	163.9	153.5	154.4
Nov	173.8	181.1	180.7	147.5	151.9	171.4	191.3	164.8	154.1	155.3

Source: Department of Labor, Bureau of Labor Statistics.

TABLE B–48.—Consumer price indexes by commodity and service groups, 1939–76

For urban wage earners and clerical workers

[1967=100]

Year or month	All items	Commodities					Services			Special indexes		
		All commodities	Food	Commodities less food			All services	Rent	Services less rent	All items less food	All items less shelter	Nondurable commodities
				All	Durable	Nondurable						
1939	41.6	40.2	34.6	47.7	48.5	44.3	43.5	56.0	38.1	47.2	39.7	38.4
1940	42.0	40.6	35.2	48.0	48.1	44.7	43.6	56.2	38.1	47.3	39.9	38.9
1941	44.1	43.3	38.4	50.4	51.4	46.7	44.2	57.2	38.6	48.7	42.4	41.6
1942	48.8	49.6	45.1	56.0	58.4	51.6	45.6	58.5	40.3	52.1	47.7	47.6
1943	51.8	54.0	50.3	58.4	60.3	53.8	46.4	58.5	42.1	53.6	51.3	51.8
1944	52.7	54.7	49.6	61.6	65.9	56.6	47.5	58.6	44.2	55.7	52.2	52.2
1945	53.9	56.3	50.7	64.1	70.9	58.6	48.2	58.8	45.1	56.9	53.6	53.7
1946	58.5	62.4	58.1	68.1	74.1	62.9	49.1	59.2	46.7	59.4	59.0	59.6
1947	66.9	75.0	70.6	76.8	80.3	72.2	51.1	61.1	49.0	64.9	68.5	71.9
1948	72.1	80.4	76.6	82.7	86.2	77.8	54.3	65.1	51.9	69.6	73.9	77.2
1949	71.4	78.3	73.5	81.5	87.4	76.3	56.9	68.0	54.5	70.3	72.6	74.9
1950	72.1	78.8	74.5	81.4	88.4	76.2	58.7	70.4	56.0	71.1	73.1	75.4
1951	77.8	85.9	82.8	87.5	95.1	82.0	61.8	73.2	59.3	75.7	79.2	82.5
1952	79.5	87.0	84.3	88.3	96.4	82.4	64.5	76.2	62.2	77.5	80.8	83.4
1953	80.1	86.7	83.0	88.5	95.7	83.1	67.3	80.3	64.8	79.0	81.0	83.2
1954	80.5	85.9	82.8	87.5	93.3	83.5	69.5	83.2	66.7	79.5	81.0	83.2
1955	80.2	85.1	81.6	86.9	91.5	83.5	70.9	84.3	68.2	79.7	80.6	82.5
1956	81.4	85.9	82.2	87.8	91.5	85.3	72.7	85.9	70.1	81.1	81.7	83.7
1957	84.3	88.6	84.9	90.5	94.4	87.6	75.6	87.5	73.3	83.8	84.4	86.3
1958	86.6	90.6	88.5	91.5	95.9	88.2	78.5	89.1	76.4	85.7	86.9	88.6
1959	87.3	90.7	87.1	92.7	97.3	89.3	80.8	90.4	79.0	87.3	87.6	88.2
1960	88.7	91.5	88.0	93.1	96.7	90.7	83.5	91.7	81.9	88.8	88.9	89.4
1961	89.6	92.0	89.1	93.4	96.6	91.2	85.2	92.9	83.9	89.7	89.9	90.2
1962	90.6	92.8	89.9	94.1	97.6	91.8	86.8	94.0	85.5	90.8	90.9	90.9
1963	91.7	93.6	91.2	94.8	97.9	92.7	88.5	95.0	87.3	92.0	92.1	92.0
1964	92.9	94.6	92.4	95.6	98.8	93.5	90.2	95.9	89.2	93.2	93.2	93.0
1965	94.5	95.7	94.4	96.2	98.4	94.8	92.2	96.9	91.5	94.5	94.6	94.6
1966	97.2	98.2	99.1	97.5	98.5	97.0	95.8	98.2	95.3	96.7	97.4	98.1
1967	100.0	100.0	100.0	100.0	100.0	100.0	100.0	100.0	100.0	100.0	100.0	100.0
1968	104.2	103.7	103.6	103.7	103.1	104.1	105.2	102.4	105.7	104.4	104.1	103.9
1969	109.8	108.4	108.9	108.1	107.0	108.8	112.5	105.7	113.8	110.1	109.0	108.9
1970	116.3	113.5	114.9	112.5	111.8	113.1	121.6	110.1	123.7	116.7	114.4	114.0
1971	121.3	117.4	118.4	116.8	116.5	117.0	128.4	115.2	130.8	122.1	119.3	117.7
1972	125.3	120.9	123.5	119.4	118.9	119.8	133.3	119.2	135.9	125.8	122.9	121.7
1973	133.1	129.9	141.4	123.5	121.9	124.8	139.1	124.3	141.8	130.7	131.1	132.8
1974	147.7	145.5	161.7	136.6	130.6	140.9	152.1	130.6	156.0	143.7	146.1	151.0
1975	161.2	158.4	175.4	149.1	145.5	151.7	166.6	137.3	171.9	157.1	159.1	163.2
1975: Jan	156.1	153.4	170.9	143.9	139.3	147.2	161.3	134.5	166.2	151.9	154.1	158.7
Feb	157.2	154.4	171.6	144.9	140.3	148.2	162.6	135.1	167.5	153.0	155.0	159.6
Mar	157.8	155.0	171.3	146.0	142.1	148.8	163.2	135.5	168.3	153.9	155.6	159.7
Apr	158.6	155.7	171.2	147.2	143.6	149.8	164.1	135.9	169.2	154.9	156.3	160.1
May	159.3	156.5	171.8	148.1	144.8	150.5	164.5	136.4	169.6	155.6	157.0	160.8
June	160.6	157.9	174.4	148.9	145.8	151.2	165.7	136.9	170.9	156.6	158.4	162.4
July	162.3	160.1	178.6	149.4	146.9	152.2	166.6	137.3	171.9	157.6	160.3	165.0
Aug	162.8	160.4	178.1	150.7	147.5	153.0	167.4	138.0	172.7	158.3	160.8	165.2
Sept	163.6	160.8	177.8	151.4	148.2	153.8	169.1	138.4	174.6	159.5	161.6	165.4
Oct	164.6	161.7	179.0	152.2	148.9	154.6	170.1	139.3	175.7	160.4	162.6	166.4
Nov	165.6	162.2	179.8	152.6	149.2	155.1	172.0	139.9	177.7	161.5	163.4	167.1
Dec	166.3	162.7	180.7	152.8	149.3	155.4	173.1	140.6	179.0	162.1	164.1	167.6
1976: Jan	166.7	162.4	180.8	152.3	149.0	154.7	174.9	141.2	181.0	162.6	164.4	167.3
Feb	167.1	162.3	180.0	152.7	149.3	155.2	176.1	142.1	182.2	163.4	164.9	167.2
Mar	167.5	162.3	178.7	153.3	150.4	155.5	177.2	142.7	183.4	164.2	165.3	166.7
Apr	168.2	163.1	179.2	154.2	151.9	156.0	177.7	143.2	184.0	165.0	166.1	167.2
May	169.2	164.2	180.0	155.5	153.5	157.0	178.4	143.8	184.7	166.0	167.1	168.2
June	170.1	165.2	180.9	156.5	154.7	157.9	179.5	144.4	185.8	167.0	168.1	169.0
July	171.1	166.0	182.1	157.1	155.8	158.1	180.7	145.0	187.2	167.9	169.0	169.7
Aug	171.9	166.6	182.4	158.0	156.4	159.1	181.8	145.6	188.4	168.9	169.7	170.4
Sept	172.6	167.0	181.6	158.9	156.9	160.4	183.2	146.2	189.8	170.0	170.4	170.7
Oct	173.3	167.4	181.6	159.6	157.8	161.0	184.1	146.9	190.8	170.8	171.0	171.0
Nov	173.8	167.7	181.1	160.3	158.0	161.9	185.1	147.5	191.8	171.6	171.6	171.3

Source: Department of Labor, Bureau of Labor Statistics.

Selected Bibliography

Andersen, Ronald and Björn Smedby. "Changes in Response to Symptoms of Illness in the United States and Sweden," *Inquiry*, June 1975, pp. 116–127.

Bancroft, Gertrude and Stuart Garfinkel. "Job Mobility in 1961," *Monthly Labor Review*, 86 (August 1963), 897–906. (U.S. Department of Labor, Bureau of Labor Statistics, Special Labor Force Report No. 35.)

Becker, Gary. *Human Capital: A Theoretical and Empirical Analysis, With Special Reference to Education*, 2nd. ed., New York: National Bureau of Economic Research, 1975.

Becker, Gary. *Economics of Discrimination*. Chicago: University of Chicago Press, 1957.

Becker, Joseph M. *Experience Rating in Unemployment Insurance: Virtue or Vice*. Kalamazoo, Michigan: The W. E. Upjohn Institute for Employment Research, 1972.

Bowen, William G. and T. Aldrich Finegan. *The Economics of Labor Force Participation*. Princeton: Princeton University Press, 1969.

Chiswick, Barry R. "The Effect of Unemployment Compensation on a Seasonal Industry: Agriculture." *Journal of Political Economy*, June 1976, pp. 591–602.

Chiswick, Barry R., J. Fackler, J. O'Neill and S. Polachek. "The Effect of Occupation on Race and Sex Differences in Hourly Earnings." *Proceedings of the American Statistical Association, Business and Economics Section*, 1974, pp. 219–228.

Chiswick, Barry R., and Jacob Mincer. "Time Series Changes in Income Inequality." *Journal of Political Economy, Supplement*, May/June, 1972, pp. s34–s66.

Davis, Karen. *National Health Insurance: Benefits, Costs, and Consequences*. Washington, D.C.: The Brookings Institution, 1975.

Enterline, Philip, *et. al.* "Effects of Free Medical Care on Medical Practice, The Quebec Experience." *New England Journal of Medicine*, May 1973, pp. 1152–1155.

Fechter, Alan. *Public Employment Programs*. Washington, D.C.: American Enterprise Institute, 1975.

Feldstein, Martin. "Temporary Layoffs in the Theory of Unemployment."

Journal of Political Economy, October 1976, pp. 937–958.

Feldstein, Martin. "The Welfare Loss of Excess Health Insurance." *Journal of Political Economy*, March 1973, pp. 251–280.

Flaim, Paul O. "Discouraged Workers and Changes in Unemployment." *Monthly Labor Review* 96 (1973), pp. 8–16.

Fuchs, Victor, ed. *Essays in the Economics of Health and Medical Care*. New York: National Bureau of Economic Research, 1972.

Fuchs, Victor. "Differences in Hourly Earnings Between Men and Women." *Monthly Labor Review*, U.S. Department of Labor, Bureau of Labor Statistics, May 1971.

Gallaway, Lowell E. *The Retirement Decision: An Exploratory Essay*. Research Report No. 9, Division of Research and Statistics, Social Security Administration, 1965.

Garfinkel, Irwin. "Income Transfer Programs and Work Effort: A Review." *Studies in Public Welfare*, Paper No. 13, Joint Economic Committee, February 18, 1975.

Gramlich, Edward M. "The Distributional Effects of Higher Unemployment." *Brookings Papers on Economic Activity* 2 (1974), pp. 293–336.

Grossman, Michael. *Demand for Health*. Occasional Paper 119, National Bureau of Economic Research, 1972.

Holen, Arlene and Stanley Horowitz. "The Effects of Unemployment Insurance and Eligibility Enforcement on Unemployment." *Journal of Law and Economics*, October 1974, pp. 403–432.

Johnson, George E., and Frank P. Stafford. "The Earnings and Promotion of Women Faculty." *American Economic Review*, December 1974, pp. 888–903.

Johnson, George and James Tomola, "An Impact Evaluation of Public Employment Programs." Technical Analysis Paper, A.S.P.E.R., Department of Labor, 1974, mimeo.

Kosters, Marvin and Finis Welch. "The Effects of Minimum Wages on the Distribution of Changes in Aggregate Employment." *American Economic Review*, June 1972, pp. 323–332.

Landes, William. "The Economics of Fair Employment Laws." *Journal of Political Economy*, July 1968, pp. 507–552.

Lloyd, Cynthia B., ed. *Sex, Discrimination, and the Division of Labor*. New York: Columbia University Press, 1975.

Mincer, Jacob and Solomon Polachek. "Family Investments in Human Capital." *Journal of Political Economy, Supplement*, March/April 1974, pp. s76–s108.

Mincer, Jacob. "The Distribution of Labor Income: A Survey with Special Reference to the Human Capital Approach." *Journal of Economic Literature*, March 1970, pp. 1–26.

Mincer, Jacob. "Labor Force Participation of Married Women: A Study of Labor Supply." in C. Christ, ed., *Aspects of Labor Economics*. Princeton: Princeton University Press, 1962.

Munts, Raymond and Irwin Garfinkel. *The Work Disincentive Effects of Unemployment Insurance*. Kalamazoo, Michigan: The W. E. Upjohn Institute for Employment Research, 1974.

O'Neill, June. "The Sex Differential in Earnings and Labor Market Discrimination Against Women." *Journal of Contemporary Business,* Summer 1973, pp. 41–52.

O'Neill, June. "Returns from Social Security Contributions." Paper presented at American Economic Association meeting, Atlantic City, New Jersey, 1976.

Projector, Dorothy S., and Judith Bretz. "Measurement of Transfer Income in the Current Population Survey," in James D. Smith, ed. *The Personal Distribution of Income and Wealth.* New York: National Bureau of Economic Research, 1975.

Rees, Albert. *Economics of Work and Pay.* New York: Harper and Row, 1973.

Report of the Panel on Social Security Financing to the Committee on Finance, United States Senate, 94th Congress, First Session.

Report of the Quadrennial Advisory Council on Social Security, House Document, No. 94–75, 94th Congress, First Session.

Rosett, Richard, ed. *The Role of Health Insurance in the Health Services Sector.* New York: New York, National Bureau of Economic Research, 1976.

Ross, Heather L., and Isabel V. Sawhill. *Time of Transition: The Growth of Families Headed by Women.* Washington, D.C.: Urban Institute, 1975.

Storey, James R. "Welfare in the 70's: A National Study of Benefits Available in 100 Local Areas." *Studies in Public Welfare,* Paper No. 15, Joint Economic Committee, July 22, 1974.

Suter, Larry E., and Herman P. Miller. "Income Differences Between Men and Career Women." *American Journal of Sociology,* January 1973, pp. 962–974.

The Family, Poverty, and Welfare Programs, Paper No. 12, *Part I: Factors Influencing Family Instability; Part II: Household Patterns and Government Policies,* two volumes of studies prepared for the use of the Subcommittee on Fiscal Policy of the Joint Economic Committee, November 1974.

U.S. Bureau of the Census, *Current Population Reports,* Series P-60, No. 101, "Money Income in 1974 of Families and Persons in the United States"; and No. 102, "Characteristics of the Population Below the Poverty Level: 1974."

von Furstenberg, G. M., A. P. Horowitz and B. Harrison, eds. *Patterns of Racial Discrimination, Vol. II, Employment and Income.* Lexington, Mass.: D. C. Heath, 1974.

Vroman, Wayne. *Older Worker Earnings and the 1965 Social Security Amendments,* Research Report No. 38, Office of Research and Statistics, Social Security Administration, 1971.

White, Kerr L. "International Comparisons of Medical Care." *Scientific American,* August 1975, pp. 17–25.

Index